Herbert Schildt

Windows NT
Programming Handbook

Osborne McGraw-Hill
Berkeley New York St. Louis San Francisco Auckland Bogotá Hamburg London Madrid Mexico City
Milan Montreal New Delhi Panama City Paris São Paulo Singapore Sydney Tokyo Toronto

ACQUISITIONS EDITOR
Jeffrey M. Pepper

ASSOCIATE EDITOR
Vicki Van Ausdall

TECHNICAL EDITOR
Asael Dror
John Mueller

PROJECT EDITOR
Wendy Rinaldi

COPY EDITOR
Joe Ferrie

PROOFREADER
Jeff Barash

INDEXER
Sheryl Schildt

COMPUTER DESIGNER
Jani Beckwith

SERIES DESIGN
Seventeenth Street Studios

COVER DESIGN
Bay Graphics

Osborne **McGraw-Hill**
2600 Tenth Street
Berkeley, California 94710
U.S.A.

For information on software, translations, or book distributors outside of the U.S.A., please write to Osborne **McGraw-Hill** at the above address.

Windows NT Programming Handbook

Copyright © 1993 by McGraw-Hill, Inc. All rights reserved. Printed in the United States of America. Except as permitted under the Copyright Act of 1976, no part of this publication may be reproduced or distributed in any form or by any means, or stored in a database or retrieval system, without the prior written permission of the publisher, with the exception that the program listings may be entered, stored, and executed in a computer system, but they may not be reproduced for publication.

1234567890 DOC 99876543

ISBN 0-07-881873-7

Information has been obtained by Osborne **McGraw-Hill** from sources believed to be reliable. However, because of the possibility of human or mechanical error by our sources, Osborne **McGraw-Hill**, or others, Osborne **McGraw-Hill** does not guarantee the accuracy, adequacy, or completeness of any information and is not responsible for any errors or omissions or the results obtained from use of such information.

Contents at a Glance

Contents

Preface

Windows NT is *the* operating system that is designed to take personal computing into the next century. It is flexible, powerful, and, to be honest, it can be complex to program for. It is also one of the most thoroughly thought-out operating systems in existence and is logically consistent from one subsystem to the next. Therefore, once you have mastered its essentials and created a reserve of reusable code fragments, it is a pleasure to work with. In fact, if you have been programming for a system such as DOS, then you will find Windows NT's attention to consistency a marked improvement.

One of the joys of writing about Windows NT is that it provides a nearly limitless range of topics to discuss. As soon as I finished one chapter, the next chapter's topic would immediately suggest itself. However, this blessing can also be a curse—it is difficult to *stop* writing about this exciting system! There is so much to say about Windows NT that the hardest part of the task of writing this book was deciding which topics would be included and which would have to wait for subsequent books. I made the selections according to the following criteria. All programming essentials are discussed. In my opinion, a Windows NT handbook simply must discuss the basics. Conversion from 16-bit Windows to Windows NT is covered. Since many programmers will be converting older, 16-bit Windows code to the new 32-bit Windows NT system, it seemed important to discuss this procedure. Finally, several features unique to Windows NT are highlighted. These include consoles and thread-based multitasking.

Whether you are converting older Windows programs to NT, or writing Windows-style programs for the first time, this book will help you accomplish your goals. It contains all the information you need to begin writing Windows NT programs. It also lays a firm foundation upon which you may build your knowledge of Windows NT in those specialized areas that apply to your own programming situation. Finally, it contains special 16-bit Conversion Notes which help fast-track the conversion process.

Who Is This Book For?

This book is for any programmer that wants to learn to write programs for Windows NT. It *does not* assume that you have written 16-bit Windows programs. However, it does assume that you are an accomplished C (or C++) programmer. If you are new to C, I suggest that you first take some time to learn it because many Windows NT constructs make use of rather sophisticated C programming techniques. Specifically, you should have no trouble using pointers, structures, or unions. The code in the book is straight C code; no C++ features are used, so you don't need to know C++.

Although this book *does not* assume that you are familiar with the essentials of operating system theory, Windows NT is sufficiently sophisticated that you will have an easier time learning to program for it if you have some background or experience with operating system basics.

One last point: If you have never written a Windows-style program before, be patient! Windows-style programs are much different from the type of programs that you have been writing. However, by the end of Chapter 4, the overall structure of a Windows NT program should be clear and the creation of Windows NT programs will be no trouble.

What Programming Tools You Will Need

The code in this book was written, compiled, and tested using the Microsoft Windows NT Developers Kit C/C++ compiler. You will need either this compiler or another C/C++ compiler that is designed to produce Windows NT-compatible object code.

HS
May 3, 1993
Mahomet IL

Diskette Offer

There are many useful and interesting functions, classes, and programs contained in this book. If you're like me, you probably would like to use them, but hate typing them into the computer. When I key in routines from a book it always seems that I type something wrong and spend hours trying to get the program to work. This is especially true for Windows NT programs, which tend to be long. For this reason, I am offering the source code on diskette for all the functions and programs contained in this book for $24.95. Just fill in the order blank on the next page and mail it, along with your payment, to the address shown. Or, if you're in a hurry, just call (217) 586-4021 (the number of my consulting office) and place your order by telephone. (Visa and Mastercard accepted.)

Please send me _____ copies, at $24.95 each, of the programs in *Windows NT Programming Handbook* on an IBM compatible diskette.

Foreign orders only: Checks must be drawn on a U.S. bank and please add $5 shipping and handling.

_____

Name

_____

Address

_____   _____   _____

City   State   Zip

_____

Telephone

Diskette size (check one): 5 1/4" _____   3 1/2" _____
Method of payment: Check _____   Visa _____   MC _____
Credit card number: _____
Expiration date: _____
Signature: _____

Send to:
Herbert Schildt
398 County Rd 2500 N
Mahomet, IL 61853
or phone: (217) 586-4021
     FAX: (217) 586-4997
This offer subject to change or cancellation at any time.

Chapter 1

Windows NT Overview

tHIS book is, first and foremost, a practical "how to" guide to Windows NT programming. As such, it is not overly concerned with the theoretical aspects of Windows NT, except as they directly relate to writing programs. Instead, this book provides a hands-on approach that will have you writing Windows NT programs as soon as possible.

The preceding paragraph notwithstanding, before you can become a Windows NT programmer, it is necessary that you understand in a general way how Windows NT operates, what design concepts it embodies, and how it manages your computer. It is also important to understand how Windows NT differs from its predecessors: DOS and Windows. Therefore, this chapter presents an overview of Windows NT and discusses ways in which it relates to and differs from DOS and Windows.

If you have never written a Windows program before, then most of the information in this book will be new to you. Just be patient. If you proceed methodically, you will become an accomplished Windows NT programmer by the time you finish this book. If you have programmed for Windows, then you will be able to advance more quickly, but be careful. There are some differences between Windows NT and Windows that will affect the way that you write programs.

All the examples in this book are written in C, and this book assumes that you are familiar with the C language. C is *the* language of Windows NT. Put bluntly, if you want to program for Windows NT, you must be a C programmer. If you don't know C, take some time to learn it now.

note: *For a complete (and readable) discussion of the theoretical aspects and underpinnings of Windows NT, I suggest Helen Custer's* Inside Windows NT *(Microsoft Press, 1993, Redmond, WA).*

What Is Windows NT?

Windows NT is the next generation operating system, intended to operate PCs well into the next century. Windows NT was designed to be a portable operating system, able to easily span several diverse hardware platforms, including single and multiple processor environments. It can easily be extended or enhanced as hardware evolves.

As you read this book, you may notice that perhaps the single most important characteristic of Windows NT is that it is a full, 32-bit operating system. By moving to a complete 32-bit implementation, Windows NT has left behind many of the quirks and problems associated with the older 16-bit systems.

A primary design goal of Windows NT was compatibility with other PC-based operating systems and with the programs designed to run under them. That is, Windows NT was designed to allow downward compatibility with the large base of existing PC applications. Towards this end, Windows NT contains emulators that allow it to automatically (and seamlessly) execute programs written for the following operating systems:

◆ DOS

◆ Windows (including 16-bit applications)

◆ OS/2

◆ POSIX (Portable Operating System Interface based on UNIX)

Windows NT automatically creates the right environment for the type of program you run. For example, when you execute a DOS program, Windows NT automatically creates a windowed command prompt in which to run the program.

Another design consideration of Windows NT was security. Windows NT provides an environment that meets the DoD C2 security classification. This level of security provides for password-protected log on, resource access control and ownership, and an activity log that provides an audit trail of certain activities. Also, memory is cleared before it is reused by another user; and memory used by one program is protected from memory used by another. It is not possible for one program to "corrupt" another or to interrogate the contents of its variables.

Windows NT also was intended to meet or exceed current performance standards. Where this was not possible, such as when emulating another operating environment, a maximum performance loss of ten percent or less was achieved.

One other important aspect of Windows NT is that it can run on computers with multiple CPUs. While few of these computers exist at the time of this writing, they will become more common. When they are available, Windows NT will be there to support them.

How Windows NT Works

Windows NT can effectively and efficiently operate your computer, provide compatibility with other operating systems, and allow for extensibility, because it is organized using a *client/server* model. As you may know, there are several ways to organize an operating system. The client/server model is distinct from the other common approaches in the way it organizes and executes its code. To understand how, let's begin by first defining two important terms: user mode and kernel mode.

User and Kernel Modes

All but the most primitive operating systems define two modes of execution. Application programs run in one mode, and system code runs in the other. In short, the purpose of having two modes is to enforce the control of the operating system over the computer. This scheme prevents an application program from improperly accessing a system resource.

When you write an application program, it executes in *user mode*. A user mode program cannot directly interact with the hardware of the computer or even with the lower levels of the operating system. Instead, it interacts only with the operating system interface. In this way, an application program is both managed and prevented from inappropriately calling a low-level system routine or directly accessing a hardware resource (such as a port). Therefore, user mode has access to the hardware and the low-level system services only through the kernel interface.

By contrast, the operating system kernel runs in *kernel mode*. In kernel mode, a system service has access to all system services and to the hardware itself. Kernel mode has full access to the machine and typically runs at the highest priority setting.

In most traditional operating systems, the entire operating system runs in kernel mode, and application programs run in user mode. For a traditional operating system, this means that things like the file system, the memory manager, and the I/O processor all run in kernel mode.

Windows NT breaks from the traditional organization in the following way: it moves most of the operating system service out of the kernel. Therefore, the kernel for Windows NT is very small, and the services moved out of the kernel now execute in user mode! As you will see, moving most system services out of the kernel makes it possible to update, modify, or enhance a service without altering the operating system kernel. This makes Windows NT extensible and portable. It also makes it easy to support several different operating systems. Because the services are no longer running in kernel mode, but rather in user mode, they are called *servers*.

Because most of the system services are moved out of the kernel, you might wonder what is left. First, the Windows NT kernel contains the scheduler, which manages the executing tasks in the system. It also contains all hardware interface code. Most importantly, it contains the code that communicates with the servers.

Understanding the Client/Server Model

Because Windows NT moves most of its system services out of kernel mode and transforms them into servers running in user mode, you might think that a Windows NT application program would be free to interact with these servers directly. However, this is not the case. Even though Windows NT servers run in user mode, they are still fully protected and isolated from application programs. The way this protection is provided is the essence of the client/server model.

The client/server approach is based upon the passing of messages between the application program and the servers it uses. In short, the only way that an application program (that is, the client) can access a system service (that is, the server) is to pass a message to the kernel. The kernel then passes this message to the appropriate server, which processes the message and sends a response back to the kernel. The kernel then returns the information to the application program. Thus, an application program can never directly communicate with a server. All communication is routed through the kernel and any improper access is screened out. In this way, the operating system still retains complete control of the computer.

To better understand the client/server relationship, let's use an example. Assume an application program wants to open a file. The program sends a message, to the kernel, that it wants to open a file. The kernel routes this message to the file server. The file server opens the file and obtains a handle to it. This handle is then sent to the kernel, which passes it back to the application program. This scheme is depicted in Figure 1-1. By using the client/server approach, it is still possible to protect and control access to low-level system services while reducing the size of the kernel.

The client/server model offers several advantages over the traditional approach. First, it allows the various servers to be maintained and updated without altering the kernel. In essence, new servers can be "dropped in" as needed without altering the low-level portions of Windows NT. Second, by keeping the kernel small, it helps make the kernel portable. Finally, the client/server approach makes it easier to provide compatibility with other operating systems. To understand why, consider this: because the servers run in user mode and are not part of the kernel, they can easily be changed. Further, there may be multiple servers for the same services, each one emulating a different operating system. Thus, when a program designed for a different operating system is run, its requests for kernel services can easily and automatically be routed to the correct server. It is this approach that allows Windows NT to support DOS, OS/2, POSIX, and Windows programs.

Understanding Processes and Threads

As you almost certainly know, Windows NT is a multitasking operating system. As such, it can run two or more programs concurrently. On systems with only one processor, the programs share the CPU and do not, technically, run simultaneously, although, because of the speed of the computer, they appear to. However, Windows NT can be run on computers that have two or more CPUs. When this is the case, programs may, indeed, actually execute simultaneously. Since you can't always know what type of computer your program will be executed on, it is best to assume that true, concurrent execution is always occurring.

Unlike some other operating systems, Windows NT supports two forms of multitasking: process-based and thread-based. A *process* is a program that is executing. Because Windows NT can multitask processes, it can run more than one program at a time. This is the traditional form of multitasking, with which you are probably familiar.

Windows NT's second form of multitasking is thread-based. A *thread* is a dispatchable unit of executable code. The name comes from the concept of a "thread of execution." All processes have at least one thread. However, a Windows NT process may have several.

Because Windows NT multitasks threads and each process can have more than one thread, you might assume that it is possible for one process to have

Figure 1-2

How the client/server model works

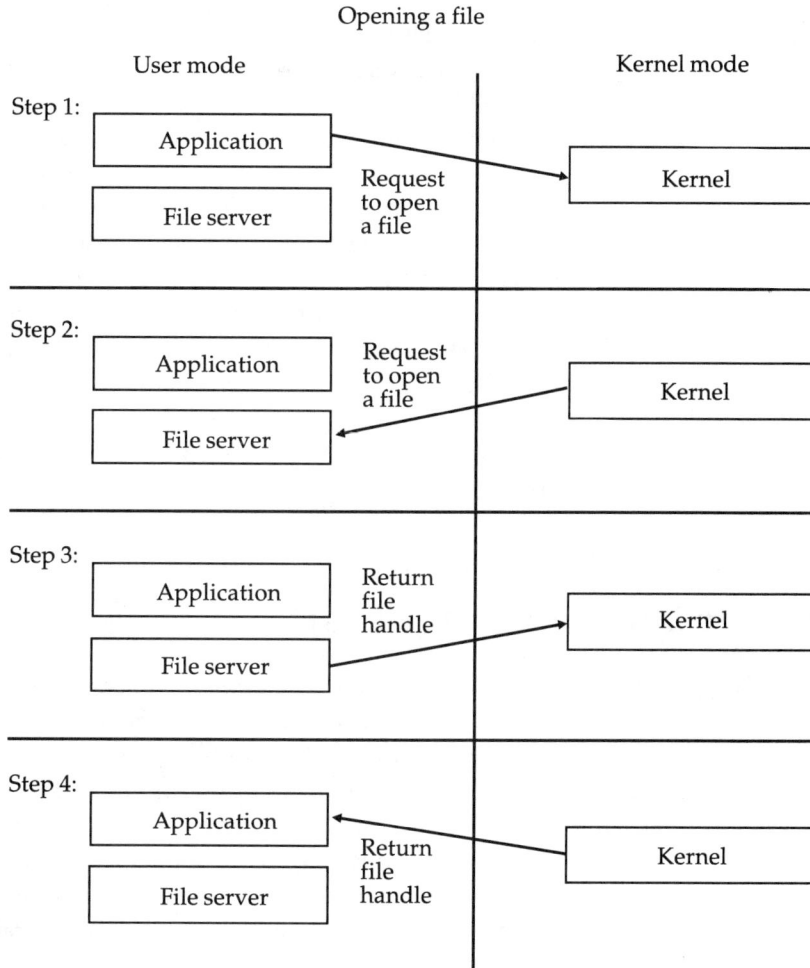

Opening a file

User mode | Kernel mode

Step 1:

Application → Kernel

Request to open a file

File server

Step 2:

Application

Request to open a file

Kernel → File server

File server

Step 3:

Application

Return file handle

File server → Kernel

File server

Step 4:

Application ← Kernel

Return file handle

File server

two or more pieces of itself executing simultaneously. As it turns out, this assumption is correct. When working with Windows NT, it is possible to multitask both programs and pieces of a single program.

The Windows NT Call-Based Interface

If you come from a DOS background, then you know that you interface to DOS using various software interrupts. For example, the standard DOS interrupt is 0x21. While using a software interrupt to access DOS services is perfectly acceptable (given the limited scope of the DOS operating system), it is completely inadequate as a means of interfacing to a full-featured, multitasking operating system like Windows NT. Instead, Windows NT, like Windows before it, uses a *call-based interface* to access the operating system.

The Windows NT call-based interface uses a rich set of system defined functions to access operating system features. Collectively, these functions are called the *Application Programming Interface,* or API for short. The API contains several hundred functions which your application program calls in order to communicate with Windows NT. These functions provide all necessary operating system related activities, such as memory allocation, screen output, and windows creation.

Dynamic Link Libraries (DLLs)

Because the API consists of several hundred functions, you might be thinking that a large amount of code is linked into every program that is compiled for Windows NT, causing each program to contain much duplicate code. However, this is not the case. Instead, the Windows NT API functions are contained in *Dynamic Link Libraries,* or DLLs for short, to which each program has access when it is executed. Here is how dynamic linking works.

The Windows NT API functions are stored in a relocatable format within a DLL. During the compilation phase, when your program calls an API function, the linker does not add the code for that function to the executable version of your program. Instead, it adds loading instructions for that function, such as what DLL it resides in and the function name. When your program is executed, the necessary API routines are also loaded by the Windows NT loader. In this way, the application program does not need to contain the actual API code while stored on disk. The code is added only when loaded into memory for execution.

Dynamic linking has some very important benefits. First, since virtually all programs will use the API functions, DLLs prevent disk space from being wasted by the significant amount of duplicated object code that would be created if the API functions were actually added to each program's executable file on disk. Second, updates and enhancements to Windows NT can be accomplished by changing the dynamic link library routines. Existing application programs do not need to be recompiled. Third, using the dynamic link approach makes the emulation of other operating systems an easier task.

Windows Versus Windows NT

While Windows NT is the next step in the Windows product line, which began with Windows' original release in 1985, it represents a major step forward in operating system design. However, from the point of view of the application programmer, the approach to programming will be the same.

The good news is that if you are familiar with Windows, you will have no trouble learning to use or program Windows NT. From the user's point of view, Windows NT looks just like Windows. The Program Manager, the File Manager, and the accessories are all there and operate, more or less, in the same way. For the purpose of this book, the more important good news is that you program for Windows NT in much the same way that you did for Windows. Windows NT preserves the name space of the original Windows API functions. When Windows NT added functionality, it did so by adding new functions. While there are some differences between Windows and Windows NT, for the most part these differences are easy to accommodate. Also, old Windows programs run fine under Windows NT, so you won't have to port all of your applications at once.

Although to the user and, to a large extent, to the application programmer, Windows and Windows NT look the same, there are some differences. The most important of these are summarized here.

User Differences

From the user's point of view, Windows NT adds substantial functionality, including the ability to transparently run DOS programs. When you run a DOS program, a windowed command prompt interface is automatically created. Further, this windowed command prompt is fully integrated into the overall Windows NT graphical interface.

Because Windows NT supports security, it includes several security-related features. First, it contains user accounts, which can be maintained with differing access privileges. You must log on to Windows NT into a user account. Also, pressing CTRL-ALT-DEL no longer reboots your computer. Instead, it simply takes you to the log in screen.

Windows NT also includes a number of accessories and administrative tools not supported by Windows.

Programming Differences

From the programmer's point of view, there are two main differences between Windows and Windows NT. First, Windows NT supports full 32-bit addressing and uses virtual memory. Windows uses a 16-bit segmented addressing mode. For many application programs these differences will have little effect. For others, the effect will be substantial. Frankly, while the transition may not be painless, you will find the Windows NT 32-bit memory model much easier to program for.

The second difference concerns the way that multitasking is accomplished. Windows uses a non-preemptive approach to task switching. This means that a Windows task must manually return control to the scheduler in order for another task to run. In other words, a Windows program retains control of the CPU until it decides to give it up. Therefore, an ill-behaved program could monopolize the CPU. By contrast, Windows NT uses preemptive, time-slice based tasking. In this scheme, tasks are automatically preempted by Windows NT, and the CPU is then assigned to the next task (if one exists). Preemptive multitasking is generally the superior method, because it allows the operating system to fully control tasking, and it prevents one task from dominating the system. Most programmers view the move to preemptive multitasking as a step forward.

In addition to the two major changes just described, Windows NT differs from Windows in some other, less dramatic ways, which are described here.

INPUT QUEUES

Another difference between Windows and Windows NT is found in the *input queue*. (Input queues hold messages, such as a keypress or mouse activity, until they can be sent to your program.) In Windows, there is just one input queue for all tasks running in the system. However, Windows NT supplies each thread with its own input queue. The advantage to each thread having its own queue is that no one process can reduce system performance by responding to its messages slowly.

Although multiple input queues are an important addition, this change has no direct impact on how you program for Windows NT.

DLLS

Although both Windows and Windows NT use a DLL-based API to provide access to the operating system, the actual content of the DLLs differ. (Generally, these differences do not matter from a programming point of view.) In Windows, the DLL actually contains the API functions, which are linked to an executable program when it is run. However, in Windows NT, the DLLs contain short pieces of code called *stubs*. Each stub transforms the application's function call into a message, which is then passed to the kernel. The kernel then passes this message to the appropriate server. After the server completes its necessary activities as requested by the message, the result is returned to the kernel, which then passes it back to the application program via the DLL stub. Although the mechanism differs substantially between Windows and Windows NT, it does not affect the way that you program for Windows NT.

CONSOLES

In the past, text-based (that is, non-windowed) applications were fairly inconvenient to use from Windows. However, Windows NT supports a special type of window called a *console*. A console window provides a standard text-based, command prompt interface. However, aside from being text-based, a console acts and can be manipulated like other windows. The addition of the text-based console not only allows non-windowed applications to run in a full windows environment, but also makes it more convenient for you to create short, throw-away utility programs. Perhaps more importantly, the inclusion of consoles in Windows NT is a final acknowledgment that some text-based applications make sense, and now they can be managed as part of the overall Windows environment. In essence, the addition of console windows completes the Windows application environment.

FLAT ADDRESSING

Windows NT applications have available to them 4 gigabytes of virtual memory in which to run! Further, this address space is *flat*. Unlike Windows, DOS, and other 8086-family operating systems which use segmented memory, Windows NT treats memory as linear. And, because Windows NT virtualizes memory, each application has as much memory as it could reasonably (and possibly) want. While the change to flat addressing is mostly transparent to the programmer, it does relieve much of the tedium and frustration of dealing with the old, segmented approach.

CHANGES TO MESSAGES AND PARAMETER TYPES

Because of the shift in Windows NT to 32-bit addressing, some messages passed to a Windows NT program will be organized differently than they are when passed to a Windows program. Also, the parameter types used to declare a window function have changed because of the move to 32-bit addressing. The specific changes to the messages and parameters will be discussed later in this book, as they are used.

What Software Is Needed

At the time of this writing, the only way that you can program for Windows NT is to use Microsoft's *Windows NT Developers Kit*. (This is formally called the *WIN32 Software Developers Kit for Windows NT,* but almost no one actually refers to it by this rather long name!) This development kit includes a C/C++ compiler that can compile all of the programs in this book.

By the time you read this book, it is possible (in fact, likely) that you will be able to use other compilers to create Windows NT code. The programs in this book should be able to be compiled by any Windows NT compatible compiler. However, the specific compiler options and make file instructions may differ if you use a different compiler.

The examples in this book are written in standard C so that they can be compiled by the widest variety of compilers. However, because most contemporary compilers also support the C++ extensions, there is no reason why your own programs cannot be written in C++.

Terminology

To avoid confusion, for the remainder of this book the following terms will be used. The 16-bit version of Windows will be referred to as *16-bit Windows*. Windows NT will be called precisely that. When discussing both environments generically, or when the difference doesn't matter, the term *Windows* will be used.

Conversion Notes

Since many readers will be converting 16-bit Windows applications to Windows NT, conversion notes are included when appropriate. While conversion of 16-bit applications to Windows NT is not fundamentally difficult, several important differences will be highlighted.

Chapter 2

Windows NT Programming

Overview

T H I S chapter introduces Windows NT programming. It has two main purposes. First, it discusses how a program must interact with Windows NT and what rules must be followed by every Windows NT application. Second, it develops an application skeleton that will be used as a basis for all other Windows NT programs. As you will see, all Windows NT programs share several common traits. It is these shared attributes that will be contained in the application skeleton.

As the preceding chapter mentioned, although similar in spirit, there are significant differences between 16-bit Windows (such as Windows 3.1) and Windows NT. These differences will be discussed as they occur. Pay special attention to the differences if you will be porting older applications.

To begin, this chapter presents the Windows NT programming perspective.

note: *If you already know how to write programs for 16-bit Windows, then this and the next few chapters contain many fundamental Windows programming concepts and techniques with which you are already familiar. (In fact, 16-bit Windows and Windows NT programs are, on the surface, almost identical.) However, you should at least skim through these chapters, because there are differences between 16-bit Windows and Windows NT that you need to understand.*

Windows NT Programming Perspective

The goal of Windows NT (and Windows in general) is to enable a person who has basic familiarity with the system to sit down and run virtually any application without prior training. In theory, if you can run one Windows program, you can run them all. Of course, in actuality, most useful programs will still require some sort of training in order to be used effectively, but at least this instruction can be restricted to *what* the program *does,* not *how* the user must *interact* with it. In fact, much of the code in a Windows application is there just to support the user interface.

At this point it is very important for you to understand that not every program that runs under Windows NT will necessarily present the user with a Windows style interface. However, only those programs written to take advantage of Windows will look and feel like Windows programs. While you can override the basic Windows design philosophy, you had better have a good reason to do so, because the users of your programs will, most often, be very disturbed. Quite honestly, if you are writing application programs for Windows NT, they should conform to the accepted Windows programming philosophy.

Windows NT is graphics oriented, which means that it provides a *Graphical User Interface* (GUI). While graphics hardware and video modes are quite diverse, many of the differences are handled by Windows. This means that, for the most part, your program does not need to worry about what type of graphics hardware or video mode is being used.

Let's look at a few of the more important features of Windows NT.

The Desktop Model

With few exceptions, the point of a window-based user interface is to provide on the screen the equivalent of a desktop. On a desk may be found several different pieces of paper, one on top of another, often with fragments of different pages visible beneath the top page. The equivalent of the desktop in Windows NT is the screen. The equivalents of pieces of paper are windows on the screen. On a desk you may move pieces of paper about, maybe switching which piece of paper is on top or how much of another is exposed to view. Windows NT allows the same type of operations on its windows. By selecting a window, you can make it current, which means putting it on top of all other windows. You can enlarge or shrink a window, or move it about on the screen. In short, Windows lets you control the surface of the screen the way you control the surface of your desk.

The Mouse

Windows NT allows the use of the mouse for almost all control, selection, and drawing operations. Of course, to say that it *allows* the use of the mouse is an understatement. The fact is that the Windows NT interface was *designed for the mouse*—it *allows* the use of the keyboard! Although it is certainly possible for an application program to ignore the mouse, it does so only in violation of a basic Windows design principle.

Icons and Graphic Images

Windows NT allows (but does not require) the use of icons and bit-mapped graphic images. The theory behind the use of icons and graphic images is found in the old adage: a picture is worth a thousand words.

An icon is a small symbol that is used to represent some function or program that can be activated by moving the mouse to the icon and double-clicking on it. A graphic image is generally used simply to convey information quickly to the user.

Menus and Dialog Boxes

Aside from standard windows, Windows NT also provides special purpose windows. The most common of these are the menu and dialog boxes. Briefly, a *menu* is, as you would expect, a special window that contains only a menu from which the user makes a selection. However, instead of having to provide the menu selection functions in your program, you simply create a standard menu using built-in menu selection functions.

A *dialog box* is a special window that allows more complex interaction with the application than that allowed by a menu. For example, your application might use a dialog box to input a filename. With few exceptions, non-menu input is accomplished via a dialog box.

How Windows NT and Your Program Interact

When you write a program for many operating systems, it is your program that initiates interaction with the operating system. For example, in a DOS program, it is the program that requests such things as input and output. Put differently, programs written in the "traditional way" call the operating system. The operating system does not call your program. However, in large measure, Windows NT works in the opposite way. It is Windows NT that calls your program. The process works like this: a Windows NT program waits until it is sent a *message* by Windows. The message is passed to your program through a special function that is called by Windows. Once a message is received, your program is expected to take an appropriate action. While your program may call one or more Windows NT API functions when responding to a message, it is still Windows NT that initiates the activity. More than anything else, it is the message-based interaction with Windows NT that dictates the general form of all Windows NT programs.

There are many different types of messages that Windows NT may send your program. For example, each time the mouse is clicked on a window belonging to your program, a "mouse-clicked" message will be sent to your program. Another type of message is sent each time a window belonging to your program must be redrawn. Still another message is sent each time the user presses a key when your program is the focus of input. Keep one fact firmly in mind: as far as your program is concerned, messages arrive randomly. This is why Windows NT programs resemble interrupt-driven programs. You can't know what message will be next.

The Windows NT API

In general, the Windows environment is accessed through a call-based interface called the API (Application Program Interface). The several hundred API functions provide all the system services performed by Windows NT. There is a subset of the API called the GDI (Graphics Device Interface), which is the part of Windows that provides device-independent graphics support. It is the GDI functions that make it possible for a Windows application to run on a variety of different hardware configurations.

For the most part, the API functions supplied by the original, 16-bit versions of Windows and those supplied with Windows NT are compatible. Indeed, for the most part the functions are called by the same name and are used in the same way. However, even though similar in spirit and purpose, the two APIs differ because, as mentioned in Chapter 1, Windows NT supports full, 32-bit addressing, while 16-bit Windows supports only the 16-bit, segmented memory model. This difference has caused the API functions to be widened to accept 32-bit arguments and return 32-bit values. Also, a few API functions have had to be altered to accommodate the 32-bit architecture. If you are new to Windows programming in general, then these changes will not affect you significantly. However, if you will be porting code from 16-bit Windows to Windows NT, then you will need to examine carefully the arguments you pass to each API function.

Because Windows NT supports full 32-bit addressing, it makes sense that integers are also 32 bits long. This means that types **int** and **unsigned** will be 32 bits, not 16 bits long as is the case for 16-bit Windows. If you want to use a 16-bit integer, it must be declared as **short**. (Portable **typedef** names are provided by Windows NT for these types, as you will see shortly.) This means that if you will be porting code from the 16-bit environment, you will need to check your use of integers, because they will automatically be expanded from 16 to 32 bits, and side effects may result.

Another result of 32-bit addressing is that pointers no longer need to be declared as **near** or **far**. Any pointer can access any part of memory. In Windows NT, both **far** and **near** are defined as nothing. This means you can leave **far** and **near** in your programs when porting to Windows NT, but they will have no effect.

The Components of a Window

Before moving on to specific aspects of Windows NT programming, a few important terms need to be defined. Figure 2-1 shows a standard window with each of its elements pointed out.

All windows have a border that defines the limits of the window and is used to resize the window. At the top of the window are several items. On the far left is the system menu icon (or box, as it is commonly called). Clicking on this box causes the system menu to be displayed. To the right of the system menu

Figure 2-1

The elements of a standard window

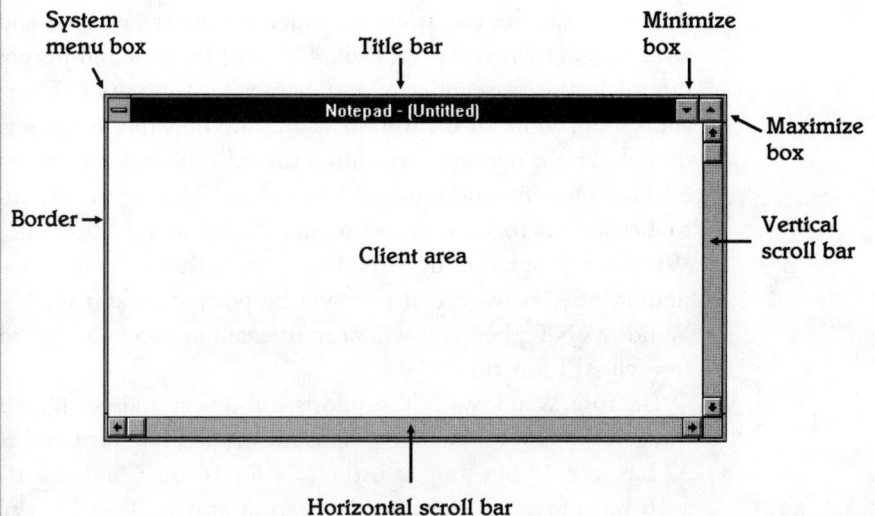

box is the window's title. At the far right are the minimize and maximize boxes. The client area is the part of the window in which your program activity takes place. Most windows also have horizontal and vertical scroll bars that are used to move text through the window.

Some Windows NT Application Basics

Before developing the Windows NT application skeleton, some basic concepts common to all Windows NT programs need to be discussed.

WinMain()

All Windows NT programs begin execution with a call to **WinMain()**. (Windows programs do not have a **main()** function.) **WinMain()** has some special properties that differentiate it from other functions in your application. First, it must be declared using the **WINAPI** calling convention. By default, functions in your C or C++ programs use the C calling convention. However, it is possible to compile a function so that it uses a different calling convention. For example, a common alternative is to use the Pascal calling convention. For various technical reasons, the calling convention Windows NT uses to call **WinMain()** is **WINAPI**. The return type of **WinMain()** should be **int**.

16-bit Conversion Note In 16-bit Windows, the calling convention used for **WinMain()** was **FAR PASCAL**. However, this should be changed to **WINAPI** when porting existing applications to Windows NT.

The Window Function

All Windows NT programs must contain a special function that is not called by your program, but is called by Windows NT. This function is generally called the *window function*. The window function is called by Windows NT when it needs to pass a message to your program. It is through this function that Windows NT communicates with your program. The window function receives the message in its parameters. All window functions must be declared as returning type **LRESULT CALLBACK**. The type **LRESULT** is a **typedef** that (at the time of this writing) is another name for **LONG**. The **CALLBACK** calling convention is used with those functions that will be called by Windows NT. In Windows terminology, any function that is called by Windows is referred to as a *callback function*.

16–bit Conversion Note 16–bit Windows code specifies the window function as **FAR PASCAL**. However, while Windows NT still allows this definition, for the sake of portability, you should use **CALLBACK** for all of your new Windows NT code. This will allow changes made to Windows NT in the future to be transparent to your code.

In addition to receiving the messages sent by Windows NT, the window function must initiate any actions indicated by a message. Typically, a window function's body consists of a **switch** statement that links a specific response to each message that the program will respond to. Your program need not respond to every message that Windows NT will send. For messages that your program doesn't care about, you can let Windows NT provide default processing. Since there are over 100 different messages that Windows NT can generate, it is common for most messages to simply be processed by Windows NT and not by your program.

All messages are 32-bit integer values. Further, all messages are linked with any additional information that the message requires.

Window Classes

When your Windows NT program first begins execution, it will need to define and register a *window class*. (Here, the word *class* is not being used in its C++ sense. Rather, it means *style* or *type*.) When you register a window class, you are telling Windows NT about the form and function of the window. However, registering the window class does not cause a window to come into existence. To actually create a window requires additional steps.

The Message Loop

As explained earlier, Windows NT (and Windows in general) communicates with your program by sending it messages. All Windows NT applications must establish a *message loop* inside the **WinMain()** function. This loop reads any pending message from the application's message queue and then dispatches that message back to Windows NT, which then calls your program's window function with that message as a parameter. This may seem to be an overly complex way of passing messages, but it is, nevertheless, the way that all Windows programs must function. (Part of the reason for this is to return control to Windows NT so that the scheduler can allocate CPU time as it sees fit, rather than waiting for your application's time slice to end.)

Windows Data Types

As you will soon see, Windows NT programs do not make extensive use standard C/C++ data types, such as **int** or **char** ★. Instead, most data types used by Windows NT have been **typdef**ed within the **windows.h** file and/or its related files. This file is supplied by Microsoft (and any other company that makes a Windows NT C/C++ compiler) and must be included in all Windows NT programs. Some of the most common types are **HANDLE, HWND, BYTE, WORD, DWORD, UINT, LONG, BOOL, LPSTR**, and **LPCSTR. HANDLE** is a 32-bit integer that is used as a handle. As you will see, there are a number of handle types, but they all are the same size as **HANDLE.** A *handle* is simply a value that identifies some resource. For example, **HWND** is a 32-bit integer that is used as a window handle. Also, all handle types begin with an *H.* **BYTE** is an 8-bit unsigned character. **WORD** is a 16-bit unsigned short integer. **DWORD** is an unsigned long integer. **UINT** is an unsigned 32-bit integer. **LONG** is another name for **long. BOOL** is an integer. This type is used to indicate values that are either true or false. **LPSTR** is a pointer to a string, and **LPCSTR** is a **const** pointer to a string.

In addition to the basic types described above, Windows NT defines several structures. The two that are needed by the skeleton program are **MSG** and **WNDCLASS**. The **MSG** structure holds a Windows NT message and **WNDCLASS** is a structure that defines a window class. These structures will be discussed later in this chapter.

▬▬▬

16-bit Conversion Note **UINT** is a 32-bit unsigned integer when compiling Windows NT programs. It becomes a 16-bit unsigned integer if you compile your code for 16-bit Windows.

A Windows NT Skeleton

Now that the necessary background information has been covered, it is time to develop a minimal Windows NT application. As stated, all Windows NT programs have certain things in common. In this section a Windows NT skeleton is developed that provides these necessary features. In the world of Windows programming, application skeletons are commonly used, because there is a substantial "price of admission" when creating a Windows program. Unlike DOS programs that you may have written, in which a minimal program is about five lines long, a minimal Windows program is approximately 50 lines long. Therefore, application skeletons are commonly used in developing Windows applications.

A minimal Windows NT program contains two functions: **WinMain()** and the window function. The **WinMain()** function must perform the following general steps:

1. Define a window class

2. Register that class with Windows NT

3. Create a window of that class

4. Display the window

5. Begin running the message loop

The window function must respond to all relevant messages. Since the skeleton program does nothing but display its window, the only message that it must respond to is the one that tells the application that the user has terminated the program.

Before discussing the specifics, let us examine the following program, which is a minimal Windows NT skeleton. It creates a standard window that includes a title. The window also contains the system menu and is, therefore, capable of being minimized, maximized, moved, resized, and closed. It also contains the standard minimized and maximized icons.

```
/* A minimal Windows NT skeleton. */

/* The following definition causes stricter type checking.
   This is optional, but suggested because it will help
   catch potential type mismatch errors--especially
   when porting from 16-bit Windows. */
```

```
#define STRICT
"
#include <windows.h>

LRESULT CALLBACK WindowFunc(HWND, UINT, WPARAM, LPARAM);

char szWinName[] = "MyWin"; /* name of window class */

int WINAPI WinMain(HINSTANCE hThisInst, HINSTANCE hPrevInst,
                   LPSTR lpszArgs, int nWinMode)
{
  HWND hwnd;
  MSG msg;
  WNDCLASS wcl;

  /* Define a window class. */
  wcl.hInstance = hThisInst; /* handle to this instance */
  wcl.lpszClassName = szWinName; /* window class name */
  wcl.lpfnWndProc = WindowFunc; /* window function */
  wcl.style = 0; /* default style */

  wcl.hIcon = LoadIcon(NULL, IDI_APPLICATION); /* icon style */
  wcl.hCursor = LoadCursor(NULL, IDC_ARROW); /* cursor style */
  wcl.lpszMenuName = 0; /* no menu */

  wcl.cbClsExtra = 0; /* no extra */
  wcl.cbWndExtra = 0; /* information needed */

  /* Make the window light gray. */
  wcl.hbrBackground = GetStockObject(LTGRAY_BRUSH);

  /* Register the window class. */
  if(!RegisterClass (&wcl)) return 0;

  /* Now that a window class has been registered, a window
     can be created. */
  hwnd = CreateWindow(
    szWinName, /* name of window class */
    "Windows NT Skeleton", /* title */
    WS_OVERLAPPEDWINDOW, /* window style--normal */
    CW_USEDEFAULT, /* X coordinate--let Windows decide */
    CW_USEDEFAULT, /* Y coordinate--let Windows decide */
    CW_USEDEFAULT, /* width--let Windows decide */
```

```
        CW_USEDEFAULT, /* height--let Windows decide */
         NULL, /* handle of parent window--there isn't one */
         NULL, /* no menu */
         hThisInst, /* handle of this instance of the program */
         NULL /* no additional arguments */
      );

      /* Display the window. */
      ShowWindow(hwnd, nWinMode);
      UpdateWindow(hwnd);

      /* Create the message loop. */
      while(GetMessage(&msg, NULL, 0, 0))
      {
        TranslateMessage(&msg); /* allow use of keyboard */
        DispatchMessage(&msg); /* return control to Windows */
      }
      return msg.wParam;
    }


/* This function is called by Windows NT and is passed
   messages from the message queue.
*/
LRESULT CALLBACK WindowFunc(HWND hwnd, UINT message, WPARAM wParam,
                LPARAM lParam)
{
  switch(message) {
    case WM_DESTROY: /* terminate the program */
      PostQuitMessage(0);
      break;
    default:
      /* Let Windows NT process any messages not specified in
         the preceding switch statement. */
      return DefWindowProc(hwnd, message, wParam, lParam);
  }
  return 0;
}
```

Let's go through this program step by step.

First, all Windows NT programs must include the header **windows.h**. As stated, this file contains the API function prototypes and various types and definitions used by Windows NT. For example, the data types **HWND** and **WNDCLASS** are defined in **windows.h**. As the comment before the **#define** statement indicates, by defining the macro **STRICT**, you cause the compiler to perform stronger type checking. (It must be defined before you include **windows.h**.) You will want to define this macro when you first begin to develop Windows NT programs, or if you are porting old 16-bit Windows applications. This option may not be available if you are using a compiler other than Microsoft's. If it isn't, then simply leave out the satement.

The window function used by the program is called **WindowFunc()**. It is declared as a callback function, because this is the function that Windows NT calls to communicate with the program.

As stated, program execution begins with **WinMain()**. **WinMain()** is passed four parameters. **hThisInst** and **hPrevInst** are handles. **hThisInst** refers to the current instance of the program. Remember, Windows NT is a multitasking system, so it is possible that more than one instance of your program may be running at the same time. **hPrevInst** will always be NULL. (In 16-bit Windows programs, **hPrevInst** would be non-zero if there were other instances of the program currently executing, but this no longer applies to Windows NT.) The **lpszArgs** parameter is a pointer to a string that holds any command line arguments specified when the application was begun. The **nWinMode** parameter contains a value that determines if the window will be displayed when your program begins execution or shown only in its iconic form.

Inside the function, three variables are created. The **hwnd** variable will hold a value that identifies the program's window. The **msg** structure variable will hold window messages, and the **wcl** structure variable will be used to define the window class.

16-bit Conversion Note As mentioned above, the **hPrevInst** parameter will always be NULL in a Windows NT program. The reason for this is because of a fundamental change between 16-bit Windows and Windows NT. In 16-bit Windows, multiple instances of a program share window classes and various other bits of data. Therefore, it was important for an application to know if another version of itself was running in the system. However, in Windows NT each process is isolated from the next, and there is no automatic sharing of window classes and the like. The only reason that the **hPrevInst** exists in Windows NT is for the sake of compatibility.

Defining the Window Class

The first two actions that **WinMain()** takes is to define a window class and then register it. A window class is defined by filling in the fields defined by the **WNDCLASS** structure. Its fields are shown here:

```
UINT style; /* type of window */
WNDPROC lpfnWndProc; /* address to window func */
int cbClsExtra; /* extra class info */
int cbWndExtra; /* extra window info */
HINSTANCE hInstance; /* handle of this instance */
HICON hIcon; /* handle of minimized icon */
HCURSOR hCursor; /* handle of mouse cursor */
HBRUSH hbrBackground; /* background color */
LPCSTR lpszMenuName; /* name of main menu */
LPCSTR lpszClassName; /* name of window class */
```

As you can see by looking at the program, the **hInstance** field is assigned the current instance handle as specified by **hThisInst**. The name of the window class is pointed to by **lpszClassName**, which points to the string "MyWin" in this case. The address of the window function is assigned to **lpfnWndProc**. No default style is specified. No extra information is needed.

■■■■

16-bit Conversion Note In 16-bit Windows, each window class must be registered only once. Therefore, if another instance of the program is running, then the current instance must not define and register the window class. To avoid this possibility, the value of **hPrevInst** is tested. If it is non-zero, then the window class has already been registered by a previous instance. If not, then the window class is defined and registered. However, this test is no longer needed by Windows NT and is not included in any of the examples in this book. However, for downward compatibility with 16-bit Windows, you may wish to include it, and doing so causes no harm.

All Windows applications need to define a default shape for the mouse cursor and for the minimized icon. An application can define its own custom version of these resources, or it may use one of the built-in styles, as the skeleton does. The style of the minimized icon is loaded by the API function **LoadIcon()**, whose prototype is shown here:

HICON LoadIcon(HANDLE *hInst*, LPCSTR *lpszName*);

This function returns a handle to an icon. Here, *hInst* specifies the handle of the module that contains the icon, and its name is specified in *lpszName*. However, to use one of the built-in icons, you must use NULL for the first parameter and specify one of the following macros for the second:

Icon Macro	Shape
IDI_APPLICATION	Default icon
IDI_ASTERISK	Information icon
IDI_EXLAMATION	Exclamation point icon
IDI_HAND	Stop sign
IDI_QUESTION	Question mark icon

To load the mouse cursor, use the API **LoadCursor()** function. This function has the following prototype:

HCURSOR LoadCursor(HANDLE *hInst*, LPCSTR *lpszName*);

This function returns a handle to a cursor resource. Here, *hInst* specifies the handle of the module that contains the mouse cursor and its name is specified in *lpszName*. However, to use one of the built-in cursors, you must use NULL for the first parameter and specify one of the built-in cursors using its macros for the second parameter. Some of the most common built-in cursors are shown here:

Cursor Macro	Shape
IDC_ARROW	Default arrow pointer
IDC_CROSS	Crosshairs
IDC_IBEAM	Vertical I-beam
IDC_WAIT	Hourglass

The background color of the window created by the skeleton is specified as light gray, and a handle to this *brush* is obtained using the API function **GetStockObject()**. A brush is a resource that paints the screen using a predetermined size, color, and pattern. The function **GetStockObject()** is used to obtain a handle to a number of standard display objects, including brushes, pens (which draw lines), and character fonts. It has this prototype:

HGDIOBJ GetStockObject(int *object*);

The function returns a handle to the object specified by *object*. Here are some of the built-in brushes available to your program:

Macro Name	Background Type
BLACK_BRUSH	Black
DKGRAY_BRUSH	Dark gray
HOLLOW_BRUSH	See through window
LTGRAY_BRUSH	Light gray
WHITE_BRUSH	White

You may use these macros as parameters to **GetStockObject()** to obtain a brush. Once the window class has been fully specified, it is registered with Windows NT using the API function **RegisterClass()**, whose prototype is shown here:

ATOM RegisterClass(LPWNDCLASS *lpWClass*);

The function returns a value that identifies the window class. **ATOM** is a **typedef** of **int**. Each window class is given a unique value. The type **LPWNDCLASS** is a pointer to a **WNDCLASS** structure. Therefore, *lpWClass* must be the address of a **WNDCLASS** structure.

▬▬▬

16-bit Conversion Note The return value of **RegisterClass()** for 16-bit Windows was a Boolean value indicating success (true) or failure (false). This has been changed in Windows NT to a value that identifies the class.

Creating a Window

Once a window class has been defined and registered, your application can actually create a window of that class using the API function **CreateWindow()**, whose prototype is shown here:

```
HWND CreateWindow(
     LPCSTR lpszClassName, /* name of window class */
     LPCSTR lpszWinName, /* title of window */
     DWORD dwStyle, /* type of window */
     int X, int Y, /* upper-left coordinates */
     int Width, int Height, /* dimensions of window */
```

```
        HWND hParent, /* handle of parent window */
        HMENU hMenu, /* handle of main menu */
        HINSTANCE hThisInst, /* handle of creator */
        LPVOID lpszAdditional /* pointer to additional info */
);
```

As you can see by looking at the skeleton program, many of the parameters to **CreateWindow()** may be defaulted or specified as NULL. In fact, most often the *X, Y, Width,* and *Height* parameters will simply use the macro **CW_USEDEFAULT**, which tells Windows NT to select an appropriate size and location for the window. If the window has no parent, which is the case in the skeleton, then *hParent* must be specified as NULL. (You may also use the macro **HWND_DESKTOP** for this parameter.) If the window does not contain a main menu, then *hMenu* must be NULL. Also, if no additional information is required, as is most often the case, then *lpszAdditional* is NULL.

The remaining four parameters must be explicitly set by your program. First, *lpszClassName* must point to the name of the window class. (This is the name you gave it when it was registered.) The title of the window is a string pointed to by *lpszWinName.* This can be a null string, but usually a window will be given a title. The style (or type) of window actually created is determined by the value of *dwStyle.* The macro **WS_OVERLAPPEDWINDOW** specifies a standard window that has a system menu, a border, minimize, and maximize boxes. While this style of window is the most common, you can construct one to your own specifications. To accomplish this, you simply OR together the various style macros that you want. Some other common styles are shown here:

Style Macro	Window Feature
WS_OVERLAPPED	Overlapped window with border
WS_MAXIMIZEBOX	Maximize box
WS_MINIMIZEBOX	Minimize box
WS_SYSMENU	System menu
WS_HSCROLL	Horizontal scroll bar
WS_VSCROLL	Vertical scroll bar

The *hThisInst* parameter must contain the current instance handle of the application.

The **CreateWindow()** function returns the handle of the window it creates or NULL if the window cannot be created.

Once the window has been created, it is still not displayed on the screen. To cause the window to be displayed, call the **ShowWindow()** API function. This function has the following prototype:

BOOL ShowWindow(HWND *hwnd,* int *nHow*);

The handle of the window to display is specified in *hwnd.* The display mode is specified in *nHow.* The first time the window is displayed, you will want to pass **WinMain()**'s **nWinMode** as the *nHow* parameter. Remember, the value of **nWinMode** determines whether the window will be displayed as an icon or as an active window when the program begins execution. Subsequent calls can display (or remove) the window as necessary. Some common values for *nHow* are shown here:

Display Macro	Effect
SW_HIDE	Removes the window
SW_MINIMIZE	Minimizes the window into an icon
SW_MAXIMIZE	Maximizes the window
SW_RESTORE	Returns a window to normal size

The **ShowWindow()** function returns the previous display status of the window. If the window was displayed, then non-zero is returned. If the window was not displayed, then zero is returned.

Although not technically necessary for the skeleton, a call to **UpdateWindow()** is included, because it is needed by virtually every Windows NT application that you will create. It essentially tells Windows NT to send a message to your application that the main window needs to be updated. (This message will be discussed in the next chapter.)

The Message Loop

The final part of the skeletal **WinMain()** is the message loop. The *message loop* is a part of all Windows applications. Its purpose is to receive and process messages sent by Windows NT. When an application is running, it is continually being sent messages. These messages are stored in the application's message queue until they can be read and processed. Each time your application is ready to read another message, it must call the API function **GetMessage()**, which has this prototype:

BOOL GetMessage(LPMSG *msg,* HWND *hwnd,* UINT *min,* UINT *max*);

The message will be received by the structure pointed to by *msg*. All Window messages are of structure type **MSG**, shown here:

```
/* Message structure */
typedef struct tagMSG
  {
    HWND hwnd; // window that message is for
    UINT message; // message
    WPARAM wParam; // message-dependent info
    LPARAM lParam; // more message-dependent info
    DWORD time; // time message posted
    POINT pt; // X,Y location of mouse
  } MSG;
```

In **MSG**, the handle of the window for which the message is intended is contained in **hwnd**. All Windows NT messages are 32-bit integers and the message is contained in **message**. Additional information relating to each message is passed in **wParam** and **lParam**. The type **WPARAM** is a **typedef** for **UINT**, and **LPARAM** is a **typedef** for **LONG**.

16–bit Conversion Note The **message** field of **MSG** is 16 bits long in 16-bit Windows, but it is widened to 32 bits for Windows NT. Also, the **wParam** field, which is 16 bits in 16-bit Windows, has been widened to 32 bits in Windows NT. Be aware of these change when porting code.

The time the message was sent is specified in milliseconds since the application began execution in the **time** field.

The structure **POINT** is defined like this:

```
typedef struct tagPOINT {
  LONG x, y;
} POINT;
```

The **pt** field will contain the coordinates of the mouse when the message was sent.

16–bit Windows Conversion Note In 16-bit Windows, the **x** and **y** in the **POINT** structure are declared as integers. However, in Windows NT, they are widened to **LONG**.

If there are no messages in the application's message queue, then a call to **GetMessage()** will pass control back to Windows NT. (We will explore messages in greater detail in the next chapter.)

The *hwnd* parameter to **GetMessage()** specifies the window for which messages will be obtained. It is possible (even likely) that an application will contain several windows, and you may only want to receive messages for a specific window. If you want to receive all messages directed at your application, this parameter must be NULL.

The remaining two parameters to **GetMessage()** specify a range of messages that will be received. Generally, you want your application to receive all messages. To accomplish this, specify both *min* and *max* as 0, as the skeleton does.

GetMessage() returns zero when the user terminates the program, causing the message loop to terminate. Otherwise it returns non-zero.

Inside the message loop two functions are called. The first is the API function **TranslateMessage()**. This function translates virtual key codes generated by Windows NT into actual characters. (Virtual keys are discussed later in this book.) Although not necessary for all applications, most call **TranslateMessage()** , because it is needed to allow full integration of the keyboard into your application program.

Once the message has been read and translated, it is dispatched back to Windows NT using the **DispatchMessage()** API function. Windows NT then holds this message until it can pass it to the program's window function.

Once the message loop terminates, the **WinMain()** function ends by returning the value of **msg.wParam** to Windows NT. This value contains the return code generated when your program terminates.

The Window Function

The second function in the application skeleton is its window function. In this case the function is called **WindowFunc()**, but it could have any name you like. The window function is passed the first four members of the **MSG** structure as parameters. For the skeleton, the only parameter that is used is the message itself. However, in the next chapter you will learn more about the parameters to this function.

The skeleton's window function responds to only one message explicitly: **WM_DESTROY**. This message is sent when the user terminates the program. When this message is received, your program must execute a call to the API function **PostQuitMessage()**. The argument to this function is an exit code that is returned in **msg.wParam** inside **WinMain()**. Calling **PostQuitMessage()** causes a **WM_QUIT** message to be sent to your application, which causes **GetMessage()** to return false and thus stops your program.

Any other messages received by **WindowFunc()** are passed along to Windows NT, via a call to **DefWindowProc()**, for default processing. This step is necessary because all messages must be dealt with in one fashion or another.

Using a Definition File

If you are familiar with 16-bit Windows programming, then you have used *definition files*. For 16-bit Windows, all programs need to have a definition file associated with them. A definition file is simply a text file that specifies certain information and settings needed by your 16-bit Windows program. However, because of the 32-bit architecture of Windows NT (and other improvements), definition files are not needed for Windows NT programs. However, there is no harm in supplying a definition file; if you want to include one for the sake of downward compatibility with 16-bit Windows, then you are free to do so.

If you are new to Windows programming in general and you don't know what a definition file is, the following discussion will give you a brief overview.

All definition files use the extension .DEF. For example, the definition file for the skeleton program could be called SKEL.DEF. Here is a definition file that you can use to provide downward compatibility to 16-bit Windows.

```
NAME Windows NT Skeleton
DESCRIPTION 'Skeleton Program'
EXETYPE WINDOWS
CODE PRELOAD MOVEABLE DISCARDABLE
DATA PRELOAD MOVEABLE MULTIPLE
HEAPSIZE 8192
STACKSIZE 8192
EXPORTS WindowFunc
```

This file specifies the name of the program and its description, both of which are optional. It also states that the executable file will be compatible with Windows (rather than DOS, for example). The CODE statement tells Windows to load all of the program at startup (PRELOAD), that the code may be moved in memory (MOVEABLE), and that the code may be removed from memory and reloaded if (and when) necessary (DISCARDABLE). The file also states that your program's data must be loaded upon execution and may be moved about in memory. It also specifies that each instance of the program has its own data (MULTIPLE). Next, the size of the heap and stack allocated to the program is specified. Finally, the name of the window function is exported. Exporting allows Windows to call the function.

remember: *Definition files are not needed when programming for Windows NT. However, they cause no harm and may be included for downward compatibility with 16-bit Windows.*

Compiling the Skeleton Program

The exact commands and methods that you use to compile a Windows NT program will differ depending upon two things. First, the exact commands will differ between different compilers. Second, over time, the actual compilation commands will evolve as a compiler changes. Therefore, the following information is only a guide. You will need to check your compiler's user manual for the precise information.

At the time of this writing, the following command sequence will compile and link the Windows NT skeleton program using the Microsoft Software Developer's Kit (SDK) C/C++ compiler. (This sequence assumes that the skeleton is called SKEL.C.)

```
cl386 skel.c -c -Di386=1 -DWIN32 -D_X86_=1
link skel.obj -subsystem:windows -entry:WinMainCRTStartup
    -out:skel.exe libc.lib ntdll.lib kernel32.lib user32.lib
    gdi32.lib winspool.lib comdlg32.lib
```

Because most Windows NT programs are more complicated than the simple skeleton, it is generally best to use a make file for each program you develop. Towards this end, the following make file will compile the skeleton program, assuming that you are using the Microsoft SDK for Windows NT.

```
# Make File for Windows NT
#
# For Microsoft's Windows NT Software Developers Kit
# (SDK) Compiler and associated tools.
#
!include <ntwin32.mak>
all: skel.exe

skel.obj: skel.c
 $(cc) $(cflags) $(cvars) skel.c

skel.exe: skel.obj
    $(link) $(guiflags) -out:skel.exe skel.obj $(guilibs)
```

At the time of this writing, the make program supplied in the Windows NT SDK is called NMAKE. (For information about using the make program supplied by your compiler, consult your user manuals.)

Naming Conventions

Before finishing this chapter, a short comment on naming functions and variables needs to be made. If you are new to Windows NT programming, several of the variable and parameter names in the skeleton program and their descriptions probably seemed rather unusual. The reason for this is that they follow a set of naming conventions that was invented by Microsoft for Windows programming. For functions, the name consists of a verb followed by a noun. The first character of the verb and noun are capitalized.

For variable names, Microsoft chose to use a rather complex system of embedding the data type into a variable's name. To accomplish this, a lowercase type prefix is added to the start of the variable's name. The name, itself, is begun with a capital letter. The type prefixes are shown in Table 2-1. Frankly, the use of type prefixes is controversial and is not universally supported. Many Windows programmers use this method, many do not. This method will be used by the Windows NT programs in this book when it seems reasonable to do so. However, you are free to use any naming convention you like.

Prefix	Data Type
b	Boolean (one byte)
c	Character (one byte)
dw	Long unsigned integer
f	16-bit bitfield
h	Handle
l	Long integer
lp	Long pointer
n	Short integer
p	Short pointer
pt	Long integer holding screen coordinates
w	Short unsigned integer
sz	Pointer to null-terminated string
lpsz	Long pointer to null-terminated string
rgb	Long integer holding RGB color values

Table 2-2
Variable Type Prefix Characters

Chapter 3

Processing Messages

a s explained in Chapter 2, Windows NT communicates with your application by sending it messages. For this reason, the processing of these messages is at the core of all Windows NT applications. In the previous chapter you learned how to create a skeletal Windows NT application. In this chapter, that skeleton will be expanded to receive and process several common messages.

What Are Messages?

There are a large number of Windows NT messages. Each message is represented by a unique 32-bit integer value. In the header file **windows.h** there are standard names for these messages. Generally, you will use the macro name, not the actual integer value, when referring to a message. Here are some common Windows NT message macros:

    WM_CHAR
    WM_PAINT
    WM_MOVE
    WM_LBUTTONUP
    WM_LBUTTONDOWN

Two other values accompany each message and contain information related to the specific message. One of these values is of type **WPARAM**, the other is of type **LPARAM**. For Windows NT, both of these types translate into 32-bit integers. These values are called **wParam** and **lParam**, respectively. They typically hold things like cursor or mouse coordinates; the value of a key press; or a system related value, such as character size. As each message is discussed, the meaning of the values contained in **wParam** and **lParam** will be described.

16-bit Conversion Note In 16–bit windows, **wParam** is a 16-bit value. However, in Windows NT, it is a 32-bit value. This change causes a few messages to be different between the two versions of Windows. These differences will be noted as needed.

As mentioned in Chapter 2, the function that actually processes Windows NT messages is your program's window function. As you should recall, this function is passed four parameters: the handle of the window that the message is for, the message itself, and the last two parameters are **wParam** and **lParam**.

Sometimes two pieces of information are encoded into the two words that comprise the **wParam** and **lParam** parameters. To provide easy access to each half of **wParam** and **lParam**, Windows NT defines two macros called **LOWORD** and **HIWORD**. They return the low-order and high-order words of a long integer, respectively. They are used like this:

    x = LOWORD(lParam);

    x = HIWORD(lParam);

You will see these macros in use later in this chapter.

Responding to a Key Press

One of the most common Windows NT messages is generated when a key is pressed. This message is called **WM_CHAR.** It is important to understand that your application never receives keystrokes, per se, directly from the keyboard. Instead, each time a key is pressed, a **WM_CHAR** message is sent to the active window. To see how this process works, this section extends the skeletal application developed in Chapter 2 so that it processes keystroke messages.

Each time a **WM_CHAR** is sent, **wParam** contains the ASCII value of the key pressed. **LOWORD(lParam)** contains the number of times the key has been repeated as a result of the key being held down. The bits of **HI-WORD(lParam)** are encoded as shown here:

15: Set if the key is being released; cleared if the
key had been released and is now being pressed.

14: Set if the key was pressed before the message was sent; cleared if it was not pressed.

13: Set if the ALT key is also being pressed; cleared if ALT is not pressed.

12: Used by Windows NT.

11: Used by Windows NT.

10: Used by Windows NT.

9: Used by Windows NT.

8: Set if the key pressed is a function key or an extended key; cleared otherwise.

7—0: Manufacturer–dependent key code.

For our purposes, the only value that is important at this time is **wParam**, since it holds the key that was pressed. However, notice how detailed the information is that Windows NT supplies about the state of the system. Of course, you are free to use as much or as little of this information as you like.

To process a **WM_CHAR** message, you must add it to the **switch** statement inside your program's window function. For example, here is a window function that processes a keystroke by displaying it on the screen.

```
char str[80] = ""; /* holds output string */

LRESULT CALLBACK WindowFunc(HWND hwnd, UINT message, WPARAM wParam,
            LPARAM lParam)
{
  HDC hdc;

  switch(message) {
    case WM_CHAR: /* process keystroke */
      hdc = GetDC(hwnd); /* get device context */
      TextOut(hdc, 1, 1, "  ", 2); /* erase old character */
      sprintf(str, "%c", (char) wParam); /* stringize character */
      TextOut(hdc, 1, 1, str, strlen(str)); /* output char */
      ReleaseDC(hwnd, hdc); /* release device context */
```

```
        break;
    case WM_DESTROY: /* terminate the program */
        PostQuitMessage(0);
        break;
    default:
        /* Let Windows NT process any messages not specified in
           the preceding switch statement. */
        return DefWindowProc(hwnd, message, wParam, lParam);
    }
    return 0;
}
```

The purpose of the code inside the **WM_CHAR** case is very simple: it simply echoes the key to the screen! You are probably surprised that it takes so many lines of code to accomplish this seemingly trivial feat. There are two reasons for this. First, Windows NT is multitasking and you cannot output a character if your program is not the focus of output—for example, if another task has overlaid your window. The second reason is that another part of your program may have overlaid your window. In either situation, before performing output, your program must first acquire permission. This is done by calling **GetDC()**. This obtains a *device context*. For now, don't worry about what this means. It will be discussed in the next section. However, once you obtain a device context, you may write to the screen. At the end of the process, the device context is released using **ReleaseDC()**. Your program must release the device context when it is done with it. If it doesn't, the device context cannot be granted to another program or to your own program when requested again. Both **GetDC()** and **ReleaseDC()** are API functions. Their prototypes are shown here:

HDC GetDC(HWND *hwnd*);

int ReleaseDC(HWND *hwnd*, HDC *hdc*);

GetDC() returns a device context associated with the window whose handle is specified by *hwnd*. The type **HDC** specifies a handle to a device context.

ReleaseDC() returns true if the device context was released, false otherwise. The *hwnd* parameter is the handle of the window for which the device context is released. The *hdc* parameter is the handle of the device context obtained through the call to **GetDC()**.

The function that actually outputs the character is the API function **TextOut()**. Its prototype is shown here:

BOOL TextOut(HDC *DC*, int *x*, int *y*, LPCSTR *lpstr*,
int *ncount*);

The type **BOOL** is an integer that holds true/false values. The **TextOut()** function outputs the string pointed to by *lpstr* at the screen coordinates specified by *x, y*. The length of the string is specified in *ncount*. The **TextOut()** function returns non–zero if successful, zero otherwise.

In the function, each time a **WM_CHAR** message is received, the character that is typed by the user is converted, using **sprintf()**, into a string one character long and then displayed using **TextOut()** at location 1, 1. (The string **str** is global because it will need to keep its value between function calls in later examples.) In a window, the upper left corner of the client area is location 0, 0. Window coordinates are always relative to the window, not the screen. Therefore, as characters are entered, they are displayed in the upper left corner no matter where the window is physically located on the screen.

The reason for the first call to **TextOut()** is to erase whatever previous character was just displayed. Because Windows NT is a graphics–based system, characters are of different sizes, and the overwriting of one character by another does not necessarily cause all of the previous character to be erased. For example, if you typed a **w** followed by an **i,** part of the **w** would still be displayed if it wasn't manually erased. (Try commenting out the first call to **TextOut()** and observe what happens.)

It is important to understand that no Windows NT API function will allow output beyond the borders of a window. Output will automatically be clipped to prevent the boundaries from being crossed.

At first you might think that using **TextOut()** to output a character is not an efficient application of the function. The fact is that Windows NT (and Windows, in general) does not contain a function that simply outputs a character. As you will see, Windows NT performs much of its user interaction through dialog and menu boxes. For this reason it only contains a few functions that output text to the client area.

Here is the entire skeleton that processes keystrokes.

```
/* A minimal Windows NT skeleton that processes the
   WM_CHAR message. */

/* The following definition causes stricter type checking.
   This is optional, but suggested because it will help
   catch potential type mismatch errors--especially
   when porting from 16-bit Windows. */
#define STRICT
```

```
#include <windows.h>
#include <string.h>
#include <stdio.h>

LRESULT CALLBACK WindowFunc(HWND, UINT, WPARAM, LPARAM);

char szWinName[] = "MyWin"; /* name of window class */

char str[80] = ""; /* holds output string */

int WINAPI WinMain(HINSTANCE hThisInst, HINSTANCE hPrevInst,
                   LPSTR lpszArgs, int nWinMode)
{
  HWND hwnd;
  MSG msg;
  WNDCLASS wcl;

  /* Define a window class. */
  wcl.hInstance = hThisInst; /* handle to this instance */
  wcl.lpszClassName = szWinName; /* window class name */
  wcl.lpfnWndProc = WindowFunc; /* window function */
  wcl.style = 0; /* default style */

  wcl.hIcon = LoadIcon(NULL, IDI_APPLICATION); /* icon style */
  wcl.hCursor = LoadCursor(NULL, IDC_ARROW); /* cursor style */
  wcl.lpszMenuName = NULL; /* no menu */

  wcl.cbClsExtra = 0; /* no extra */
  wcl.cbWndExtra = 0; /* information needed */

  /* Make the window light gray. */
  wcl.hbrBackground = GetStockObject(LTGRAY_BRUSH);

  /* Register the window class. */
  if(!RegisterClass (&wcl)) return 0;

  /* Now that a window class has been registered, a window
     can be created. */
  hwnd = CreateWindow(
    szWinName, /* name of window class */
    "Windows NT Skeleton", /* title */
    WS_OVERLAPPEDWINDOW, /* window style--normal */
    CW_USEDEFAULT, /* X coordinate--let Windows decide */
```

```
      CW_USEDEFAULT, /* Y coordinate--let Windows decide */
      CW_USEDEFAULT, /* width--let Windows decide */
      CW_USEDEFAULT, /* height--let Windows decide */
      NULL, /* handle of parent window--there isn't one */
      NULL, /* no menu */
      hThisInst, /* handle of this instance of the program */
      NULL /* no additional arguments */
    );

    /* Display the window. */
    ShowWindow(hwnd, nWinMode);
    UpdateWindow(hwnd);

    /* Create the message loop. */
    while(GetMessage(&msg, NULL, 0, 0))
    {
      TranslateMessage(&msg); /* allow use of keyboard */
      DispatchMessage(&msg); /* return control to Windows */
    }
    return msg.wParam;
}


/* This function is called by Windows NT and is passed
   messages from the message queue.
*/
LRESULT CALLBACK WindowFunc(HWND hwnd, UINT message, WPARAM wParam,
                LPARAM lParam)
{
  HDC hdc;

  switch(message) {
    case WM_CHAR: /* process keystroke */
      hdc = GetDC(hwnd); /* get device context */
      TextOut(hdc, 1, 1, "  ", 2); /* erase old character */
      sprintf(str, "%c", (char) wParam); /* stringize character */
      TextOut(hdc, 1, 1, str, strlen(str)); /* output char */
      ReleaseDC(hwnd, hdc); /* release device context */
      break;
    case WM_DESTROY: /* terminate the program */
      PostQuitMessage(0);
      break;
    default:
      /* Let Windows NT process any messages not specified in
         the preceding switch statement. */
```

```
        return DefWindowProc(hwnd, message, wParam, lParam);
    }
    return 0;
}
```

Device Contexts

The program in the previous section had to obtain a device context prior to outputting to the window. Also, that device context had to be released prior to the termination of that function. It is now time to understand what a device context is. A device context is an output path from your Windows NT application, through the appropriate device driver, to the client area of your window. The device context also fully defines the state of the device driver.

Before your application can output information to the client area of the window, a device context must be obtained. Until this is done, there is no linkage between your program and the window relative to output. As mentioned earlier, several things can occur that will temporarily prevent a device context from being obtained. For example, another application may prevent the device context from being granted to your application. In any event, remember that it is necessary to obtain a device context prior to performing any output to a window. Since **TextOut()**, and other output functions, require a handle to a device context, this is a self-enforcing rule.

Processing the WM_PAINT Message

Before continuing, again run the program from the previous section and enter a few characters. Next, minimize and then restore the window. As you will see, the last character typed is not displayed after the window is restored. Also, if the window is overwritten by another window and then redisplayed, the character is not redisplayed. The reason for this is simple: in general, Windows NT does not keep a record of what a window contains. Instead, it is your program's job to maintain the contents of a window. To help your program accomplish this, each time the contents of a window must be redisplayed, your program will be sent a **WM_PAINT** message. (This message will also be sent when your window is first displayed.) Each time your program receives this message it must redisplay the contents of the window. In this section, you will add a message response function that processes the **WM_PAINT** message.

note:

For various technical reasons, when the window is moved or resized, its contents are redisplayed. However, this will not occur when the window is minimized or overwritten and then redisplayed.

Before explaining how to respond to a **WM_PAINT** message it might be useful to explain why Windows NT does not automatically rewrite your window. The answer is short and to the point. In many situations, it is easier for your program, which has intimate knowledge of the contents of the window, to rewrite it than it would be for Windows NT to do so. While the merits of this approach have been much debated by programmers, you should simply accept it, because it is unlikely to change.

The first step to processing a **WM_PAINT** message is to add its **case** to the **switch** statement inside the window function, as shown here:

```
case WM_PAINT: /* process a repaint request */
  hdc = BeginPaint(hwnd, &paintstruct); /* get DC */
  TextOut(hdc, 1, 1, str, strlen(str)); /* output string */
  EndPaint(hwnd, &paintstruct); /* release DC */
  break;
```

Let's look at this closely. First, notice that a device context is obtained using a call to **BeginPaint()** instead of **GetDC()**. For various reasons, when you process a **WM_PAINT** message, you must obtain a device context using **BeginPaint()**, which has this prototype:

HDC BeginPaint(HWND *hwnd*, LPPAINTSTRUCT *lpPS*);

The second parameter is a pointer to a structure of type **PAINTSTRUCT**, which is defined like this:

```
typedef struct tagPAINTSTRUCT {
  HDC hdc; // handle to device context
  BOOL fErase; // true if background has been erased
  RECT rcPaint; // coordinates of region to redraw
  BOOL fRestore;  // reserved
  BOOL fIncUpdate; // reserved
  BYTE rgbReserved[16]; // reserved
} PAINTSTRUCT;
```

The type **RECT** is a structure that specifies the upper left and lower right coordinates of a rectangular region. This structure is shown here:

```
typedef tagRECT {
  LONG left, top; // upper left
  LONG right, bottom; // lower right
} RECT;
```

In **PAINTSTRUCT**, the **rcPaint** element contains the coordinates of the region of the window that needs to be repainted. For now, you will not need to use the contents of this structure, because you can assume that the entire window must be redisplayed. Once the device context has been obtained, the character is displayed. Next, the device context is released with a call to **EndPaint()**. (You cannot use **ReleaseDC()** with **BeginPaint()**.)

Here is the full program that now processes **WM_PAINT** messages:

```c
/* A minimal Windows NT skeleton that adds
   a WM_PAINT message. */

/* The following definition causes stricter type checking.
   This is optional, but suggested because it will help
   catch potential type mismatch errors--especially
   when porting from 16-bit Windows. */
#define STRICT

#include <windows.h>
#include <string.h>
#include <stdio.h>

LRESULT CALLBACK WindowFunc(HWND, UINT, WPARAM, LPARAM);

char szWinName[] = "MyWin"; /* name of window class */

char str[80] = "Windows NT Sample"; /* holds output string */

int WINAPI WinMain(HINSTANCE hThisInst, HINSTANCE hPrevInst,
                   LPSTR lpszArgs, int nWinMode)
{
  HWND hwnd;
  MSG msg;
  WNDCLASS wcl;

  /* Define a window class. */
  wcl.hInstance = hThisInst; /* handle to this instance */
  wcl.lpszClassName = szWinName; /* window class name */
  wcl.lpfnWndProc = WindowFunc; /* window function */
```

```
wcl.style = 0; /* default style */

wcl.hIcon = LoadIcon(NULL, IDI_APPLICATION); /* icon style */
wcl.hCursor = LoadCursor(NULL, IDC_ARROW); /* cursor style */
wcl.lpszMenuName = NULL; /* no menu */

wcl.cbClsExtra = 0; /* no extra */
wcl.cbWndExtra = 0; /* information needed */

/* Make the window light gray. */
wcl.hbrBackground = GetStockObject(LTGRAY_BRUSH);

/* Register the window class. */
if(!RegisterClass (&wcl)) return 0;

/* Now that a window class has been registered, a window
   can be created. */
hwnd = CreateWindow(
  szWinName, /* name of window class */
  "Windows NT Skeleton", /* title */
  WS_OVERLAPPEDWINDOW, /* window style--normal */
  CW_USEDEFAULT, /* X coordinate--let Windows decide */
  CW_USEDEFAULT, /* Y coordinate--let Windows decide */
  CW_USEDEFAULT, /* width--let Windows decide */
  CW_USEDEFAULT, /* height--let Windows decide */
  NULL, /* handle of parent window--there isn't one */
  NULL, /* no menu */
  hThisInst, /* handle of this instance of the program */
  NULL /* no additional arguments */
);

/* Display the window. */
ShowWindow(hwnd, nWinMode);
UpdateWindow(hwnd);

/* Create the message loop. */
while(GetMessage(&msg, NULL, 0, 0))
{
  TranslateMessage(&msg); /* allow use of keyboard */
  DispatchMessage(&msg); /* return control to Windows */
}
return msg.wParam;
}
```

```
/* This function is called by Windows NT and is passed
   messages from the message queue.
*/
LRESULT CALLBACK WindowFunc(HWND hwnd, UINT message, WPARAM wParam,
                LPARAM lParam)
{
  HDC hdc;
  PAINTSTRUCT paintstruct;

  switch(message) {
    case WM_CHAR: /* process keystroke */
      hdc = GetDC(hwnd); /* get device context */
      TextOut(hdc, 1, 1, "  ", 2); /* erase old character */
      sprintf(str, "%c", (char) wParam); /* stringize character */
      TextOut(hdc, 1, 1, str, strlen(str)); /* output char */
      ReleaseDC(hwnd, hdc); /* release device context */
      break;
    case WM_PAINT: /* process a repaint request */
      hdc = BeginPaint(hwnd, &paintstruct); /* get DC */
      TextOut(hdc, 1, 1, str, strlen(str)); /* output string */
      EndPaint(hwnd, &paintstruct); /* release DC */
      break;
    case WM_DESTROY: /* terminate the program */
      PostQuitMessage(0);
      break;
    default:
      /* Let Windows NT process any messages not specified in
         the preceding switch statement. */
      return DefWindowProc(hwnd, message, wParam, lParam);
  }
  return 0;
}
```

Before continuing, enter, compile, and run this program. Try typing a few characters and then minimizing and restoring the window. As you will see, each time the window is redisplayed, the last character you typed is automatically redrawn. Notice that the global array **str** is initialized to **Windows NT Sample** and that this is displayed when the program begins execution. The reason for this is that when a window is created, a **WM_PAINT** message is automatically generated.

While the handling of the **WM_PAINT** message in the skeleton is quite simple, it must be emphasized that most real world versions of this will be more complex because most windows contain considerably more output.

Since it is your program's responsibility to restore the window if it is resized or overwritten, you must always provide some mechanism to accomplish this. In real world programs, this is usually accomplished one of three ways. First, your program can simply regenerate the output by computational means. This is most feasible when no user input is used. Second, your program can maintain a virtual screen that you simply copy to the window each time it must be redrawn. Finally, in some instances, you can keep a record of events and replay the events when the window needs to be redrawn. Which approach is best depends completely upon the application. Most of the examples in this book won't bother to redraw the window, because doing so typically involves substantial additional code which often just muddies the point of an example. However, your programs will need to restore their windows in order to be conforming Windows NT applications.

Responding to Mouse Messages

Since Windows is, to a great extent, a mouse-based operating system, all Windows programs should respond to mouse input. Because the mouse is so important, there are several different types of mouse messages. This section examines the two most common. These are **WM_LBUTTONDOWN** and **WM_RBUTTONDOWN**, which are generated when the left button and right button are pressed, respectively.

To begin, you must add the responses to the two mouse messages to the **switch** statement in the window function, as shown here:

```
case WM_RBUTTONDOWN: /* process right button */
  hdc = GetDC(hwnd); /* get DC */
  strcpy(str, "Right button is down.");
  TextOut(hdc, LOWORD(lParam), HIWORD(lParam),
          str, strlen(str));
  ReleaseDC(hwnd, hdc); /* Release DC */
  break;
case WM_LBUTTONDOWN: /* process left button */
  hdc = GetDC(hwnd); /* get DC */
  strcpy(str, "Left button is down.");
  TextOut(hdc, LOWORD(lParam), HIWORD(lParam),
          str, strlen(str));
  ReleaseDC(hwnd, hdc); /* Release DC */
  break;
```

When either button is pressed, the mouse's current X, Y location is specified in **LOWORD(lParam)** and **HIWORD(lParam)**, respectively. The mouse message response functions use these coordinates as the location to display their output. That is, each time you press a mouse button, a message will be displayed at the location of the mouse pointer.

Here is the complete skeleton that responds to the mouse messages.

```c
/* A minimal Windows NT skeleton that responds
   to mouse messages. */

/* The following definition causes stricter type checking.
   This is optional, but suggested because it will help
   catch potential type mismatch errors--especially
   when porting from 16-bit Windows. */
#define STRICT

#include <windows.h>
#include <string.h>
#include <stdio.h>

LRESULT CALLBACK WindowFunc(HWND, UINT, WPARAM, LPARAM);

char szWinName[] = "MyWin"; /* name of window class */

char str[80] = "Windows NT Sample"; /* holds output string */

int WINAPI WinMain(HINSTANCE hThisInst, HINSTANCE hPrevInst,
                   LPSTR lpszArgs, int nWinMode)
{
  HWND hwnd;
  MSG msg;
  WNDCLASS wcl;

  /* Define a window class. */
  wcl.hInstance = hThisInst; /* handle to this instance */
  wcl.lpszClassName = szWinName; /* window class name */
  wcl.lpfnWndProc = WindowFunc; /* window function */
  wcl.style = 0; /* default style */

  wcl.hIcon = LoadIcon(NULL, IDI_APPLICATION); /* icon style */
  wcl.hCursor = LoadCursor(NULL, IDC_ARROW); /* cursor style */
  wcl.lpszMenuName = NULL; /* no menu */
```

```
wcl.cbClsExtra = 0; /* no extra */
wcl.cbWndExtra = 0; /* information needed */

/* Make the window light gray. */
wcl.hbrBackground = GetStockObject(LTGRAY_BRUSH);

/* Register the window class. */
if(!RegisterClass (&wcl)) return 0;

/* Now that a window class has been registered, a window
   can be created. */
hwnd = CreateWindow(
  szWinName, /* name of window class */
  "Windows NT Skeleton", /* title */
  WS_OVERLAPPEDWINDOW, /* window style--normal */
  CW_USEDEFAULT, /* X coordinate--let Windows decide */
  CW_USEDEFAULT, /* Y coordinate--let Windows decide */
  CW_USEDEFAULT, /* width--let Windows decide */
  CW_USEDEFAULT, /* height--let Windows decide */
  NULL, /* handle of parent window--there isn't one */
  NULL, /* no menu */
  hThisInst, /* handle of this instance of the program */
  NULL /* no additional arguments */
);

/* Display the window. */
ShowWindow(hwnd, nWinMode);
UpdateWindow(hwnd);

/* Create the message loop. */
while(GetMessage(&msg, NULL, 0, 0))
{
  TranslateMessage(&msg); /* allow use of keyboard */
  DispatchMessage(&msg); /* return control to Windows */
}
  return msg.wParam;
}

/* This function is called by Windows NT and is passed
   messages from the message queue.
*/
LRESULT CALLBACK WindowFunc(HWND hwnd, UINT message, WPARAM wParam,
```

```
                   LPARAM lParam)
{
  HDC hdc;
  PAINTSTRUCT paintstruct;

  switch(message) {
    case WM_CHAR: /* process keystroke */
      hdc = GetDC(hwnd); /* get device context */
      TextOut(hdc, 1, 1, "  ", 2); /* erase old character */
      sprintf(str, "%c", (char) wParam); /* stringize character */
      TextOut(hdc, 1, 1, str, strlen(str)); /* output char */
      ReleaseDC(hwnd, hdc); /* release device context */
      break;
    case WM_PAINT: /* process a repaint request */
      hdc = BeginPaint(hwnd, &paintstruct); /* get DC */
      TextOut(hdc, 1, 1, str, strlen(str)); /* output string */
      EndPaint(hwnd, &paintstruct); /* release DC */
      break;
    case WM_RBUTTONDOWN: /* process right button */
      hdc = GetDC(hwnd); /* get DC */
      strcpy(str, "Right button is down.");
      TextOut(hdc, LOWORD(lParam), HIWORD(lParam),
              str, strlen(str));
      ReleaseDC(hwnd, hdc); /* Release DC */
      break;
    case WM_LBUTTONDOWN: /* process left button */
      hdc = GetDC(hwnd); /* get DC */
      strcpy(str, "Left button is down.");
      TextOut(hdc, LOWORD(lParam), HIWORD(lParam),
              str, strlen(str));
      ReleaseDC(hwnd, hdc); /* Release DC */
      break;
    case WM_DESTROY: /* terminate the program */
      PostQuitMessage(0);
      break;
    default:
       /* Let Windows NT process any messages not specified in
          the preceding switch statement. */
      return DefWindowProc(hwnd, message, wParam, lParam);
  }
  return 0;
}
```

Figure 3-1 shows sample output from this program.

Figure 3-1

Sample output
from the
application
skeleton

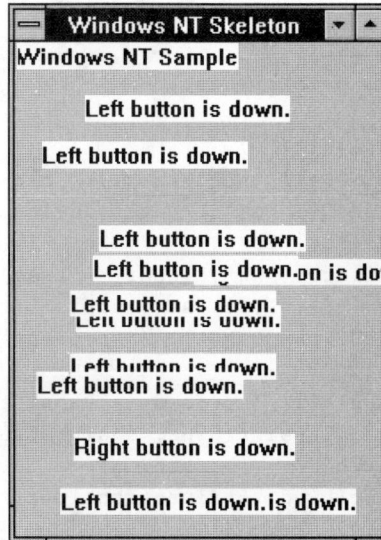

A Closer Look at the Mouse Messages

Each time a **WM_LBUTTONDOWN** or a **WM_RBUTTONDOWN** message is generated, several pieces of information are also supplied in the **wParam** parameter. It may contain any combination of the following values:

    MK_CONTROL
    MK_SHIFT
    MK_MBUTTON
    MK_RBUTTON
    MK_LBUTTON

If the CTRL key is pressed when a mouse button is pressed, then **wParam** will contain **MK_CONTROL**. If the SHIFT key is pressed when a mouse button is pressed, then **wParam** will contain **MK_SHIFT.** If the right button is down when the left button is pressed, then **wParam** will contain **MK_RBUTTON**. If the left button is down when the right button is pressed, then **wParam** will contain **MK_LBUTTON**. If the middle button (if it exists) is down when one of the other buttons is pressed, then **wParam** will contain **MK_MBUTTON**. Before moving on, you might want to try experimenting with these messages. Remember, more than one of these values may be present.

Generating a WM_PAINT Message

It is possible for your program to cause a **WM_PAINT** message to be generated. At first, you might wonder why your program would need to generate a **WM_PAINT** message since, it seems, that it can repaint its window whenever it wants. However, this is a false assumption. Remember, updating a window is a costly process in terms of time. Because Windows NT is a multitasking system that might be running other programs that are also demanding CPU time, you should let Windows NT decide when it is best to perform output to your window by sending a **WM_PAINT** message. This allows Windows to better manage the system and efficiently allocate CPU time to all the tasks in the system. Using this approach, your program simply holds all output until this message is received and then updates the window.

In the previous application skeletons, the **WM_PAINT** message was only received when the window was resized or uncovered. However, if all output is held until a **WM_PAINT** message is received, then to achieve interactive I/O, there must be some way to tell Windows NT that it needs to send a **WM_PAINT** message to your window whenever output is pending. As expected, Windows NT includes such a feature. Thus, when your program has information to output, it simply requests that a **WM_PAINT** message be sent when Windows NT is ready to do so.

To cause Windows NT to send a **WM_PAINT** message, your program will call the **InvalidateRect()** API function. Its prototype is shown here:

BOOL InvalidateRect(HWND *hwnd,* CONST RECT **lpRect,*
    BOOL *bErase*);

Here, *hwnd* is the handle of the window that you want to send the **WM_PAINT** message to. The **RECT** structure pointed to by *lpRect* specifies the coordinates within the window that must be redrawn. If this value is NULL, then the entire window will be specified. If *bErase* is true, then the background will be erased. If it is 0, then the background is left unchanged. The function returns non-zero if successful; zero otherwise. (In general, this function will always succeed.)

When **InvalidateRect()** is called, it tells Windows NT that the window is invalid and must be redrawn. This, in turn, causes Windows NT to send a **WM_PAINT** message to the window.

Here is a reworked version of the previous application skeleton that performs all output by generating a **WM_PAINT** message. The other message response functions simply prepare the information to be displayed and then call **InvalidateRect()**.

```
/* A minimal Windows NT skeleton that routes all output
   through the WM_PAINT message. */

/* The following definition causes stricter type checking.
   This is optional, but suggested because it will help
   catch potential type mismatch errors--especially
   when porting from 16-bit Windows. */
#define STRICT

#include <windows.h>
#include <string.h>
#include <stdio.h>

LRESULT CALLBACK WindowFunc(HWND, UINT, WPARAM, LPARAM);

char szWinName[] = "MyWin"; /* name of window class */

char str[80] = "Windows NT Sample"; /* holds output string */

int X = 1, Y = 1; /* screen location */

int WINAPI WinMain(HINSTANCE hThisInst, HINSTANCE hPrevInst,
                   LPSTR lpszArgs, int nWinMode)
{
  HWND hwnd;
  MSG msg;
  WNDCLASS wcl;

  /* Define a window class. */
  wcl.hInstance = hThisInst; /* handle to this instance */
  wcl.lpszClassName = szWinName; /* window class name */
  wcl.lpfnWndProc = WindowFunc; /* window function */
  wcl.style = 0; /* default style */

  wcl.hIcon = LoadIcon(NULL, IDI_APPLICATION); /* icon style */
```

```
wcl.hCursor = LoadCursor(NULL, IDC_ARROW); /* cursor style */
wcl.lpszMenuName = NULL; /* no menu */

wcl.cbClsExtra = 0; /* no extra */
wcl.cbWndExtra = 0; /* information needed */

/* Make the window light gray. */
wcl.hbrBackground = GetStockObject(LTGRAY_BRUSH);

/* Register the window class. */
if(!RegisterClass (&wcl)) return 0;

/* Now that a window class has been registered, a window
   can be created. */
hwnd = CreateWindow(
  szWinName, /* name of window class */
  "Windows NT Skeleton", /* title */
  WS_OVERLAPPEDWINDOW, /* window style--normal */
  CW_USEDEFAULT, /* X coordinate--let Windows decide */
  CW_USEDEFAULT, /* Y coordinate--let Windows decide */
  CW_USEDEFAULT, /* width--let Windows decide */
  CW_USEDEFAULT, /* height--let Windows decide */
  NULL, /* handle of parent window--there isn't one */
  NULL, /* no menu */
  hThisInst, /* handle of this instance of the program */
  NULL /* no additional arguments */
);

/* Display the window. */
ShowWindow(hwnd, nWinMode);
UpdateWindow(hwnd);

/* Create the message loop. */
while(GetMessage(&msg, NULL, 0, 0))
{
  TranslateMessage(&msg); /* allow use of keyboard */
  DispatchMessage(&msg); /* return control to Windows */
}
return msg.wParam;
}

/* This function is called by Windows NT and is passed
   messages from the message queue.
*/
```

```
LRESULT CALLBACK WindowFunc(HWND hwnd, UINT message, WPARAM wParam,
                 LPARAM lParam)
{
  HDC hdc;
  PAINTSTRUCT paintstruct;

  switch(message) {
    case WM_CHAR: /* process keystroke */
      X = Y = 1; /* display chars in upper left corner */
      sprintf(str, "%c", (char) wParam); /* stringize character */
      InvalidateRect(hwnd, NULL, 1); /* paint the screen */
      break;
    case WM_PAINT: /* process a repaint request */
      hdc = BeginPaint(hwnd, &paintstruct); /* get DC */
      TextOut(hdc, X, Y, str, strlen(str)); /* output string */
      EndPaint(hwnd, &paintstruct); /* release DC */
      break;
    case WM_RBUTTONDOWN: /* process right button */
      strcpy(str, "Right button is down.");
      X = LOWORD(lParam); /* set X,Y to current */
      Y = HIWORD(lParam); /* mouse location */
      InvalidateRect(hwnd, NULL, 1); /* paint the screen */
      break;
    case WM_LBUTTONDOWN: /* process left button */
      strcpy(str, "Left button is down.");
      X = LOWORD(lParam); /* set X,Y to current */
      Y = HIWORD(lParam); /* mouse location */
      InvalidateRect(hwnd, NULL, 1); /* paint the screen */
      break;
    case WM_DESTROY: /* terminate the program */
      PostQuitMessage(0);
      break;
    default:
      /* Let Windows NT process any messages not specified in
         the preceding switch statement. */
      return DefWindowProc(hwnd, message, wParam, lParam);
  }
  return 0;
}
```

Notice that the program adds two new global variables called **X** and **Y** that hold the location at which the text will be displayed when a **WM_PAINT** message is received.

As you can see, by channelling all output through **WM_PAINT**, the program has actually become smaller and, in some ways, easier to understand. Also, as stated at the start of this section, the program allows Windows NT to decide when it is most appropriate to update the window.

note: *Many Windows applications route all (or most) output through* **WM_PAINT**, *for the reasons already stated. However, the previous programs are not technically wrong in outputting text within their message response functions. It is just that this approach may not be the best for all purposes.*

Generating Timer Messages

The last message that will be discussed here is **WM_TIMER.** Using Windows NT, it is possible to establish a timer that will interrupt your program at periodic intervals. Each time the timer goes off, it sends a **WM_TIMER** message to your window function. Using a timer is a good way to "wake up your program" every so often. This is particularly useful when your program is running as a background task.

To start a timer, use the **SetTimer()** API function, whose prototype is shown here:

UINT SetTimer(HWND *hwnd*, UINT *nID*, UINT *wLength*,
         TIMERPROC *lpTFunc*);

Here, *hwnd* is the handle of the window that uses the timer. The value of *nID* specifies a value that will be associated with this timer. (More than one timer can be active.) The value of *wLength* specifies the length of the period, in milliseconds. That is, *wLength* specifies how much time there is between interrupts. The function pointed to by *lpTFunc* is the timer function that will be called when the timer goes off. This must be a callback function that uses a prototype similar to that used by the window function. It must return **VOID CALLBACK** and take the same type of parameters as the window function. However, if the value of *lpTFunc* is NULL, as it commonly is, then your program's window function will be used for this purpose. In this case, each time the timer goes off, a **WM_TIMER** message is put into the message queue for your program, and your program's window function processes it like any other message. This is the approach used by the example that follows. The function returns *nID* if successful. If the timer cannot be allocated, zero is returned.

Once a timer has been started, it continues to interrupt your program until either you terminate the application or your program executes a call to the **KillTimer()** API function, whose prototype is shown here:

BOOL KillTimer(HWND *hwnd,* UINT *nID*);

Here, *hwnd* is the window that contains the timer and *nID* is the value that identifies that particular timer.

Each time a **WM_TIMER** message is generated, the value of **wParam** contains the ID of the timer and **lParam** contains the time that the event occurred.

To demonstrate the use of a timer, the following program uses a timer to create a clock. It uses the ANSI C standard time functions to obtain and display the current system time and date. Each time the timer goes off, which is approximately once each second, the time is updated. Thus, the time displayed is accurate to within 1 second.

```c
/* A clock program. */

/* The following definition causes stricter type checking.
   This is optional, but suggested because it will help
   catch potential type mismatch errors--especially
   when porting from 16-bit Windows. */
#define STRICT

#include <windows.h>
#include <string.h>
#include <stdio.h>
#include <time.h>

LRESULT CALLBACK WindowFunc(HWND, UINT, WPARAM, LPARAM);

char szWinName[] = "WinNTClock"; /* name of window class */

char str[80] = ""; /* holds output string */

int X = 1, Y = 1; /* screen location */

int WINAPI WinMain(HINSTANCE hThisInst, HINSTANCE hPrevInst,
                   LPSTR lpszArgs, int nWinMode)
{
  HWND hwnd;
  MSG msg;
```

```
WNDCLASS wcl;

/* Define a window class. */
wcl.hInstance = hThisInst; /* handle to this instance */
wcl.lpszClassName = szWinName; /* window class name */
wcl.lpfnWndProc = WindowFunc; /* window function */
wcl.style = 0; /* default style */

wcl.hIcon = LoadIcon(NULL, IDI_APPLICATION); /* icon style */
wcl.hCursor = LoadCursor(NULL, IDC_ARROW); /* cursor style */
wcl.lpszMenuName = NULL; /* no menu */

wcl.cbClsExtra = 0; /* no extra */
wcl.cbWndExtra = 0; /* information needed */

/* Make the window light gray. */
wcl.hbrBackground = GetStockObject(WHITE_BRUSH);

/* Register the window class. */
if(!RegisterClass (&wcl)) return 0;

/* Now that a window class has been registered, a window
   can be created. */
hwnd = CreateWindow(
  szWinName, /* name of window class */
  "Clock", /* title */
  WS_OVERLAPPEDWINDOW, /* window style--normal */
  CW_USEDEFAULT, /* X coordinate--let Windows decide */
  CW_USEDEFAULT, /* Y coordinate--let Windows decide */
  CW_USEDEFAULT, /* width--let Windows decide */
  CW_USEDEFAULT, /* height--let Windows decide */
  NULL, /* handle of parent window--there isn't one */
  NULL, /* no menu */
  hThisInst, /* handle of this instance of the program */
  NULL /* no additional arguments */
);

/* Display the window. */
ShowWindow(hwnd, nWinMode);

/* start a timer -- interrupt once per second */
SetTimer(hwnd, 1, 1000, NULL);

UpdateWindow(hwnd);
```

```
  /* Create the message loop. */
  while(GetMessage(&msg, NULL, 0, 0))
  {
    TranslateMessage(&msg); /* allow use of keyboard */
    DispatchMessage(&msg); /* return control to Windows */
  }

  KillTimer(hwnd, 1); /* stop the timer */

  return msg.wParam;
}


/* This function is called by Windows NT and is passed
   messages from the message queue.
*/
LRESULT CALLBACK WindowFunc(HWND hwnd, UINT message, WPARAM wParam,
              LPARAM lParam)
{
  HDC hdc;
  PAINTSTRUCT paintstruct;
  struct tm *newtime;
  time_t t;

  switch(message) {
    case WM_PAINT: /* process a repaint request */
      hdc = BeginPaint(hwnd, &paintstruct); /* get DC */
      TextOut(hdc, X, Y, str, strlen(str)); /* output string */
      EndPaint(hwnd, &paintstruct); /* release DC */
      break;
    case WM_TIMER: /* timer went off */
      /* get the new time */
      t = time(NULL);
      newtime = localtime(&t);

      /* display the new time */
      strcpy(str, asctime(newtime));
      str[strlen(str)-1] = '\0'; /* remove /r/n */
      InvalidateRect(hwnd, NULL, 0); /* update screen */
      break;
    case WM_DESTROY: /* terminate the program */
      PostQuitMessage(0);
      break;
    default:
```

```
        /* Let Windows NT process any messages not specified in
           the preceding switch statement. */
        return DefWindowProc(hwnd, message, wParam, lParam);
    }
    return 0;
}
```

Sample output from this program is shown in Figure 3-2.

Now that you have learned how a Windows NT program processes messages, you can move on to creating message boxes and menus, which are the subjects of the next chapter.

Figure 3-2

The clock window

Chapter 4

Message Boxes and Menus

OW that you know how to construct a basic Windows NT skeleton and receive and process messages, it is time to begin exploration of Windows NT's user interface components. Although you can write a Windows NT application that appears just like a DOS application, doing so is not in the spirit of Windows programming. In order for your Windows NT applications to conform to Windows' general design principles, you will need to communicate with the user using several different types of special windows. There are three basic types of user interface windows: message boxes, menus, and dialog boxes. This chapter discusses message boxes and menus. (The next chapter examines dialog boxes.) As you will see, the basic style of each of these windows is predefined by Windows NT. You need only supply the specific information that relates to your application.

Keep in mind that message boxes and menus are usually *child windows* of your original application windows. This means that they are owned by your application and are dependent upon it.

Message Boxes

By far, the simplest interface window is the message box. A message box displays a message to the user and waits for an acknowledgment. It is possible to construct message boxes that allow the user to select between a few basic alternatives, but in general, the purpose of a message box is simply to inform the user that some event has taken place.

To create a message box, use the **MessageBox()** API function. Its prototype is shown here:

int MessageBox(HWND *hwnd*, LPCSTR *lpText*, LPCSTR *lpCaption*,
        UINT *wMBType*);

Here, *hwnd* is the handle to the parent window. The *lpText* parameter is a pointer to a string that will appear inside the message box. The string pointed to by *lpCaption* is used as the caption for the box. The value of *wMBType* determines the exact nature of the message box, including what type of buttons will be present. Some of its most common values are shown in Table 4–1. These macros are defined by including **windows.h**, and you can OR together two or more of these macros so long as they are not mutually exclusive. **Message-Box()** returns the user's response to the box. The possible return values are shown here:

Button Pressed	Return Value
Abort	IDABORT
Retry	IDRETRY
Ignore	IDIGNORE
Cancel	IDCANCEL
No	IDNO
Yes	IDYES
OK	IDOK

These macros are defined by including **windows.h**. Remember, depending upon the value of *wMBType,* only certain buttons will be present.

Value	Effect
MB_ABORTRETRYIGNORE	Displays Abort, Retry, and Ignore push buttons
MB_ICONEXCLAMATION	Displays exclamation-point icon
MB_ICONHAND	Displays a stop sign icon
MB_ICONINFORMATION	Displays an information icon
MB_ICONQUESTION	Displays a question mark icon
MB_ICONSTOP	Same as MB_ICONHAND
MB_OK	Displays OK push button
MB_OKCANCEL	Displays OK and Cancel push buttons
MB_RETRYCANCEL	Displays Retry and Cancel push buttons
MB_YESNO	Displays Yes and No push buttons
MB_YESNOCANCEL	Displays Yes, No, and Cancel push buttons

Table 4-1
Some Common Values for wMBType

To display a message box, simply call the **MessageBox()** function. Windows NT will display it at its first opportunity. You do not need to obtain a device context or generate a **WM_PAINT** message. **MessageBox()** handles all of these details for you.

Here is a simple example that displays a message box when you press a mouse button:

```
/* A minimal Windows NT skeleton that demonstrates
   message boxes. */

/* The following definition causes stricter type checking.
   This is optional, but suggested because it will help
   catch potential type mismatch errors--especially
   when porting from 16-bit Windows. */
#define STRICT

#include <windows.h>
#include <string.h>
#include <stdio.h>

LRESULT CALLBACK WindowFunc(HWND, UINT, WPARAM, LPARAM);

char szWinName[] = "MyWin"; /* name of window class */

char str[80] = "Windows NT Sample"; /* holds output string */

int X = 1, Y = 1; /* screen location */

int WINAPI WinMain(HINSTANCE hThisInst, HINSTANCE hPrevInst,
                   LPSTR lpszArgs, int nWinMode)
{
  HWND hwnd;
  MSG msg;
  WNDCLASS wcl;

  /* Define a window class. */
  wcl.hInstance = hThisInst; /* handle to this instance */
  wcl.lpszClassName = szWinName; /* window class name */
  wcl.lpfnWndProc = WindowFunc; /* window function */
  wcl.style = 0; /* default style */

  wcl.hIcon = LoadIcon(NULL, IDI_APPLICATION); /* icon style */
  wcl.hCursor = LoadCursor(NULL, IDC_ARROW); /* cursor style */
```

```
    wcl.lpszMenuName = NULL; /* no menu */

    wcl.cbClsExtra = 0; /* no extra */
    wcl.cbWndExtra = 0; /* information needed */

    /* Make the window light gray. */
    wcl.hbrBackground = GetStockObject(LTGRAY_BRUSH);

    /* Register the window class. */
    if(!RegisterClass (&wcl)) return 0;

    /* Now that a window class has been registered, a window
       can be created. */
    hwnd = CreateWindow(
      szWinName, /* name of window class */
      "Using Message Boxes", /* title */
      WS_OVERLAPPEDWINDOW, /* window style--normal */
      CW_USEDEFAULT, /* X coordinate--let Windows decide */
      CW_USEDEFAULT, /* Y coordinate--let Windows decide */
      CW_USEDEFAULT, /* width--let Windows decide */
      CW_USEDEFAULT, /* height--let Windows decide */
      NULL, /* handle of parent window--there isn't one */
      NULL, /* no menu */
      hThisInst, /* handle of this instance of the program */
      NULL /* no additional arguments */
    );

    /* Display the window. */
    ShowWindow(hwnd, nWinMode);
    UpdateWindow(hwnd);

    /* Create the message loop. */
    while(GetMessage(&msg, NULL, 0, 0))
    {
      TranslateMessage(&msg); /* allow use of keyboard */
      DispatchMessage(&msg); /* return control to Windows */
    }
    return msg.wParam;
}

/* This function is called by Windows NT and is passed
   messages from the message queue.
*/
LRESULT CALLBACK WindowFunc(HWND hwnd, UINT message, WPARAM wParam,
```

```
                    LPARAM lParam)
{
  HDC hdc;
  PAINTSTRUCT paintstruct;
  int response;

  switch(message) {
    case WM_CHAR: /* process keystroke */
      X = Y = 1; /* display chars in upper left corner */
      sprintf(str, "%c", (char) wParam); /* stringize character */
      InvalidateRect(hwnd, NULL, 1); /* paint the screen */
      break;
    case WM_PAINT: /* process a repaint request */
      hdc = BeginPaint(hwnd, &paintstruct); /* get DC */
      TextOut(hdc, X, Y, str, strlen(str)); /* output string */
      EndPaint(hwnd, &paintstruct); /* release DC */
      break;
    case WM_RBUTTONDOWN: /* process right button */
      response = MessageBox(hwnd, "Press One:", "Right Button",
                  MB_ABORTRETRYIGNORE);
      switch(response) {
        case IDABORT:
          MessageBox(hwnd, "", "Abort", MB_OK);
          break;
        case IDRETRY:
          MessageBox(hwnd, "", "Retry", MB_OK);
          break;
        case IDIGNORE:
          MessageBox(hwnd, "", "Ignore", MB_OK);
          break;
      }
      break;
    case WM_LBUTTONDOWN: /* process left button */
      response = MessageBox(hwnd, "Continue?", "Left Button",
                  MB_ICONHAND | MB_YESNO);
      switch(response) {
        case IDYES:
          MessageBox(hwnd, "Press Button", "Yes", MB_OK);
          break;
        case IDNO:
          MessageBox(hwnd, "Press Button", "No", MB_OK);
          break;
      }
      break;
```

```
      case WM_DESTROY: /* terminate the program */
        PostQuitMessage(0);
        break;
      default:
        /* Let Windows NT process any messages not specified in
           the preceding switch statement. */
        return DefWindowProc(hwnd, message, wParam, lParam);
    }
    return 0;
}
```

Each time a mouse button is pressed, a message box is displayed. For example, pressing the right button displays the message box shown in Figure 4-1.

As you will see, when you press the right button a message box displays the buttons Abort, Retry, and Ignore. Depending upon your response, a second message box will be displayed that indicates which button you pressed. Pressing the left mouse button causes a message box to be displayed that contains a stop sign. This box allows a Yes or a No response.

Before continuing, experiment with message boxes, trying different types.

Introducing Menus

In Windows the most common element of control is the menu. Virtually all main windows have some type of menu associated with them. Because menus are so common and important in Windows applications, Windows NT provides substantial built-in support for them. As you will see, adding a menu to a window involves these relatively few steps:

1. Define the form of the menu in a resource file.

2. Load the menu when your program creates its main window.

3. Process menu selections.

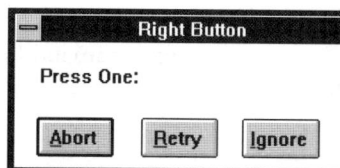

Figure 4-1

A sample message box

In Windows NT, the top level of a menu is displayed across the top of the window. Submenus are displayed as popup menus. (You should be accustomed to this approach because it is used by virtually all Windows programs.)

Before beginning, it is necessary to explain what resources and resource files are.

Using Resources

Windows NT defines several common types of objects as *resources*. Resources are, essentially, objects that are used by your program, but are defined outside your program. They include things such as menus, icons, dialog boxes, and bitmapped graphics. Since a menu is a resource, you need to understand resources before you can add a menu to your program.

A resource is created separately from your program, but is added to the .EXE file when your program is linked. Resources are contained in *resource files*, which have the extension .RC. In general, the filename should be the same as that of your program's .EXE file. For example, if your program is called PROG.EXE, then its resource file should be called PROG.RC.

Depending upon the resource, some are specified as text using a standard text editor. Text resources are typically defined within the resource file. Others, such as icons, are most easily generated using a resource editor, but they still must be referred to in the .RC file that is associated with your application. The sample resource files in this chapter are simply text files, because menus are text-based resources.

Resource files are not C or C++ files. Instead, they contain a special resource language, or *script,* that must be compiled using a *resource compiler*. The resource compiler converts an .RC file into a .RES file, which may be linked with your program.

Compiling .RC Files

Once you have created an .RC file, you compile it into a .RES file using the resource compiler, which is called RC.EXE. Exactly how you compile a resource file will depend upon what compiler you are using. If you are using the Microsoft Windows NT SDK, then to compile a resource file called SKEL.RC, you will use a command line similar to this:

```
RC SKEL.RC
```

Other manufactures may require a slightly different command syntax or options.

The output of the resource compiler will be a .RES file. Normally, it is this file that you will link with your program to build the final Windows NT application. (For instructions on exactly how to link .RES files, consult your compiler's user manual.) However, at the time of this writing, an intermediate step is required when using the Windows NT SDK. This step converts the .RES file into an .RBJ file, which is then linked with your application. Therefore, if you are using the Microsoft Windows NT SDK, you must use CVTRES.EXE to convert a .RES to an .RBJ file. For example, this line converts SKEL.RES into SKEL.RBJ:

```
CVTRES -i386 SKEL.RES -o SKEL.RBJ
```

remember: *The conversion of a .RES file into an .RBJ file is a temporary step that will not be necessary in the future.*

Once you have compiled your resource, you then link the .RES file with your program. Or, if you are using the Microsoft Windows NT SDK, you link the .RBJ file with your program. For example, if using the Microsoft SDK, this LINK command will be used to link SKEL.RBJ to your program:

```
link32 skel.obj skel.rbj -subsystem:windows -entry:WinMainCRTStartup
    -out:skel.exe libc.lib ntdll.lib kernel32.lib user32.lib
    gdi32.lib winspool.lib comdlg32.lib
```

Creating a Simple Menu

Before a menu can be included, you must define its content in a resource file. All menu definitions have this general form:

MenuName MENU *[Options]*
{
    menu items
}

Here, *MenuName* is the name of the menu. (It may also be an integer value identifying the menu, but all examples in this book will use the name when referring to the menu.) The keyword **MENU** tells the resource compiler that a menu is being created. There are several options which can be specified when creating the menu. They are shown in Table 4-2. (Again, these macros are defined by including **windows.h**.) However, for Windows NT, the only option that has an effect is **DISCARDABLE**. The others are allowed for compatibility with 16-bit Windows resource files, but ignored otherwise. The examples in this book simply use the default settings and specify no options.

There are two types of items that can be used to define the menu: **MENUITEM**s and **POPUP**s. A **MENUITEM** specifies a final selection. A **POPUP** specifies a popup submenu, which may, in itself, contain other **MENUITEM**s or **POPUP**s. The general form of these two statements is shown here:

MENUITEM "*ItemName*", *MenuID* [, *Options*]

POPUP "*PopupName*" [, *Options*]
{
    menu items
}

Here, *ItemName* is the name of the menu selection, such as "Help" or "File". *MenuID* is a unique integer associated with a menu item that will be sent to your Windows NT application when a selection is made. Typically, these values are defined as macros inside a header file that is included in both your application code and in the .RC resource file. *PopupName* is the name of the popup menu. For both cases, the values for *Options* (defined by including **windows.h**) are shown in Table 4-3.

Option	Meaning
DISCARDABLE	Menu may be removed from memory when no longer needed
FIXED	Menu is fixed in memory
LOADONCALL	Menu is loaded when used
MOVEABLE	Menu may be moved in memory
PRELOAD	Menu is loaded when your program begins execution

Table 4-2
The MENU Options

Option	Meaning
CHECKED	A check mark is displayed next to the name. (Not applicable to top level menus.)
GRAYED	The name is shown in gray and may not be selected.
HELP	May be associated with a help selection. This applies to MENUITEMs only.
INACTIVE	The option may not be selected.
MENUBARBREAK	For menu bar, causes a horizontal bar to separate this item from the previous. For popup menus, causes the item to be put in a different column. In this case, the item is separated using a bar.
MENUBREAK	Same as MENUBARBREAK except that no separator bar is used.

Table 4-3
The MENUITEM and POPUP Options

Here is an example of a simple menu that you should enter into your computer at this time. Call the file MENU.RC.

```
; Sample menu resource file.
#include "menu.h"

MYMENU MENU
{
  POPUP "&One"
  {
    MENUITEM "&Alpha", IDM_ALPHA
    MENUITEM "&Beta", IDM_BETA
  }
  POPUP "&Two"
  {
    MENUITEM "&Gamma", IDM_GAMMA
    POPUP "&Delta"
    {
      MENUITEM "&Epsilon", IDM_EPSILON
      MENUITEM "&Zeta", IDM_ZETA
    }
    MENUITEM "&Eta", IDM_ETA
    MENUITEM "&Theta", IDM_THETA
  }
  MENUITEM "&Help", IDM_HELP
}
```

This menu, called **MYMENU**, contains three top level, menu bar options: One, Two, and Help. The One and Two options contain popup submenus. The Delta option activates a popup submenu of its own. Notice that options that activate submenus do not have menu ID values associated with them. Only actual menu items have ID numbers. In this menu, all menu ID values are specified as macros beginning with **IDM**. (These macros are defined in the header file **menu.h**.) What names you give these values is arbitrary.

An **&** in an item's name causes the key that it precedes to become the shortcut key associated with that option. That is, once that menu is active, pressing that key causes that menu item to be selected. It doesn't have to be the first key in the name, but it should be unless a conflict with another name exists.

note:

You can embed comments into a resource file on a line-by-line basis by beginning them with a semicolon, as the first line of the resource file shows. You may also use C and C++ style comments.

The **menu.h** header file, which is included in MENU.RC, contains the macro definitions of the menu ID values. It is shown here. Enter it at this time.

```
#define IDM_ALPHA      100
#define IDM_BETA       101
#define IDM_GAMMA      102
#define IDM_DELTA      103
#define IDM_EPSILON    104
#define IDM_ZETA       105
#define IDM_ETA        106
#define IDM_THETA      107
#define IDM_HELP       108
```

This file defines the menu ID values that will be returned when the various menu items are selected. This file will also be included in the program that uses the menu. Remember, the actual names and values that you give the menu items are arbitrary. However, each value must be unique. The valid range for ID values is 0 through 65,565.

Including a Menu in Your Program

Once you have created a menu, you include that menu in a program by specifying its name when you create the window's class. Specifically, you assign the **lpszMenuName** field a pointer to a string that contains the name of the menu. For example, to load the menu **MYMENU**, you would use this line when defining the window's class:

```
wcl.lpszMenuName = "MYMENU"; // main menu
```

Responding to Menu Selections

Each time the user makes a menu selection, your program's window function is sent a **WM_COMMAND** command message. When that message is received, the value of **LOWORD(wParam)** corresponds to the menu item's ID constant. (That is, **LOWORD(wParam)** contains the value you associated with the item when you defined the menu in its .RC file.) Since **WM_COMMAND** is sent whenever a menu item is selected and the value associated with that item is contained in **LOWORD(wParam)**, you will need to use a nested **switch** statement to determine which item was selected. For example, this fragment responds to a selection made from **MYMENU**.

```
switch(message) {
  case WM_COMMAND:
    switch(LOWORD(wParam)) {
      case IDM_ALPHA: MessageBox(hwnd, "Alpha", "", MB_OK);
        break;
      case IDM_BETA: MessageBox(hwnd, "Beta", "", MB_OK);
        break;
      case IDM_GAMMA: MessageBox(hwnd, "Gamma", "", MB_OK);
        break;
      case IDM_EPSILON: MessageBox(hwnd, "Epsilon", "", MB_OK);
        break;
      case IDM_ZETA: MessageBox(hwnd, "Zeta", "", MB_OK);
        break;
      case IDM_ETA: MessageBox(hwnd, "Eta", "", MB_OK);
        break;
      case IDM_THETA: MessageBox(hwnd, "Theta", "", MB_OK);
        break;
      case IDM_HELP: MessageBox(hwnd, "No Help", "Help", MB_OK);
        break;
    }
    break;
```

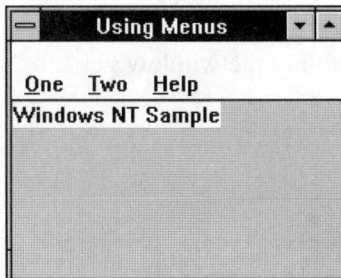

Figure 4-2

Sample output from the menu example

For the sake of illustration, the response to each selection simply displays an acknowledgment of that selection on the screen. However, in real applications, the response to menu selections will generally be more complex.

A Sample Menu Program

Here is a program that demonstrates the menu created in the previous section. Enter it at this time, calling it MENU.C. When you run the program, your screen will look like that shown in Figure 4-2.

```c
/* A minimal Windows NT skeleton that demonstrates
   menus. */

/* The following definition causes stricter type checking.
   This is optional, but suggested because it will help
   catch potential type mismatch errors--especially
   when porting from 16-bit Windows. */
#define STRICT

#include <windows.h>
#include <string.h>
#include <stdio.h>
#include "menu.h"

LRESULT CALLBACK WindowFunc(HWND, UINT, WPARAM, LPARAM);

char szWinName[] = "MyWin"; /* name of window class */

char str[80] = "Windows NT Sample"; /* holds output string */

int X = 1, Y = 1; /* screen location */
```

```c
int WINAPI WinMain(HINSTANCE hThisInst, HINSTANCE hPrevInst,
                   LPSTR lpszArgs, int nWinMode)
{
  HWND hwnd;
  MSG msg;
  WNDCLASS wcl;

  /* Define a window class. */
  wcl.hInstance = hThisInst; /* handle to this instance */
  wcl.lpszClassName = szWinName; /* window class name */
  wcl.lpfnWndProc = WindowFunc; /* window function */
  wcl.style = 0; /* default style */

  wcl.hIcon = LoadIcon(NULL, IDI_APPLICATION); /* icon style */
  wcl.hCursor = LoadCursor(NULL, IDC_ARROW); /* cursor style */

  /* specify name of menu resource */
  wcl.lpszMenuName = "MYMENU"; /* main menu */

  wcl.cbClsExtra = 0; /* no extra */
  wcl.cbWndExtra = 0; /* information needed */

  /* Make the window light gray. */
  wcl.hbrBackground = GetStockObject(LTGRAY_BRUSH);

  /* Register the window class. */
  if(!RegisterClass (&wcl)) return 0;

  /* Now that a window class has been registered, a window
     can be created. */
  hwnd = CreateWindow(
    szWinName, /* name of window class */
    "Using Menus", /* title */
    WS_OVERLAPPEDWINDOW, /* window style--normal */
    CW_USEDEFAULT, /* X coordinate--let Windows decide */
    CW_USEDEFAULT, /* Y coordinate--let Windows decide */
    CW_USEDEFAULT, /* width--let Windows decide */
    CW_USEDEFAULT, /* height--let Windows decide */
    NULL, /* handle of parent window--there isn't one */
    NULL, /* no menu */
    hThisInst, /* handle of this instance of the program */
    NULL /* no additional arguments */
  );
```

```c
  /* Display the window. */
  ShowWindow(hwnd, nWinMode);
  UpdateWindow(hwnd);

  /* Create the message loop. */
  while(GetMessage(&msg, NULL, 0, 0))
  {
    TranslateMessage(&msg); /* allow use of keyboard */
    DispatchMessage(&msg); /* return control to Windows */
  }
  return msg.wParam;
}

/* This function is called by Windows NT and is passed
   messages from the message queue.
*/
LRESULT CALLBACK WindowFunc(HWND hwnd, UINT message, WPARAM wParam,
                LPARAM lParam)
{
  HDC hdc;
  PAINTSTRUCT paintstruct;
  int response;

  switch(message) {
    case WM_COMMAND:
      switch(LOWORD(wParam)) {
        case IDM_ALPHA: MessageBox(hwnd, "Alpha", "", MB_OK);
          break;
        case IDM_BETA: MessageBox(hwnd, "Beta", "", MB_OK);
          break;
        case IDM_GAMMA: MessageBox(hwnd, "Gamma", "", MB_OK);
          break;
        case IDM_EPSILON: MessageBox(hwnd, "Epsilon", "", MB_OK);
          break;
        case IDM_ZETA: MessageBox(hwnd, "Zeta", "", MB_OK);
          break;
        case IDM_ETA: MessageBox(hwnd, "Eta", "", MB_OK);
          break;
        case IDM_THETA: MessageBox(hwnd, "Theta", "", MB_OK);
          break;
```

```
      case IDM_HELP: MessageBox(hwnd, "No Help", "Help", MB_OK);
        break;
    }
    break;
  case WM_CHAR: /* process keystroke */
    X = Y = 1; /* display chars in upper left corner */
    sprintf(str, "%c", (char) wParam); /* stringize character */
    InvalidateRect(hwnd, NULL, 1); /* paint the screen */
    break;
  case WM_PAINT: /* process a repaint request */
    hdc = BeginPaint(hwnd, &paintstruct); /* get DC */
    TextOut(hdc, X, Y, str, strlen(str)); /* output string */
    EndPaint(hwnd, &paintstruct); /* release DC */
    break;
  case WM_RBUTTONDOWN: /* process right button */
    response = MessageBox(hwnd, "Press One:", "Right Button",
            MB_ABORTRETRYIGNORE);
    switch(response) {
      case IDABORT:
        MessageBox(hwnd, "", "Abort", MB_OK);
        break;
      case IDRETRY:
        MessageBox(hwnd, "", "Retry", MB_OK);
        break;
      case IDIGNORE:
        MessageBox(hwnd, "", "Ignore", MB_OK);
        break;
    }
    break;
  case WM_LBUTTONDOWN: /* process left button */
    response = MessageBox(hwnd, "Continue?", "Left Button",
            MB_ICONHAND | MB_YESNO);
    switch(response) {
      case IDYES:
        MessageBox(hwnd, "Press Button", "Yes", MB_OK);
        break;
      case IDNO:
        MessageBox(hwnd, "Press Button", "No", MB_OK);
        break;
    }
    break;
```

```
    case WM_DESTROY: /* terminate the program */
      PostQuitMessage(0);
      break;
    default:
      /* Let Windows NT process any messages not specified in
         the preceding switch statement. */
      return DefWindowProc(hwnd, message, wParam, lParam);
  }
  return 0;
}
```

Adding Menu Accelerator Keys

Before leaving menus, one more feature relating to them will be discussed. This feature is the accelerator key. *Accelerator keys* are special keystrokes that you define which, when pressed, automatically select a menu option even though the menu in which that option resides is not displayed. Put differently, you can select an item directly by pressing an accelerator key, bypassing the menu entirely. The term *accelerator key* is an accurate description, because pressing one is generally a faster way to select a menu item than by first activating its menu and then selecting the item.

To define accelerator keys relative to a menu you must add an accelerator key table to your resource file. All accelerator table definitions have this general form:

TableName ACCELERATORS
{
    Key1, MenuID1 [,type] [Option]
    Key2, MenuID2 [,type] [Option]
    Key3, MenuID3 [,type] [Option]
    .

    .

    .

    Keyn, MenuIDn [,type] [Option]
}

Here, *TableName* is the name of the accelerator table. *Key* is the keystroke that selects the item and *MenuID* is the ID value associated with the desired item. The *type* specifies whether the key is a standard key (the default) or a virtual key (discussed shortly). The options may be one of the following macros: **NOINVERT**, **ALT**, **SHIFT**, and **CONTROL**. **NOINVERT** causes no top level menu to be displayed when an item is selected. **ALT** specifies an ALT key. **SHIFT** specifies a SHIFT key. **CONTROL** specifies a CTRL key.

The value of *Key* will be either a quoted character, an ASCII integer value corresponding to a key, or a virtual key code. If a quoted character is used, then it is assumed to be an ASCII character. If it is an integer value, then you must tell the resource compiler explicitly that this is an ASCII character by specifying *type* as **ASCII**. If it is a virtual key, then *type* must be **VIRTKEY**.

If the key is an uppercase quoted character, then its corresponding menu item will be selected if it is pressed while holding down SHIFT. If it is a lowercase character, then its menu item will be selected if the key is pressed by itself. If the key is specified as a lowercase character and **ALT** is specified as an option, then pressing ALT and the character will select the item. Finally, if you want the user to press CTRL and the character to select an item, specify the key in uppercase and precede it with a ^.

A virtual key is a system-independent code for a variety of keys. Virtual keys include the function keys F1 through F12, the arrow keys, and various non-ASCII keys. They are defined by macros in the header file **windows.h** (or one of its derivatives). All virtual key macros begin with **VK_**. The function keys are **VK_F1** through **VK_F12**, for example. You should refer to **windows.h** for the other virtual key code macros. To use a virtual key as an accelerator, simply specify its macro for the *key* and specify **VIRTKEY** for its *type*. You may also specify **ALT**, **SHIFT**, or **CONTROL** to achieve the desired key combination.

Here are some examples:

```
"A", IDM_x               ; select by pressing Shift-A
"a", IDM_x               ; select by pressing a
"^A", IDM_x              ; select by pressing Ctrl-A
"a", IDM_x, ALT          ; select by pressing Alt-A
```

Here is the **menu.rc** resource file that also contains accelerator key definitions for the menu specified in the previous section:

```
; Sample menu resource file
#include "menu.h"
#include <windows.h>

MYMENU MENU
{
```

```
    POPUP "&One"
    {
      MENUITEM "&Alpha\tF2", IDM_ALPHA
      MENUITEM "&Beta\tF3", IDM_BETA
    }
    POPUP "&Two"
    {
      MENUITEM "&Gamma\tShift-G", IDM_GAMMA
      POPUP "&Delta"
      {
        MENUITEM "&Epsilon\tCntl-E", IDM_EPSILON
        MENUITEM "&Zeta\tCntl-Z", IDM_ZETA
      }
      MENUITEM "&Eta\tCntl-F4", IDM_ETA
      MENUITEM "&Theta\tF5", IDM_THETA
    }
    MENUITEM "&Help", IDM_HELP
  }

; Define menu accelerators
MYMENU ACCELERATORS
{
  VK_F2, IDM_ALPHA, VIRTKEY
  VK_F3, IDM_BETA, VIRTKEY
  "G", IDM_GAMMA
  "^E", IDM_EPSILON
  "^Z", IDM_ZETA
  VK_F4, IDM_ETA, VIRTKEY, CONTROL
  VK_F5, IDM_THETA, VIRTKEY
  VK_F1, IDM_HELP, VIRTKEY
}
```

Notice that the menu definition has been enhanced to display which accelerator key selects which option. Each item is separated from its accelerator key using a tab. The header file **windows.h** is included, because it defines the virtual key macros.

Loading the Accelerator Table

Even though the accelerators are contained in the same resource file as the menu, they must be loaded separately using another API function called **LoadAccelerators()**, whose prototype is shown here:

HACCEL LoadAccelerators(HANDLE *ThisInst*, LPCSTR *Name*);

where *ThisInst* is the handle of the application and *Name* is the name of the accelerator table. The function returns a handle to the accelerator table or NULL if the table cannot be loaded.

You must call **LoadAccelerators()** soon after the window is created. For example, this shows how to load the **MYMENU** accelerator table:

```
HACCEL hAccel;

hAccel = LoadAccelerators(hThisInst, "MYMENU");
```

The value of **hAccel** will be used later to help process accelerator keys.

Although the **LoadAccelerators()** function loads the accelerator table, your program still cannot process the accelerator keys until you add another API function to the message loop. This function is called **TranslateAccelerator()**, and its prototype is shown here:

int TranslateAccelerator(HWND *hwnd*, HACCEL *hAccel*,
LPMSG *lpMess*);

Here, *hwnd* is the handle of the window for which accelerator keys will be translated. *hAccel* is the handle to the accelerator table that will be used. This is the handle returned by **LoadAccelerators()**. Finally, *lpMess* is a pointer to the message. The **TranslateAccelerator()** function returns true if an accelerator key was pressed and false otherwise. This function translates your keystrokes into the proper menu ID values.

When using **TranslateAccelerator()**, your message loop should look like this:

```
while(GetMessage(&msg, NULL, 0, 0))
{
  if(!TranslateAccelerator(hwnd, hAccel, &msg)) {
    TranslateMessage(&msg); /* allow use of keyboard */
    DispatchMessage(&msg); /* return control to Windows */
  }
}
```

To try using accelerators, make these changes to **WinMain()** from the preceding application and add the accelerator table to your resource file.

Before moving on to the next chapter, you should experiment on your own using message boxes, menus, and accelerators. Try the various options and see what they do.

Chapter 5

Using Dialog Boxes

F T E R menus, there is no more important Windows NT interface element than the dialog box. A dialog box is a type of window that provides a more flexible means by which the user can interact with your Windows NT application. In general, dialog boxes allow the user to select or enter information that would be difficult or impossible to enter using a menu.

How Dialog Boxes Interact with the User

A dialog box interacts with the user through one or more *controls*. A control is a specific type of input or output window. A control is owned by its parent window, which, for the examples presented in this chapter, is the dialog box. Windows NT supports several controls, including pushbuttons, check boxes, radio buttons, list boxes, edit boxes, combination boxes, scroll bars, and static controls. Each is briefly described here:

◆ A pushbutton is a control that the user "pushes on" (by clicking the mouse or tabbing to and then pressing ENTER) to activate some response. You have already been using pushbuttons in message boxes. For example, the OK button that we have been using in most message boxes is a pushbutton. There can be one or more pushbuttons in a dialog box.

◆ A check box contains one or more items that are either checked or not checked. If the item is checked, it means that it is selected. In a check box, more than one item may be selected.

◆ A radio button is essentially a check box in which one and only one item may be selected.

◆ A list box displays a list of items from which the user selects one (or more). List boxes are commonly used to display things such as file names.

◆ An edit box allows the user to enter a string. Edit boxes provide all necessary text editing features required by the user. Therefore, to input a string, your program simply displays an edit box and waits until the user has finished typing in the string.

◆ A combination box is a combination of a list box and an edit box.

◆ As you know, a scroll bar is used to scroll text in a window.

◆ A static control is used to output text (or graphics) that provides information to the user, but accepts no input.

In the course of explaining how to use dialog boxes with Windows, the examples in this chapter illustrate three of these controls: pushbuttons, the list box, and the edit box. Later in this book, other controls will be examined.

It is important to understand that controls both generate messages (when accessed by the user) and receive messages (from your application). A message generated by a control indicates what type of interaction the user has had with the control. A message sent to the control is essentially an instruction to which the control must respond. You will see examples of this type of message passing later in this chapter.

Modal Versus Modeless Dialog Boxes

There are two types of dialog boxes: *modal* and *modeless*. The most common dialog boxes are modal. A modal dialog box demands a response before the parent program will continue. That is, a modal dialog box will not allow you to refocus input to another part of the parent application without first responding to the dialog box.

A modeless dialog box does not prevent the parent program from running. That is, it does not demand a response before input can be focused to another part of the parent program.

Since the modal dialog box is the most common, it is the type of dialog box examined in this chapter.

Receiving Dialog Box Messages

A dialog box is a window (albeit, a special kind of window). Events that occur within it are sent to your program using the same message passing mechanism the main window uses. However, dialog box messages are not sent to your program's main window function. Instead, each dialog box that you define will need its own window function. This function must have this prototype. (Of course, the name of the function may be anything that you like.)

LRESULT CALLBACK *DFunc*(HWND *hdwnd,* UINT *message,*
WPARAM *wParam,* LPARAM *lParam*);

As you can see, this function receives the same parameters as the main window function. However, it differs from the main window function in that it returns a true or false result. Like your program's main window function, the dialog box window function will receive many messages. If it processes a message, then it must return true. If it does not respond to a message, it must return false.

In general, each control within a dialog box will be given its own resource ID. Each time that control is accessed by the user, a message will be sent to the dialog box's window function, indicating the ID of the control and the type of action the user has taken. That function will then decode the message and take appropriate actions. This process parallels the way messages are decoded by your program's main window function.

■■■

16-bit Conversion Note Because the dialog function is called by Windows, it must be exported in a .DEF file if you want your program to be downwardly compatible with 16-bit Windows.

Activating a Dialog Box

To activate a dialog box (to cause it to be displayed) you must call the **DialogBox()** API function, whose prototype is shown here:

int DialogBox(HANDLE *hThisInst,* LPCSTR *lpName,*
HWND *hwnd,* DLGPROC *lpDFunc*);

Here, *hThisInst* is a handle to the current application that is passed to your program in the instance parameter of **WinMain()**. The name of the dialog box as defined in the resource file is pointed to by *lpName*. The handle to the parent window that activates the dialog box is passed in *hwnd*. The *lpDFunc* parameter contains a pointer to the dialog box function.

16-bit Conversion Note In 16-bit Windows, the *lpDFunc* parameter to **DialogBox()** is a pointer to a *procedure-instance,* which is a short piece of code that links the dialog function with the data segment that the program is currently using. A procedure-instance is obtained using the **MakeProcInstance()** API function. However, this no longer applies to Windows NT. Instead, the *lpDFunc* parameter is a pointer to the dialog function itself.

Creating a Simple Dialog Box

For a first dialog box, a simple example will be created. This dialog box will contain three pushbuttons called Red, Green, and Cancel. When either the Red or Green button is pressed, it will activate a message box indicating the choice selected. The box will be removed from the screen when the Cancel button is pressed.

The program will have a top level menu containing three options: Dialog 1, Dialog 2, and Help. Only Dialog 1 will have a dialog box associated with it. The Dialog 2 entry is a placeholder so you can define your own dialog box as you work through the examples.

While this, and other examples in this chapter, don't do much with the information provided by the dialog box, they illustrate the central features that you will use in your own applications.

The Dialog Box Example Resource File

A dialog box is another resource that is contained in your program's resource file. Before developing a program that uses a dialog box, you will need a resource file that specifies one. Although it is possible to specify the contents of a dialog box using a text editor and enter its specifications as you do when creating a menu, this is seldom done. Instead, most programmers use a dialog editor. (The one supplied with the Microsoft Windows NT SDK is called DLGEDIT.) The main reason for this is that dialog box definitions involve the position of the various controls inside the dialog box, which is best done interactively. However, since the complete .RC files for the examples in this chapter are supplied in their text form, you should simply enter them as text. Just remember that when creating your own dialog boxes, you will want to use the dialog editor.

note:

Since, in practice, most dialog boxes are created using a dialog editor, only a brief explanation of the dialog box definition in the resource file is given.

Dialog boxes are defined within your program's resource file using the **DIALOG** statement. Its general form is shown here:

Dialog-name DIALOG [DISCARDABLE] *X, Y, Width, Height*
Features
{
   Dialog-items
}

The *Dialog-name* is the name of the dialog box. The box's upper left corner will be at *X, Y* and the box will have the dimensions specified by *Width* x *Height*. If the box may be removed from memory when not in use, then specify it as **DISCARDABLE**. One or more features of the dialog box may be specified. As you will see, two of these are the caption and the style of the box. The *Dialog-items* are the controls that comprise the dialog box.

The following file includes a menu that is used to activate the dialog box, accelerator keys, and then the dialog box itself. You should enter it into your computer at this time, calling it MYDIALOG.RC.

```
; Sample dialog box and menu resource file.
#include "mydialog.h"
#include <windows.h>

MYMENU MENU
{
  MENUITEM "Dialog &1", IDM_DIALOG1
  MENUITEM "Dialog &2", IDM_DIALOG2
  MENUITEM "&Help", IDM_HELP
}

MYMENU ACCELERATORS
{
  VK_F2, IDM_DIALOG1, VIRTKEY
  VK_F3, IDM_DIALOG2, VIRTKEY
  VK_F1, IDM_HELP, VIRTKEY
}
```

```
MYDB DIALOG 18, 18, 142, 92
CAPTION "Test Dialog Box"
STYLE DS_MODALFRAME | WS_POPUP | WS_CAPTION | WS_SYSMENU
{
   DEFPUSHBUTTON "Red", IDD_RED, 32, 40, 28, 13,
            WS_CHILD | WS_VISIBLE | WS_TABSTOP
   PUSHBUTTON "Green", IDD_GREEN, 74, 40, 30, 13,
            WS_CHILD | WS_VISIBLE | WS_TABSTOP
   PUSHBUTTON "Cancel", IDCANCEL, 52, 65, 37, 14,
            WS_CHILD | WS_VISIBLE | WS_TABSTOP
}
```

This defines a dialog box called **MYDB** that has its upper left corner at location 18, 18. Its width is 142 and its height is 92. The string after **CAPTION** becomes the title of the dialog box. The **STYLE** statement determines what type of dialog box is created. Some common style values are shown in Table 5-1. You can OR together the values that are appropriate for the style of dialog box that you desire. These style values may also used by other controls.

Value	Meaning
DS_MODALFRAME	Create modal dialog box
WS_BORDER	Include a border
WS_CAPTION	Include title bar
WS_CHILD	Create as child window
WS_POPUP	Create as popup window
WS_MAXIMIZEBOX	Include maximize box
WS_MINIMIZEBOX	Include minimize box
WS_SYSMENU	Include system menu
WS_TABSTOP	Control may be tabbed to
WS_VISIBLE	Box is visible when activated

Table 5-1
Some Common Dialog Box Style Options

Within the **MYDB** definition are defined three pushbuttons. The first is the default pushbutton. This button is automatically highlighted when the dialog box is first displayed. The general form of a pushbutton declaration is shown here:

PUSHBUTTON "*string*", *PBID, X, Y, Width, Height* [, *Style*]

Here, *string* is the text that will be shown inside the pushbutton. *PBID* is the value associated with the pushbutton. It is this value that is returned to your program when this button is pushed. The button's upper left corner will be at *X, Y* and the button will have the dimensions specified by *Width* x *Height*. The *Style* determines the exact nature of the pushbutton. The same parameters are used for default pushbuttons, as well.

The header file **mydialog.h**, which is also used by the example program, is shown here:

```
#define IDM_DIALOG1   100
#define IDM_DIALOG2   101
#define IDM_HELP      102

#define IDD_RED       103
#define IDD_GREEN     104
```

Enter this file now.

The Dialog Box Window Function

As stated earlier, events that occur within a dialog box are passed to the window function associated with that dialog box and not your program's main window function. The following dialog box window function responds to the events that occur within the **MYDB** dialog box.

```
/* A simple dialog function. */
LRESULT CALLBACK DialogFunc(HWND hdwnd, UINT message,
                            WPARAM wParam, LPARAM lParam)
{
  switch(message) {
    case WM_COMMAND:
      switch(LOWORD(wParam)) {
        case IDCANCEL:
          EndDialog(hdwnd, NULL);
```

```
          return 1;
        case IDD_RED:
          MessageBox(hdwnd, "You Picked Red", "RED", MB_OK);
          return 1;
        case IDD_GREEN:
          MessageBox(hdwnd, "You Picked Green", "GREEN", MB_OK);
          return 1;
    }
  }
  return 0;
}
```

Each time a control within the dialog box is accessed, a **WM_COMMAND** message is sent to **DialogFunc()** and **LOWORD(wParam)** contains the ID of the control affected.

DialogFunc() processes the three messages that can be generated by the box. First, if the user presses Cancel, then **IDCANCEL** is sent, causing the dialog box to be closed using a call to the API function **EndDialog()**. (**IDCANCEL** is a standard ID defined by including **windows.h**.) **EndDialog()** has this prototype:

BOOL EndDialog(HWND *hdwnd,* int *nStatus*);

Here, *hdwnd* is the handle to the dialog box and *nStatus* is a status code returned by the **DialogBox()** function. (The value of *nStatus* may be ignored, if it is not relevant to your program.) This function returns non-zero if successful and zero otherwise. (In normal situations, the function is successful.)

Pressing either of the other two buttons causes a message box to be displayed that confirms the selection.

▬▬▬

16-bit Conversion Note Remember, if you will be porting your code back to 16-bit Windows, you must add **DialogFunc()** to the EXPORTS section of your .DEF file since it is a callback function. For example, your EXPORTS statement should look like this:

EXPORTS WindowFunc DialogFunc

note: *.DEF files are not required by Windows NT, but they may be included—they are simply ignored.*

Figure 5-1

Sample output from the first dialog box program

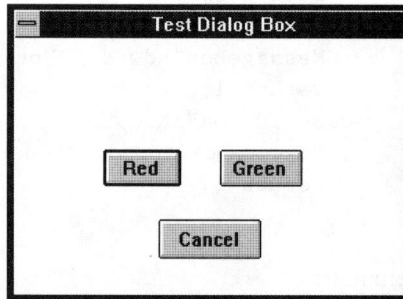

The First Dialog Box Sample Program

Here is the entire dialog box example. When the program begins execution, only the top level menu is displayed on the menu bar. By selecting Dialog 1, the user causes the dialog box to be displayed. Once the dialog box is displayed, selecting a pushbutton causes the appropriate response. A sample screen is shown in Figure 5-1.

```
/* A minimal Windows NT skeleton that demonstrates
   dialog boxes with pushbuttons. */

/* The following definition causes stricter type checking.
   This is optional, but suggested because it will help
   catch potential type mismatch errors--especially
   when porting from 16-bit Windows. */
#define STRICT

#include <windows.h>
#include <string.h>
#include <stdio.h>
#include "mydialog.h"

LRESULT CALLBACK WindowFunc(HWND, UINT, WPARAM, LPARAM);
LRESULT CALLBACK DialogFunc(HWND, UINT, WPARAM, LPARAM);

char szWinName[] = "MyWin"; /* name of window class */

HINSTANCE hInst;

int WINAPI WinMain(HINSTANCE hThisInst, HINSTANCE hPrevInst,
```

```
                    LPSTR lpszArgs, int nWinMode)
{
  HWND hwnd;
  MSG msg;
  WNDCLASS wcl;
  HANDLE hAccel;

  /* Define a window class. */
  wcl.hInstance = hThisInst; /* handle to this instance */
  wcl.lpszClassName = szWinName; /* window class name */
  wcl.lpfnWndProc = WindowFunc; /* window function */
  wcl.style = 0; /* default style */

  wcl.hIcon = LoadIcon(NULL, IDI_APPLICATION); /* icon style */
  wcl.hCursor = LoadCursor(NULL, IDC_ARROW); /* cursor style */

  /* specify name of menu resource */
  wcl.lpszMenuName = "MYMENU"; /* main menu */

  wcl.cbClsExtra = 0; /* no extra */
  wcl.cbWndExtra = 0; /* information needed */

  /* Make the window light gray. */
  wcl.hbrBackground = GetStockObject(LTGRAY_BRUSH);

  /* Register the window class. */
  if(!RegisterClass (&wcl)) return 0;

  /* Now that a window class has been registered, a window
     can be created. */
  hwnd = CreateWindow(
    szWinName, /* name of window class */
    "Dialog Boxes", /* title */
    WS_OVERLAPPEDWINDOW, /* window style--normal */
    CW_USEDEFAULT, /* X coordinate--let Windows decide */
    CW_USEDEFAULT, /* Y coordinate--let Windows decide */
    CW_USEDEFAULT, /* width--let Windows decide */
    CW_USEDEFAULT, /* height--let Windows decide */
    NULL, /* handle of parent window--there isn't one */
    NULL, /* no menu */
    hThisInst, /* handle of this instance of the program */
    NULL /* no additional arguments */
  );
```

```
    hInst = hThisInst; /* save the current instance handle */

    /* load accelerators */
    hAccel = LoadAccelerators(hThisInst, "MYMENU");

    /* Display the window. */
    ShowWindow(hwnd, nWinMode);
    UpdateWindow(hwnd);

    /* Create the message loop. */
    while(GetMessage(&msg, NULL, 0, 0))
    {
      if(!TranslateAccelerator(hwnd, hAccel, &msg)) {
        TranslateMessage(&msg); /* allow use of keyboard */
        DispatchMessage(&msg); /* return control to Windows */
      }
    }
    return msg.wParam;
}


/* This function is called by Windows NT and is passed
   messages from the message queue.
*/
LRESULT CALLBACK WindowFunc(HWND hwnd, UINT message, WPARAM wParam,
                LPARAM lParam)
{
    switch(message) {
      case WM_COMMAND:
        switch(LOWORD(wParam)) {
          case IDM_DIALOG1:
            DialogBox(hInst, "MYDB", hwnd, DialogFunc);
            break;
          case IDM_DIALOG2:
            MessageBox(hwnd, "Dialog Not Implemented", "", MB_OK);
            break;
          case IDM_HELP:
            MessageBox(hwnd, "Help", "", MB_OK);
            break;
        }
        break;
      case WM_DESTROY: /* terminate the program */
        PostQuitMessage(0);
        break;
      default:
```

```
      /* Let Windows NT process any messages not specified in
         the preceding switch statement. */
      return DefWindowProc(hwnd, message, wParam, lParam);
  }
  return 0;
}

/* A simple dialog function. */
LRESULT CALLBACK DialogFunc(HWND hdwnd, UINT message,
                            WPARAM wParam, LPARAM lParam)
{
  switch(message) {
    case WM_COMMAND:
      switch(LOWORD(wParam)) {
        case IDCANCEL:
          EndDialog(hdwnd, 0);
          return 1;
        case IDD_RED:
          MessageBox(hdwnd, "You Picked Red", "RED", MB_OK);
          return 1;
        case IDD_GREEN:
          MessageBox(hdwnd, "You Picked Green", "GREEN", MB_OK);
          return 1;
      }
  }
  return 0;
}
```

Notice the global variable **hInst**. This variable is assigned a copy of the current instance handle passed to **WinMain()**. The reason for this variable is that the dialog box needs access to the current instance handle. However, the dialog box is not created in **WinMain()**. Instead, it is created in **WindowFunc()**. Therefore, a copy of the instance parameter must be made so that it can be accessible outside of **WinMain()**.

Adding a List Box

To continue exploring dialog boxes, let's add another control to the dialog box defined in the previous program. One of the most common controls after the pushbutton is the list box.

First, add this list box description to the dialog definition in the MYDIALOG.RC resource file.

```
LISTBOX ID_LB1, 2, 10, 47, 28, LBS_NOTIFY | WS_CHILD |
        WS_VISIBLE | WS_BORDER | WS_VSCROLL | WS_TABSTOP
```

That is, your dialog box definition should now look like this:

```
MYDB DIALOG 18, 18, 142, 92
CAPTION "Test Dialog Box"
STYLE DS_MODALFRAME | WS_POPUP | WS_CAPTION | WS_SYSMENU
{
  DEFPUSHBUTTON "Red", IDD_RED, 32, 40, 28, 13,
            WS_CHILD | WS_VISIBLE | WS_TABSTOP
  PUSHBUTTON "Green", IDD_GREEN, 74, 40, 30, 13,
            WS_CHILD | WS_VISIBLE | WS_TABSTOP
  PUSHBUTTON "Cancel", IDCANCEL, 52, 65, 37, 14,
            WS_CHILD | WS_VISIBLE | WS_TABSTOP
  LISTBOX ID_LB1, 2, 10, 47, 28, LBS_NOTIFY | WS_CHILD |
            WS_VISIBLE | WS_BORDER | WS_VSCROLL | WS_TABSTOP
}
```

The **LISTBOX** statement has this general form:

LISTBOX *LBID, X, Y, Width, Height* [,*Style*]

Here, *LBID* is what identifies the list box. The box's upper left corner will be at *X, Y* and the box will have the dimensions specified by *Width* x *Height*. *Style* determines the exact nature of the list box.

You will also need to add this macro to **mydialog.h**:

```
#define ID_LB1      105
```

ID_LB1 identifies the list box specified in the dialog box definition in the resource file. It is used as an index to the message response function that responds to activity inside the list box.

Responding to a List Box

To respond to list box events requires a simple addition to the preceding program. When using a list box, you must perform two basic operations. First, you must initialize the list box when the dialog box is first displayed. This consists of sending the list box the list that it will display. (By default, the list box will be empty.) Second, once the list box has been initialized, your program will need to respond to the user selecting an item from the list.

List boxes generate various types of messages. The only one we will use is **LBN_DBLCLK**. This message is sent when the user has double-clicked on an entry in the list. This message is contained in **HIWORD(wParam)** each time a **WM_COMMAND** message is generated for a list box. Once a selection has been made, you will need to query the list box to find out which item has been selected.

Unlike a pushbutton, a list box is a control that receives messages as well as generates them. You can send a list box several different messages. However, our example only sends these two:

Macro	Purpose
LB_ADDSTRING	Add a string (selection) to the list box.
LB_GETCURSEL	Requests the index of the item selected.

LB_ADDSTRING is a message that tells the list box to add a specified string to the list. That is, the specified string becomes another selection within the box. You will see how to use this message shortly. The **LB_GETCURSEL** causes the list box to return the index of the item within the list box that the user selects. All list box indexes begin with 0.

To send a message to the list box (or any other control) use the **SendDlgItemMessage()** API function. Its prototype is shown here:

```
LONG SendDlgItemMessage(HWND hdwnd, int ID,
                UINT IDMsg, WPARAM wParam,
                LPARAM lParam);
```

SendDlgItemMessage() sends to the control (within the dialog box) whose ID is specified by *ID* the message specified by *IDMsg*. The handle of the dialog box is specified in *hdwnd*. Any additional information required by the message is specified in *wParam* and *lParam*. The additional information, if any, varies from message to message. If there is no additional information to pass to a control, the *WParam* and the *LParam* arguments should be 0. The value returned by **SendDlgItemMessage()** contains the information requested by *IDMsg*.

Initializing the List Box

Since a list box is, by default, empty, you will need to initialize it when the dialog box that contains it is first displayed. This proves to be quite simple, because each time a dialog box is activated, its window function is sent a **WM_INITDIALOG** message. Therefore, you will need to add this case to the outer **switch** statement in **DialogFunc()**.

```
case WM_INITDIALOG: // initialize list box
  SendDlgItemMessage(hdwnd, ID_LB1,
                     LB_ADDSTRING, 0, (LPARAM)"Apple");
  SendDlgItemMessage(hdwnd, ID_LB1,
                     LB_ADDSTRING, 0, (LPARAM)"Orange");
  SendDlgItemMessage(hdwnd, ID_LB1,
                     LB_ADDSTRING, 0, (LPARAM)"Pear");
  SendDlgItemMessage(hdwnd, ID_LB1,
                     LB_ADDSTRING, 0, (LPARAM)"Grape");
  return 1;
```

This code loads the list box with the strings "Apple", "Orange", "Pear", and "Grape". Each string is added to the list box by calling **SendDlgItemMessage()** with the **LB_ADDSTRING** message. The string to add is pointed to by the *lParam* parameter. (The type cast to **LPARAM** is necessary.) In this case, each string is added to the list box in the order it is sent. (However, depending upon how you construct the list box, it is possible to have the items displayed in alphabetical order.) If the number of items you send to a list box exceeds what it can display in its window, vertical scroll bars will be added automatically.

Processing a Selection

After the list box has been initialized, it is ready for use. Each time the user selects an item in the list box by double-clicking on the item, a **WM_COMMAND** message is passed to the dialog box's window function, and the **LBN_DBLCLK** message is contained in **HIWORD(wParam)**.

Once a selection has been made, you determine which item was chosen by sending the **LB_GETCURSEL** message to the list box. The list box then returns the index of the item.

To demonstrate how to process a list box selection, add this case to the inner switch inside **DialogFunc()**. Each time a selection is made, a message box will display the index of the item selected.

```
case ID_LB1: /* process list box */
  // see  if user made a selection
  if(HIWORD(wParam)==LBN_DBLCLK) {
    i = SendDlgItemMessage(hdwnd, ID_LB1,
          LB_GETCURSEL, 0, 0L);  // get index
    sprintf(str, "Index in list is: %d", i);
    MessageBox(hdwnd, str, "Selection Made", MB_OK);
  }
  return 1;
```

The Entire List Box Example

For your convenience, the entire expanded dialog box program is shown here. (Be sure to update **mydialog.h** and MYDIALOG.RC before compiling this program.)

```
/* A minimal Windows NT skeleton that demonstrates
   dialog boxes with list boxes and pushbuttons. */

/* The following definition causes stricter type checking.
   This is optional, but suggested because it will help
   catch potential type mismatch errors--especially
   when porting from 16-bit Windows. */
#define STRICT

#include <windows.h>
#include <string.h>
#include <stdio.h>
#include "mydialog.h"

LRESULT CALLBACK WindowFunc(HWND, UINT, WPARAM, LPARAM);
LRESULT CALLBACK DialogFunc(HWND, UINT, WPARAM, LPARAM);

char szWinName[] = "MyWin"; /* name of window class */
```

```
HINSTANCE hInst;

int WINAPI WinMain(HINSTANCE hThisInst, HINSTANCE hPrevInst,
                   LPSTR lpszArgs, int nWinMode)
{
  HWND hwnd;
  MSG msg;
  WNDCLASS wcl;
  HANDLE hAccel;

  /* Define a window class. */
  wcl.hInstance = hThisInst; /* handle to this instance */
  wcl.lpszClassName = szWinName; /* window class name */
  wcl.lpfnWndProc = WindowFunc; /* window function */
  wcl.style = 0; /* default style */

  wcl.hIcon = LoadIcon(NULL, IDI_APPLICATION); /* icon style */
  wcl.hCursor = LoadCursor(NULL, IDC_ARROW); /* cursor style */

  /* specify name of menu resource */
  wcl.lpszMenuName = "MYMENU"; /* main menu */

  wcl.cbClsExtra = 0; /* no extra */
  wcl.cbWndExtra = 0; /* information needed */

  /* Make the window light gray. */
  wcl.hbrBackground = GetStockObject(LTGRAY_BRUSH);

  /* Register the window class. */
  if(!RegisterClass (&wcl)) return 0;

  /* Now that a window class has been registered, a window
     can be created. */
  hwnd = CreateWindow(
    szWinName, /* name of window class */
    "Dialog Boxes", /* title */
    WS_OVERLAPPEDWINDOW, /* window style--normal */
    CW_USEDEFAULT, /* X coordinate--let Windows decide */
    CW_USEDEFAULT, /* Y coordinate--let Windows decide */
    CW_USEDEFAULT, /* width--let Windows decide */
    CW_USEDEFAULT, /* height--let Windows decide */
    NULL, /* handle of parent window--there isn't one */
    NULL, /* no menu */
    hThisInst, /* handle of this instance of the program */
```

```
    NULL /* no additional arguments */
  );

  hInst = hThisInst; /* save the current instance handle */

  /* load accelerators */
  hAccel = LoadAccelerators(hThisInst, "MYMENU");

  /* Display the window. */
  ShowWindow(hwnd, nWinMode);
  UpdateWindow(hwnd);

  /* Create the message loop. */
  while(GetMessage(&msg, NULL, 0, 0))
  {
    if(!TranslateAccelerator(hwnd, hAccel, &msg)) {
      TranslateMessage(&msg); /* allow use of keyboard */
      DispatchMessage(&msg); /* return control to Windows */
    }
  }
  return msg.wParam;
}


/* This function is called by Windows NT and is passed
   messages from the message queue.
*/
LRESULT CALLBACK WindowFunc(HWND hwnd, UINT message, WPARAM wParam,
                LPARAM lParam)
{
  switch(message) {
    case WM_COMMAND:
      switch(LOWORD(wParam)) {
        case IDM_DIALOG1:
          DialogBox(hInst, "MYDB", hwnd, DialogFunc);
          break;
        case IDM_DIALOG2:
          MessageBox(hwnd, "Dialog Not Implemented", "", MB_OK);
          break;
        case IDM_HELP:
          MessageBox(hwnd, "Help", "", MB_OK);
          break;
      }
      break;
    case WM_DESTROY: /* terminate the program */
```

```
      PostQuitMessage(0);
      break;
    default:
      /* Let Windows NT process any messages not specified in
         the preceding switch statement. */
      return DefWindowProc(hwnd, message, wParam, lParam);
  }
  return 0;
}


/* A simple dialog function. */
LRESULT CALLBACK DialogFunc(HWND hdwnd, UINT message,
                            WPARAM wParam, LPARAM lParam)
{
  long i;
  char str[80];

  switch(message) {
    case WM_COMMAND:
      switch(LOWORD(wParam)) {
        case IDCANCEL:
          EndDialog(hdwnd, 0);
          return 1;
        case IDD_RED:
          MessageBox(hdwnd, "You Picked Red", "RED", MB_OK);
          return 1;
        case IDD_GREEN:
          MessageBox(hdwnd, "You Picked Green", "GREEN", MB_OK);
          return 1;
        case ID_LB1: /* process list box */
          // see  if user made a selection
          if(HIWORD(wParam)==LBN_DBLCLK) {
            i = SendDlgItemMessage(hdwnd, ID_LB1,
                   LB_GETCURSEL, 0, 0L);  // get index

            sprintf(str, "Index in list is: %d", i);
            MessageBox(hdwnd, str, "Selection Made", MB_OK);
          }
          return 1;
      }
    case WM_INITDIALOG: // initialize list box
      SendDlgItemMessage(hdwnd, ID_LB1,
                         LB_ADDSTRING, 0, (LPARAM)"Apple");
      SendDlgItemMessage(hdwnd, ID_LB1,
```

```
                    LB_ADDSTRING, 0, (LPARAM)"Orange");
    SendDlgItemMessage(hdwnd, ID_LB1,
                    LB_ADDSTRING, 0, (LPARAM)"Pear");
    SendDlgItemMessage(hdwnd, ID_LB1,
                    LB_ADDSTRING, 0, (LPARAM)"Grape");
    return 1;
  }
  return 0;
}
```

Sample output from this program is shown in Figure 5-2.

Adding an Edit Box

The last control that we will add to the sample dialog box is the edit box. Edit boxes are particularly useful, because they allow users to enter a string of their own choosing. Before you can use an edit box, you must define one in your resource file. For this example, change MYDIALOG.RC so that it looks like this:

```
MYDB DIALOG 18, 18, 142, 92
CAPTION "Test Dialog Box"
STYLE DS_MODALFRAME | WS_POPUP | WS_CAPTION | WS_SYSMENU
{
   DEFPUSHBUTTON "Red", IDD_RED, 32, 40, 28, 13,
             WS_CHILD | WS_VISIBLE | WS_TABSTOP
   PUSHBUTTON "Green", IDD_GREEN, 74, 40, 30, 13,
             WS_CHILD | WS_VISIBLE | WS_TABSTOP
   PUSHBUTTON "Cancel", IDCANCEL, 52, 65, 37, 14,
             WS_CHILD | WS_VISIBLE | WS_TABSTOP
   PUSHBUTTON "Edit OK", IDOK, 82, 22, 30, 14,
             WS_CHILD | WS_VISIBLE | WS_TABSTOP
   LISTBOX ID_LB1, 2, 10, 47, 28, LBS_NOTIFY | WS_CHILD |
          WS_VISIBLE | WS_BORDER | WS_VSCROLL | WS_TABSTOP
   EDITTEXT ID_EB1, 61, 8, 72, 12, ES_LEFT | ES_AUTOHSCROLL |
          WS_CHILD | WS_VISIBLE | WS_BORDER | WS_TABSTOP
}
```

This version adds a pushbutton called Edit OK, which will be used to tell the program that you are done editing text in the edit box. It also adds the edit box itself. The ID for the edit box is **ID_EB1**. This definition causes a standard edit box to be created.

Figure 5-2

Sample output
that includes a
list box

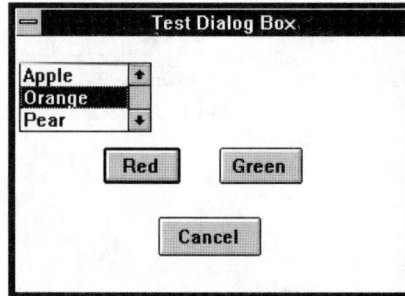

The **EDITTEXT** statement has this general form:

EDITTEXT *EDID, X, Y, Width, Height* [,*Style*]

Here, *EDID* is the value that identifies the edit box. The box's upper left corner
will be at *X, Y* and its dimensions are specified by *Width* and *Height*. *Style*
determines the exact nature of the edit box. The style macros **ES_LEFT** and
ES_AUTOHSCROLL cause the text in the box to be left justified and for
the box to include a horizontal scroll bar.

Next, add this macro definition to **mydialog.h**.

```
#define ID_EB1    106
```

Edit boxes recognize many messages and generate several of their own.
However, for the purposes of this example, there is no need for the program
to respond to any messages. As you will see, edit boxes perform the editing
function on their own. There is no need for program interaction when text is
edited. Your program simply decides when it wants to obtain the current
contents of the edit box.

To obtain the current contents of the edit box, use the API function
GetDlgItemText(). It has this prototype:

UINT GetDlgItemText(HWND *hdwnd*, int *nID*,
                    LPSTR *lpstr*, int *nMax*);

This function causes the edit box to copy the current contents of the box to
the string pointed to by *lpstr*. The handle of the dialog box is specified by *hdwnd*.

The ID of the edit box is specified by *nID*. The maximum number of characters to copy is specified by *nMax*. The function returns the length of the string.

To add an edit box to the sample program, add this **case** statement to the inner **switch** of the **DialogFunc()** function. Each time the Edit OK button is pressed, a message window will be displayed that contains the current text that is inside the edit box.

```
case IDOK: /* OK button selected */
  /* display contents of the edit box */
  GetDlgItemText(hdwnd, ID_EB1, str, 80);
  MessageBox(hdwnd, str, "Edit Box Contains", MB_OK);
  return 1;
```

The macro **IDOK** is a built-in value defined by including **windows.h**.

This chapter only scratches the surface of what you can do using dialog boxes and the various controls. Additional controls are covered later in this book. Also, you will want to experiment on your own, exploring how the various controls function and interact with your program.

Chapter 6

Creating Custom Icons,

Cursors, and Bitmaps

HIS chapter explains how to control the appearance of two important items linked with all Windows applications: the design of the icon that is displayed when an application is minimized, and the shape of the mouse cursor. How to display a bit-mapped graphic image is also discussed.

Icons, cursors, and bitmaps are resources that consist of graphical information. These resources are created using an *image editor*. (The image editor supplied with the Microsoft Windows NT SDK is called IMAGEDIT.) Once you have defined the nature of the icon, cursor, or bitmap, the image must be incorporated into the .RC file associated with your program. Finally, before the image is used, it must be loaded by your program. This chapter discusses the necessary details required to accomplish this.

Defining an Icon and a Cursor

As stated, when you create your own icons or cursors, you will need to use an image editor. For the examples that will follow, you will need both an icon and a cursor definition. You must create these using the tools supplied with your compiler. Each image must then be saved in a file.

Once you have defined the icon and cursor images, you will need to add an **ICON** and a **CURSOR** statement to your program's .RC file. These statements have these general forms:

IconName ICON [DISCARDABLE] *filename*

CursorName CURSOR [DISCARDABLE] *filename*

Here, the *IconName* is the name that identifies the icon, and *CursorName* is the name that identifies the cursor. These names are used by your program to reference the icon and cursor. If you specify **DISCARDABLE**, then your icon or cursor can be removed from memory when it is not being used. (This is optional.) The *filename* specifies the file that holds the custom icon or cursor.

For the examples that follow, you should call your icon **MYICON** and your cursor **MYCURSOR**. Store your icon in a file called ICON.ICO and your cursor in a file called CURSOR.CUR. Next, add these lines to your .RC file:

```
MYCURSOR CURSOR CURSOR.CUR
MYICON ICON ICON.ICO
```

Changing the Icon and the Cursor

As you know, all Windows NT applications first create a window class, which defines the attributes of the window, including the shape of the application's icon and mouse cursor. The handles to the icon and the mouse cursor are stored in the **hIcon** and **hCursor** fields of the **WNDCLASS** structure. So far, we have been using one of the built-in icons and cursors supplied by Windows NT. To use a custom icon and mouse cursor, you must load the new icon and the new cursor before the window class is registered. To accomplish this you must use the API functions **LoadIcon()** and **LoadCursor()**, which you learned about in Chapter 2. For example, this loads the icon identified as **MYICON** and the cursor called **MYCURSOR** and stores their handles in the appropriate fields of the **wcl WNDCLASS** structure variable:

```
wcl.hIcon = LoadIcon(hThisInst, "MYICON");
wcl.hCursor = LoadCursor(hThisInst, "MYCURSOR");
```

Here, **hThisInst** is the handle of the current instance of the program. In the previous programs in this book, these functions have been used to load default icons and cursors. Here, they will be used to load your custom icon and cursor.

A Sample Program That Demonstrates a Custom Icon and Cursor

The following program uses the custom icon and cursor defined in the resource file. The icon is displayed when the window is minimized. The cursor will be used when the mouse pointer is over the window.

Remember, before you try to compile this program, you must define a custom icon and cursor using an image editor and then add these resources to the .RC file associated with the program.

```
/* A minimal Windows NT skeleton that demonstrates
   a custom icon and mouse cursor. */

/* The following definition causes stricter type checking.
   This is optional, but suggested because it will help
   catch potential type mismatch errors--especially
   when porting from 16-bit Windows. */
#define STRICT

#include <windows.h>
#include <string.h>
#include <stdio.h>

LRESULT CALLBACK WindowFunc(HWND, UINT, WPARAM, LPARAM);

char szWinName[] = "MyWin"; /* name of window class */

int WINAPI WinMain(HINSTANCE hThisInst, HINSTANCE hPrevInst,
                   LPSTR lpszArgs, int nWinMode)
{
  HWND hwnd;
  MSG msg;
  WNDCLASS wcl;
  HANDLE hAccel;

  /* Define a window class. */
  wcl.hInstance = hThisInst; /* handle to this instance */
  wcl.lpszClassName = szWinName; /* window class name */
  wcl.lpfnWndProc = WindowFunc; /* window function */
  wcl.style = 0; /* default style */

  wcl.hIcon = LoadIcon(hThisInst, "MYICON"); /* load icon */
  wcl.hCursor = LoadCursor(hThisInst, "MYCURSOR"); /* load cursor */

  wcl.lpszMenuName = NULL; /* no main menu */

  wcl.cbClsExtra = 0; /* no extra */
  wcl.cbWndExtra = 0; /* information needed */
```

```c
/* Make the window light gray. */
wcl.hbrBackground = GetStockObject(LTGRAY_BRUSH);

/* Register the window class. */
if(!RegisterClass (&wcl)) return 0;

/* Now that a window class has been registered, a window
   can be created. */
hwnd = CreateWindow(
  szWinName, /* name of window class */
  "Custom Icon and Cursor", /* title */
  WS_OVERLAPPEDWINDOW, /* window style--normal */
  CW_USEDEFAULT, /* X coordinate--let Windows decide */
  CW_USEDEFAULT, /* Y coordinate--let Windows decide */
  CW_USEDEFAULT, /* width--let Windows decide */
  CW_USEDEFAULT, /* height--let Windows decide */
  NULL, /* handle of parent window--there isn't one */
  NULL, /* no menu */
  hThisInst, /* handle of this instance of the program */
  NULL /* no additional arguments */
);

/* Display the window. */
ShowWindow(hwnd, nWinMode);
UpdateWindow(hwnd);

/* Create the message loop. */
while(GetMessage(&msg, NULL, 0, 0))
{
  TranslateMessage(&msg); /* allow use of keyboard */
  DispatchMessage(&msg); /* return control to Windows */
}
  return msg.wParam;
}

/* This function is called by Windows NT and is passed
   messages from the message queue.
*/
LRESULT CALLBACK WindowFunc(HWND hwnd, UINT message, WPARAM wParam,
                LPARAM lParam)
{
  switch(message) {
    case WM_DESTROY: /* terminate the program */
      PostQuitMessage(0);
```

```
        break;
    default:
      /* Let Windows NT process any messages not specified in
         the preceding switch statement. */
      return DefWindowProc(hwnd, message, wParam, lParam);
  }
  return 0;
}
```

The icon is shown in Figure 6-1. Of course, your custom icon will look different.

Using a Bitmap

A bitmap is a graphic image. Since Windows is a graphics-based operating system, it makes sense that you can include graphic images in your applications. It is important to understand that you can draw graphic images, such as lines, circles, and boxes inside the client area of a window using the rich set of graphics functions contained in the Windows API. However, a bitmap, and the mechanism used to display one, is separate from those types of graphics. A bitmap is a self-contained graphical resource that your program utilizes as a single entity. A bitmap contains a bit-by-bit representation of the image that will ultimately be displayed on the screen. Put differently, a bitmap contains a complete image that your program generally displays in its totality.

Creating a Bitmap

Before continuing, you must create a bitmap resource. As with other graphical resources, you must use an image editor to create your bitmap. To use the

Figure 6-1
The customized icon

example that follows, call your bitmap file BP.BMP and then add this line to your .RC file:

```
MYBITMAP BITMAP BP.BMP
```

Displaying a Bitmap

Once you have created a bitmap and included it in your application's resource file, you may display it as many times as you want. In the example that follows, the bitmap will be displayed each time the left mouse button is pressed, at the current location of the mouse pointer.

To display a bitmap requires that you perform a number of steps. Here is the general procedure. First, you must obtain the device context, so that your program can output to the window. Then, you must load the bitmap and store its handle. You must obtain an equivalent memory device context that will hold the bitmap until it is displayed. That is, a bitmap is held in memory until it is copied to your window. To actually display the bitmap, you first select it and then call the **BitBlt()** API function, which finally displays the image.

Here is the code within your program's window function that implements the steps described in the previous paragraph. It loads a bitmap and displays it on the screen each time the left mouse button is pressed.

```
HBITMAP hBit;
HDC DC, memDC;

case WM_LBUTTONDOWN:
  DC = GetDC(hwnd); /* get device context */
  hBit = LoadBitmap(hInst, "MYBITMAP"); /* load bitmap */
  memDC = CreateCompatibleDC(DC); /* create compatible DC */
  SelectObject(memDC, hBit);
  BitBlt(DC, LOWORD(lParam), HIWORD(lParam), 64, 64,
        memDC, 0, 0, SRCCOPY); /* build image */
  ReleaseDC(hwnd, DC); /* free the device context */
  DeleteDC(memDC); /* free the memory context */
  break;
```

Let's examine this code, step by step.

Three handles are declared. The first is called **hBit**, which is a bitmap handle. This will hold the handle to the bitmap when it is loaded. Next, two device context handles are declared. **DC** is used to hold the current device context as obtained by **GetDC()**. The other, called **memDC**, holds the device context of the memory that stores the bitmap until it is drawn in the window.

Inside the **case**, a device context is obtained. This is necessary because the bitmap will be displayed in the client area of the window and no output can occur until your program is granted a device context. Next, the bitmap is loaded and its handle is stored in **hBit**, using the **LoadBitmap()** API function, whose prototype is shown here:

HBITMAP LoadBitmap(HINSTANCE *hThisInst,* LPCSTR *lpszName*);

HBITMAP is a type that holds a handle to a bitmap. The current instance is specified in *hThisInst,* and a pointer to the name of the bitmap as specified in the resource file is passed in *lpszName.* The function returns the handle to the bitmap, or NULL if an error occurs.

Next, a memory context is created that will hold the bitmap using the **CreateCompatibleDC()** API function. Its prototype is shown here:

HDC CreateCompatibleDC(HDC *hdc*);

This function returns a handle to a region of memory that is compatible with the device context of the window, specified by *hdc.* This memory will be used to construct an image before it is actually displayed. The function returns NULL if an error occurs.

Before a bitmap can be displayed, it must be selected using the **SelectObject()** API function. Since there can be several bitmaps associated with an application, you must select the one you want to display before it can actually be output to the window. The **SelectObject()** prototype is shown here:

HGDIOBJ SelectObject(HDC *hMdc,* HGDIOBJ *hObject*);

Here, *hMdc* is the memory device context that holds the object and *hObject* is the handle of that object. The function returns the handle of the previously selected object, allowing it to be reselected later, if desired.

To actually display the object once it has been selected, use the **BitBlt()** API function. Its prototype is shown here:

BOOL BitBlt(HDC *hDest,* int *X,* int *Y,* int *Width,* int *Height,*
            HDC *hSource,* int *SourceX,* int *SourceY,*
            DWORD *dwRaster*);

Here, *hDest* is the handle of the target device context, and *X* and *Y* are the upper left coordinates at which point the bitmap will be drawn. The width and height of the bitmap are specified in *Width* and *Height*. The *hSource* parameter contains the handle of the source device context, which in this case will be the memory context obtained using **CreateCompatibleDC()**. The *SourceX* and *SourceY* specify the upper left coordinates in the bitmap. These values are usually 0. The value of *dwRaster* determines how the bit-by-bit contents of the bitmap will actually be drawn on the screen. Some of its most common values are shown here:

Raster Macro	Effect
SRCCOPY	Copies bitmap as is, overwriting existing information
SRCAND	ANDs bitmap with current destination
SRCPAINT	ORs bitmap with current destination
SRCINVERT	XORs bitmap with current destination

These macros are defined by including **windows.h**. The function returns non-zero if successful and zero otherwise.

In the program, the call to **BitBlt()** displays the entire bitmap at the location at which the left mouse button was pressed, simply copying the bitmap to the window.

After the bitmap is displayed, both device contexts are released. Only a device context obtained through a call to **GetDC()** can be released using a call to **ReleaseDC()**. To release the memory device context, use **DeleteDC()**, which takes as its parameter the handle of the device context to release.

The Complete Bitmap Example Program

Here is the complete program that displays a bitmap. Sample output is shown in Figure 6-2.

remember: *Don't forget to add the global instance handle* **hInst** *if you are simply reusing the previous program.*

```
/* A minimal Windows NT skeleton that demonstrates
   a bitmap. */

/* The following definition causes stricter type checking.
```

```
        catch potential type mismatch errors--especially
        when porting from 16-bit Windows. */
#define STRICT

#include <windows.h>
#include <string.h>
#include <stdio.h>

LRESULT CALLBACK WindowFunc(HWND, UINT, WPARAM, LPARAM);

char szWinName[] = "MyWin"; /* name of window class */

HINSTANCE hInst; /* holds instance handle */

int WINAPI WinMain(HINSTANCE hThisInst, HINSTANCE hPrevInst,
                   LPSTR lpszArgs, int nWinMode)
{
  HWND hwnd;
  MSG msg;
  WNDCLASS wcl;
  HANDLE hAccel;

  /* Define a window class. */
  wcl.hInstance = hThisInst; /* handle to this instance */
  wcl.lpszClassName = szWinName; /* window class name */
  wcl.lpfnWndProc = WindowFunc; /* window function */
  wcl.style = 0; /* default style */

  wcl.hIcon = LoadIcon(hThisInst, "MYICON"); /* icon style */
  wcl.hCursor = LoadCursor(hThisInst, "MYCURSOR"); /* cursor style */

  wcl.lpszMenuName = NULL; /* no main menu */

  wcl.cbClsExtra = 0; /* no extra */
  wcl.cbWndExtra = 0; /* information needed */

  /* Make the window light gray. */
  wcl.hbrBackground = GetStockObject(LTGRAY_BRUSH);

  /* Register the window class. */
  if(!RegisterClass (&wcl)) return 0;

  /* Now that a window class has been registered, a window
     can be created. */
```

```c
  hwnd = CreateWindow(
    szWinName, /* name of window class */
    "Custom Bitmap", /* title */
    WS_OVERLAPPEDWINDOW, /* window style--normal */
    CW_USEDEFAULT, /* X coordinate--let Windows decide */
    CW_USEDEFAULT, /* Y coordinate--let Windows decide */
    CW_USEDEFAULT, /* width--let Windows decide */
    CW_USEDEFAULT, /* height--let Windows decide */
    NULL, /* handle of parent window--there isn't one */
    NULL, /* no menu */
    hThisInst, /* handle of this instance of the program */
    NULL /* no additional arguments */
  );

  hInst = hThisInst; /* initialize global instance handle */

  /* Display the window. */
  ShowWindow(hwnd, nWinMode);
  UpdateWindow(hwnd);

  /* Create the message loop. */
  while(GetMessage(&msg, NULL, 0, 0))
  {
    TranslateMessage(&msg); /* allow use of keyboard */
    DispatchMessage(&msg); /* return control to Windows */
  }
  return msg.wParam;
}

/* This function is called by Windows NT and is passed
   messages from the message queue.
*/
LRESULT CALLBACK WindowFunc(HWND hwnd, UINT message, WPARAM wParam,
                LPARAM lParam)
{
  HBITMAP hBit;
  HDC DC, memDC;

  switch(message) {
    case WM_LBUTTONDOWN:
      DC = GetDC(hwnd); /* get device context */
      hBit = LoadBitmap(hInst, "MYBITMAP"); /* load bitmap */
      memDC = CreateCompatibleDC(DC); /* create compatible DC */
      SelectObject(memDC, hBit);
```

```
        BitBlt(DC, LOWORD(lParam), HIWORD(lParam), 64, 64,
              memDC, 0, 0, SRCCOPY); /* build image */
        ReleaseDC(hwnd, DC); /* free the device context */
        DeleteDC(memDC); /* free the memory context */
        break;
      case WM_DESTROY: /* terminate the program */
        PostQuitMessage(0);
        break;
      default:
        /* Let Windows NT process any messages not specified in
           the preceding switch statement. */
        return DefWindowProc(hwnd, message, wParam, lParam);
    }
    return 0;
}
```

In the next chapter, we will again take up the topic of controls by exploring more of those supported by Windows NT.

Figure 6-2

An example of a custom bitmap

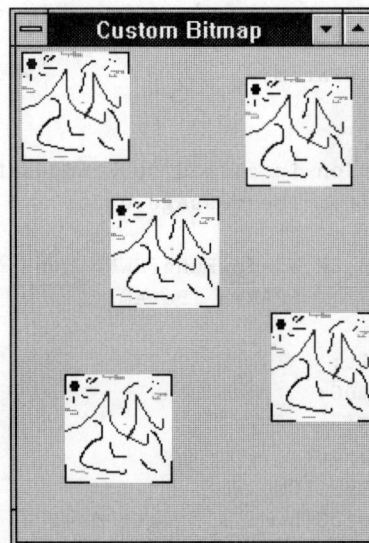

Chapter 7

A Closer Look at Controls

C O N T R O L S were introduced in Chapter 5, when dialog boxes were first discussed. This chapter continues the topic of controls by examining several more, including check boxes, radio buttons, group boxes, and static text controls. As you will see, many of the techniques that you learned when using the controls in Chapter 5 will apply to the controls discussed here.

note: *If you have not yet read Chapter 5, which covers dialog boxes, you should do so at this time, because a dialog box is used to demonstrate each control.*

Using Check Boxes

A *check box* is a control that is used to turn on or off an option. It consists of a small rectangle that can either contain an X or not. A check box has associated with it a label that describes what option the box represents. If the box contains an X, the box is said to be *checked* and the option is selected. If the box is empty, then the box is *unchecked* and the option is deselected. A check box is typically part of a dialog box and is generally defined within the dialog box's definition in your program's resource file. To add a check box to a dialog box definition, use the **CHECKBOX** command, which has this general form:

CHECKBOX "*string*", *CBID, X, Y, Width, Height* [, *Style*]

Here, *string* is the text that will be shown alongside the check box. *CBID* is the value associated with the check box. The box's upper left corner will be at *X, Y* and the box plus its associated text will have the dimensions specified by *Width* x *Height*. The *Style* determines the exact nature of the check box. If no explicit style is specified, then the check box defaults to displaying the *string* on the right and allowing the user to tab to the box. As you know from using Windows

NT, check boxes are toggles. Each time you select a check box, its state changes from checked to unchecked, and vice versa. However, this is not necessarily accomplished automatically. When you use the **CHECKBOX** resource command, you create a *manual check box*, which your program must manage by checking and unchecking the box each time it is selected. (You will see how, shortly.) However, you can have Windows NT perform this housekeeping function for you if you create an *automatic check box*. An automatic check box is created using the **AUTOCHECKBOX** resource command. It has exactly the same form as the **CHECKBOX** command. When you use an automatic check box, Windows NT automatically toggles its state (between checked and unchecked) each time it is selected.

Before continuing, you need to create the following resource file, which defines a dialog box that contains both a manual and an automatic check box. The file also defines a top level menu. Enter this file into your computer now:

```
#include "mydialog.h"
#include <windows.h>

MYMENU MENU
{
  MENUITEM "&Dialog", ID_DIALOG1
  MENUITEM "&Status", ID_STATUS
  MENUITEM "&Help", ID_HELP
}


MYMENU ACCELERATORS
{
  VK_F2, ID_DIALOG1, VIRTKEY
  VK_F3, ID_STATUS, VIRTKEY
  VK_F1, ID_HELP, VIRTKEY
}

MYDB DIALOG 18, 18, 142, 92
CAPTION "Test Dialog Box"
STYLE DS_MODALFRAME | WS_POPUP | WS_CAPTION | WS_SYSMENU
{
  PUSHBUTTON "OK", IDOK, 77, 40, 30, 13,
            WS_CHILD | WS_VISIBLE | WS_TABSTOP
  PUSHBUTTON "Cancel", IDCANCEL, 74, 65, 37, 14,
            WS_CHILD | WS_VISIBLE | WS_TABSTOP
  CHECKBOX "Check box 1" , ID_CB1, 3, 10, 48, 12
  AUTOCHECKBOX "Check box 2" , ID_CB2, 3, 22, 48, 12
}
```

You will also need to create the header file **mydialog.h**, which is shown here. This file also defines values that will be needed by examples later in this chapter.

```
#define ID_DIALOG1    100
#define ID_STATUS     101
#define ID_HELP       102

#define ID_CB1        103
#define ID_CB2        104

#define ID_CT1        105

#define ID_RB1        106
#define ID_RB2        107

#define ID_GB1        200
#define ID_GB2        201
```

Each time the user clicks on a check box or selects the check box and then presses the SPACEBAR, a **WM_COMMAND** message is sent to the dialog function and the low-order word of **wParam** contains the identifier associated with that check box. If you are using a manual check box, then you will want to respond to this command by changing the state of the box. To do this, send the check box a **BM_SETCHECK** message using the **SendDlgItemMessage()** API function. This function was discussed in Chapter 5. For your convenience, its prototype is shown here:

LONG SendDlgItemMessage(HWND *hdwnd,* int *ID,*

UINT *IDMsg,* WPARAM *wParam,*

LPARAM *lParam*);

When the **BM_SETCHECK** message is sent, the value of *wParam* determines whether the box will be checked or cleared. If *wParam* is 1, then the box will be checked. If it is 0, the box will be cleared. By default, when a dialog box is first displayed, all check boxes will be unchecked.

remember: *If you use an automatic check box, then the state of the box will be changed automatically each time it is selected. You do not need to send an automatic check box a* **BM_SETCHECK** *message.*

You can determine the status of a check box by sending it the message **BM_GETCHECK**. In this case, both *wParam* and *lParam* are 0. The check box returns 1 if the box is checked and 0 otherwise.

Here is a program that demonstrates both an automatic and a manual check box. For the sake of illustrating the difference between a manual and an automatic check box, when the manual check box is selected, it is always checked. It is not possible to uncheck the box. (That is, the manual check box cannot, in this example, be toggled.) You will see how to manage a manual check box in the next example.

```
/* A minimal Windows NT skeleton that demonstrates
   check boxes. */

/* The following definition causes stricter type checking.
   This is optional, but suggested because it will help
   catch potential type mismatch errors--especially
   when porting from 16-bit Windows. */
#define STRICT

#include <windows.h>
#include <string.h>
#include <stdio.h>
#include "mydialog.h"

LRESULT CALLBACK WindowFunc(HWND, UINT, UINT, LONG);
LRESULT CALLBACK DialogFunc(HWND, UINT, WPARAM, LPARAM);

char szWinName[] = "MyWin"; /* name of window class */

HINSTANCE hInst;

int status1=0, status2=0; /* holds status of check boxes */

int WINAPI WinMain(HINSTANCE hThisInst, HINSTANCE hPrevInst,
                   LPSTR lpszArgs, int nWinMode)
{
  HWND hwnd;
  MSG msg;
  WNDCLASS wcl;
  HANDLE hAccel;
```

```
/* Define a window class. */
wcl.hInstance = hThisInst; /* handle to this instance */
wcl.lpszClassName = szWinName; /* window class name */
wcl.lpfnWndProc = WindowFunc; /* window function */
wcl.style = 0; /* default style */

wcl.hIcon = LoadIcon(NULL, IDI_APPLICATION); /* icon style */
wcl.hCursor = LoadCursor(NULL, IDC_ARROW); /* cursor style */

/* Specify name of menu resource. */
wcl.lpszMenuName = "MYMENU"; /* main menu */

wcl.cbClsExtra = 0; /* no extra */
wcl.cbWndExtra = 0; /* information needed */

/* Make the window light gray. */
wcl.hbrBackground = GetStockObject(LTGRAY_BRUSH);

/* Register the window class. */
if(!RegisterClass (&wcl)) return 0;

/* Now that a window class has been registered, a window
   can be created. */
hwnd = CreateWindow(
  szWinName, /* name of window class */
  "Dialog Boxes", /* title */
  WS_OVERLAPPEDWINDOW, /* window style--normal */
  CW_USEDEFAULT, /* X coordinate--let Windows decide */
  CW_USEDEFAULT, /* Y coordinate--let Windows decide */
  CW_USEDEFAULT, /* width--let Windows decide */
  CW_USEDEFAULT, /* height--let Windows decide */
  NULL, /* handle of parent window--there isn't one */
  NULL, /* no menu */
  hThisInst, /* handle of this instance of the program */
  NULL /* no additional arguments */
);

hInst = hThisInst; /* save the current instance handle */

/* Load accelerators. */
hAccel = LoadAccelerators(hThisInst, "MYMENU");

/* Display the window. */
ShowWindow(hwnd, nWinMode);
```

```
  UpdateWindow(hwnd);

  /* Create the message loop. */
  while(GetMessage(&msg, NULL, 0, 0))
  {
    if(!TranslateAccelerator(hwnd, hAccel, &msg)) {
      TranslateMessage(&msg); /* allow use of keyboard */
      DispatchMessage(&msg); /* return control to Windows */
    }
  }
  return msg.wParam;
}


/* This function is called by Windows NT and is passed
   messages from the message queue.
*/
LRESULT CALLBACK WindowFunc(HWND hwnd, UINT message, WPARAM wParam,
                LPARAM lParam)
{
  char str[80];

  switch(message) {
    case WM_COMMAND:
      switch(LOWORD(wParam)) {
        case ID_DIALOG1:
          DialogBox(hInst, "MYDB", hwnd, DialogFunc);
          break;
        case ID_STATUS: /* show check box status */
          if(status1) strcpy(str, "Check box 1 is checked\n");
          else strcpy(str, "Check box 1 is not checked\n");
          if(status2) strcat(str, "Check box 2 is checked");
          else strcat(str, "Check box 2 is not checked");
          MessageBox(hwnd, str, "", MB_OK);
          break;
        case ID_HELP:
          MessageBox(hwnd, "Help", "", MB_OK);
          break;
      }
      break;
    case WM_DESTROY: /* terminate the program */
      PostQuitMessage(0);
      break;
    default:
      /* Let Windows NT process any messages not specified in
```

```
          the preceding switch statement. */
     return DefWindowProc(hwnd, message, wParam, lParam);
  }
  return 0;
}

/* A simple dialog function. */
LRESULT CALLBACK DialogFunc(HWND hdwnd, UINT message,
                            WPARAM wParam, LPARAM lParam)
{
  switch(message) {
    case WM_COMMAND:
      switch(LOWORD(wParam)) {
        case IDCANCEL:
          EndDialog(hdwnd, 0);
          return 1;
        case IDOK:
          /* update global check box status variables */
          status1 = SendDlgItemMessage(hdwnd, ID_CB1,
            BM_GETCHECK, 0, 0);  // is box checked?
          status2 = SendDlgItemMessage(hdwnd, ID_CB2,
            BM_GETCHECK, 0, 0);  // is box checked?
          EndDialog(hdwnd, 0);
          return 1;
        case ID_CB1:
          /* user selected first check box, so check it */
          SendDlgItemMessage(hdwnd, ID_CB1, BM_SETCHECK, 1, 0);
          return 1;
      }
  }
  return 0;
}
```

This program contains two global variables, called **status1** and **status2**, which hold the state of the two check boxes. These variables are set when the OK button is selected inside the dialog box. To set the state of the check boxes, select the **Dialog** main menu option. To see the status of the check boxes, select the **Status** main menu option. (The **Help** option is included only as a placeholder.)

When you run this program and select the **Dialog** main menu option, you will see the dialog box shown in Figure 7-1. Experiment with the two check boxes. Notice that the automatic check box operates normally, because Windows NT is managing it for you.

Figure 7-1

The check box
dialog box

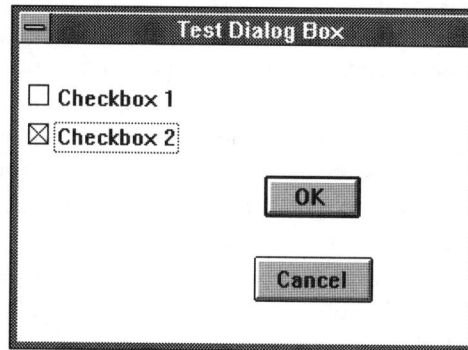

Managing Check Boxes

The check box program, as it stands, has two serious flaws. First, the state of each check box is reset each time the dialog box is displayed. That is, the previous setting of each box is lost. Secondly, while the manual check box can be set, it cannot be cleared. That is, the manual check box is not fully implemented as a toggle, the way check boxes are expected to function. In this section, you will see how to manage check boxes more effectively.

Toggling a Check Box

First, while it is far easier to simply use automatic check boxes, it is possible to implement a toggled check box by managing a manual check box. To do this means that your program will have to perform all the necessary overhead itself, instead of letting Windows NT handle it. To accomplish this, the program needs to first find out the current state of the check box and then set it to the opposite state each time the check box is selected. The following change to the dialog function accomplishes this:

```
case ID_CB1: /* this is a manually managed check box */
if(!SendDlgItemMessage(hdwnd, ID_CB1, BM_GETCHECK, 0, 0))
    SendDlgItemMessage(hdwnd, ID_CB1, BM_SETCHECK, 1, 0);
  else /* turn it off */
    SendDlgItemMessage(hdwnd, ID_CB1, BM_SETCHECK, 0, 0);
  return 1;
```

Initializing a Check Box

As mentioned, both the manual and the automatic check boxes are cleared (that is, unchecked) each time the dialog box that contains them is activated. While this might be desirable in some situations, it is not what is normally expected. Generally, check boxes retain their previous settings between activations. If you want the check boxes to reflect their previous state, then you must initialize them each time the dialog box is activated. The easiest way to do this is to send them the appropriate **BM_SETCHECK** messages when the dialog box is created. Remember, each time a dialog box is activated, it is sent a **WM_INITDIALOG** message. When this message is received, you can set the initial state of the check boxes (and anything else) inside the dialog box.

The code to initialize the check boxes is shown here. Since the state of each check box is preserved in the variables **status1** and **status2**, the contents of these variables can be used to initialize the check boxes.

```
case WM_INITDIALOG:
  /* The dialog box has just been displayed.  Set
     the check boxes appropriately. */
  SendDlgItemMessage(hdwnd, ID_CB1, BM_SETCHECK, status1, 0);
  SendDlgItemMessage(hdwnd, ID_CB2, BM_SETCHECK, status2, 0);
  return 1;
```

The entire program listing that incorporates the check box initialization and manages the manual check box is shown here. You should compare its operation to the preceding example. As you might expect, it now behaves in a way that is common to most all other Windows applications.

```
/* A minimal Windows NT skeleton that demonstrates
   check boxes with enhancements. */

/* The following definition causes stricter type checking.
   This is optional, but suggested because it will help
   catch potential type mismatch errors--especially
   when porting from 16-bit Windows. */
#define STRICT

#include <windows.h>
#include <string.h>
#include <stdio.h>
#include "mydialog.h"
```

```
LRESULT CALLBACK WindowFunc(HWND, UINT, UINT, LONG);
LRESULT CALLBACK DialogFunc(HWND, UINT, WPARAM, LPARAM);

char szWinName[] = "MyWin"; /* name of window class */

HINSTANCE hInst;

int status1=0, status2=0; /* holds status of check boxes */

int WINAPI WinMain(HINSTANCE hThisInst, HINSTANCE hPrevInst,
                   LPSTR lpszArgs, int nWinMode)
{
  HWND hwnd;
  MSG msg;
  WNDCLASS wcl;
  HANDLE hAccel;

  /* Define a window class. */
  wcl.hInstance = hThisInst; /* handle to this instance */
  wcl.lpszClassName = szWinName; /* window class name */
  wcl.lpfnWndProc = WindowFunc; /* window function */
  wcl.style = 0; /* default style */

  wcl.hIcon = LoadIcon(NULL, IDI_APPLICATION); /* icon style */
  wcl.hCursor = LoadCursor(NULL, IDC_ARROW); /* cursor style */

  /* Specify name of menu resource. */
  wcl.lpszMenuName = "MYMENU"; /* main menu */

  wcl.cbClsExtra = 0; /* no extra */
  wcl.cbWndExtra = 0; /* information needed */

  /* Make the window light gray. */
  wcl.hbrBackground = GetStockObject(LTGRAY_BRUSH);

  /* Register the window class. */
  if(!RegisterClass (&wcl)) return 0;

  /* Now that a window class has been registered, a window
     can be created. */
  hwnd = CreateWindow(
    szWinName, /* name of window class */
    "Dialog Boxes", /* title */
    WS_OVERLAPPEDWINDOW, /* window style--normal */
```

```
       CW_USEDEFAULT, /* X coordinate--let Windows decide */
       CW_USEDEFAULT, /* Y coordinate--let Windows decide */
       CW_USEDEFAULT, /* width--let Windows decide */
       CW_USEDEFAULT, /* height--let Windows decide */
       NULL, /* handle of parent window--there isn't one */
       NULL, /* no menu */
       hThisInst, /* handle of this instance of the program */
       NULL /* no additional arguments */
    );

    hInst = hThisInst; /* save the current instance handle */

    /* Load accelerators. */
    hAccel = LoadAccelerators(hThisInst, "MYMENU");

    /* Display the window. */
    ShowWindow(hwnd, nWinMode);
    UpdateWindow(hwnd);

    /* Create the message loop. */
    while(GetMessage(&msg, NULL, 0, 0))
    {
      if(!TranslateAccelerator(hwnd, hAccel, &msg)) {
        TranslateMessage(&msg); /* allow use of keyboard */
        DispatchMessage(&msg); /* return control to Windows */
      }
    }
    return msg.wParam;
}

/* This function is called by Windows NT and is passed
   messages from the message queue.
*/
LRESULT CALLBACK WindowFunc(HWND hwnd, UINT message, WPARAM wParam,
                LPARAM lParam)
{
  char str[80];

  switch(message) {
    case WM_COMMAND:
      switch(LOWORD(wParam)) {
        case ID_DIALOG1:
          DialogBox(hInst, "MYDB", hwnd, DialogFunc);
          break;
```

```
      case ID_STATUS:
        if(status1) strcpy(str, "Check box 1 is checked\n");
        else strcpy(str, "Check box 1 is not checked\n");
        if(status2) strcat(str, "Check box 2 is checked");
        else strcat(str, "Check box 2 is not checked");
        MessageBox(hwnd, str, "", MB_OK);
        break;
      case ID_HELP:
        MessageBox(hwnd, "Help", "", MB_OK);
        break;
    }
    break;
  case WM_DESTROY: /* terminate the program */
    PostQuitMessage(0);
    break;
  default:
    /* Let Windows NT process any messages not specified in
       the preceding switch statement. */
    return DefWindowProc(hwnd, message, wParam, lParam);
  }
  return 0;
}


/* A simple dialog function. */
LRESULT CALLBACK DialogFunc(HWND hdwnd, UINT message,
                            WPARAM wParam, LPARAM lParam)
{
  switch(message) {
    case WM_INITDIALOG:
      /* The dialog box has just been displayed.  Set
         the check boxes appropriately. */
      SendDlgItemMessage(hdwnd, ID_CB1, BM_SETCHECK, status1, 0);
      SendDlgItemMessage(hdwnd, ID_CB2, BM_SETCHECK, status2, 0);
      return 1;
    case WM_COMMAND:
      switch(LOWORD(wParam)) {
        case IDCANCEL:
          EndDialog(hdwnd, 0);
          return 1;
        case IDOK:
          /* update global check box status variables */
          status1 = SendDlgItemMessage(hdwnd, ID_CB1,
            BM_GETCHECK, 0, 0);  // is box checked?
          status2 = SendDlgItemMessage(hdwnd, ID_CB2,
```

```
                 BM_GETCHECK, 0, 0);  // is box checked?
            EndDialog(hdwnd, 0);
            return 1;
          case ID_CB1: /* this is a manually managed check box */
            if(!SendDlgItemMessage(hdwnd, ID_CB1, BM_GETCHECK, 0, 0))
               SendDlgItemMessage(hdwnd, ID_CB1, BM_SETCHECK, 1, 0);
            else /* turn it off */
               SendDlgItemMessage(hdwnd, ID_CB1, BM_SETCHECK, 0, 0);
            return 1;
        }
      }
      return 0;
    }
```

Adding Static Controls

A static control is one that neither receives nor generates any messages. In short, the term *static control* is simply a formal way of describing something that is displayed in a dialog box, such as a text message or a simple box used for grouping other controls. The two static controls that we will look at here are the *centered text box* and the *group box*. Both of these controls are included in the dialog definition in your program's .RC file using the commands **CTEXT** and **GROUPBOX**, respectively.

The **CTEXT** control outputs a string that is centered within a predefined area. The general form for **CTEXT** is shown here:

CTEXT "*text*", *CTID, X, Y, Width, Height* [, *Style*]

Here, *text* is the text that will be displayed. *CTID* is the value associated with the text. The text will be shown in a box whose upper left corner will be at *X, Y* and dimensions are specified by *Width* x *Height*. *Style* determines the exact nature of the text box. If no explicit style is specified, then the check box defaults to displaying the *text* centered within the box. Understand that the box itself is *not* displayed. The box simply defines the space that the text is allowed to occupy.

The **GROUPBOX** control draws a box. This box is generally used to group other controls visually. The box may contain a title. The general form for **GROUPBOX** is shown here:

GROUPBOX "*title*", *GBID, X, Y, Width, Height* [, *Style*]

Here, *title* is the title of the box. *GBID* is the value associated with the box. The upper left corner will be at *X, Y* and its dimensions are specified by *Width* x *Height*. *Style* determines the exact nature of the group box. Generally, the default setting is sufficient.

To see the effects of using these two static controls, add the following definitions to the .RC file you created for the preceding examples:

```
GROUPBOX "Checkboxes", ID_GB1, 1, 1, 51, 34
CTEXT "This is text", ID_CT1, 1, 44, 50, 24
```

After you have added these lines, recompile the preceding example, execute the program, and select the **Dialog** main menu option. The dialog box will now look like that shown in Figure 7-2.

Adding Radio Buttons

The final control that we will examine is the *radio button*. Radio buttons are used to present mutually exclusive options. A radio button consists of a label and a small circle. If the circle is empty, then the option is not selected. If the circle is filled, then the option is selected. Windows NT supports two types of radio buttons: manual and automatic. The manual radio button (like the manual check box) requires that you perform all management functions. The automatic radio button performs the management functions for you. Because managing radio buttons is more complex than managing check boxes, and because automatic radio buttons are the type generally used by applications, automatic

Figure 7-2

The dialog box with the addition of the text and group box static controls

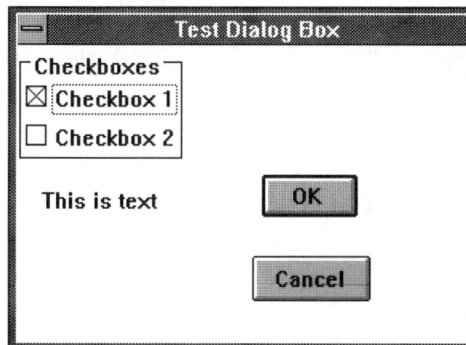

radio buttons are the only type examined here.

Like other controls, automatic radio buttons are defined in your program's resource file, within a dialog definition. To create an automatic radio button, use the **AUTORADIOBUTTON** resource command, which has this general form:

AUTORADIOBUTTON "*string*", *RBID, X, Y, Width, Height* [, *Style*]

Here, *string* is the text that will be shown alongside the button. *RBID* is the value associated with the radio button. The button's upper left corner will be at *X, Y* and the button plus its associated text will be bounded by the dimensions specified by *Width* x *Height*. *Style* determines the exact nature of the radio button. If no explicit style is specified, then the button defaults to displaying the *string* on the right and allowing the user to tab to the button.

As stated, radio buttons are generally used to create groups of mutually exclusive options. When you use automatic radio buttons to create such a group, then Windows NT automatically manages the buttons in a mutually exclusive manner. That is, each time you select one button, the previously selected button is turned off. Also, it is not possible to select more than one button at any one time. All the automatic radio buttons defined within a **DIALOG** definition constitute a mutually exclusive group.

A radio button (even an automatic one) may be set to a known state by your program by sending it the **BM_SETCHECK** message using the **SendDlgItemMessage()** API function. The value of *wParam* determines whether the button will be checked or cleared. If *wParam* is 1, then the button will be checked. It it is 0, the box will be cleared. By default, all buttons are cleared.

note: *Even using automatic radio buttons, it is possible to manually set more than one button or to clear all buttons. However, normal Windows style dictates that radio buttons be used in a mutually exclusive fashion, with one (and only one) option selected. It is strongly suggested that you do not violate this rule.*

You can obtain the status of a radio button by sending it the **BM_GETCHECK** message. The button returns 1 if the button is selected and 0 if it is not.

To add radio buttons to the example program, first add these lines to your resource file. Notice that another group box is added to surround the radio buttons. This is not necessary, of course, but such groupings are common in dialog boxes.

```
AUTORADIOBUTTON "Radio 1", ID_RB1, 60, 10, 48, 12
AUTORADIOBUTTON "Radio 2", ID_RB2, 60, 22, 48, 12
GROUPBOX "Radio Group", ID_GB2, 58, 1, 51, 34
```

Here is the entire sample program, expanded to accommodate the two radio buttons. Notice that since the radio buttons are automatic, there are only a few additions to the program. First, the state of the radio buttons is stored in two global variables, **rbstatus1** and **rbstatus2**. The values of these variables are used to set the initial button states when the dialog box is activated and to display the status of the buttons when the **Status** main menu option is selected.

```c
/* A minimal Windows NT skeleton that demonstrates
   radio buttons. */

/* The following definition causes stricter type checking.
   This is optional, but suggested because it will help
   catch potential type mismatch errors--especially
   when porting from 16-bit Windows. */
#define STRICT

#include <windows.h>
#include <string.h>
#include <stdio.h>
#include "mydialog.h"

LRESULT CALLBACK WindowFunc(HWND, UINT, UINT, LONG);
LRESULT CALLBACK DialogFunc(HWND, UINT, WPARAM, LPARAM);

char szWinName[] = "MyWin"; /* name of window class */

HINSTANCE hInst;

int cbstatus1=0, cbstatus2=0; /* holds status of check boxes */
int rbstatus1=1, rbstatus2=0; /* holds status of radio buttons */

int WINAPI WinMain(HINSTANCE hThisInst, HINSTANCE hPrevInst,
                   LPSTR lpszArgs, int nWinMode)
{
  HWND hwnd;
  MSG msg;
```

```
WNDCLASS wcl;
HANDLE hAccel;

/* Define a window class. */
wcl.hInstance = hThisInst; /* handle to this instance */
wcl.lpszClassName = szWinName; /* window class name */
wcl.lpfnWndProc = WindowFunc; /* window function */
wcl.style = 0; /* default style */

wcl.hIcon = LoadIcon(NULL, IDI_APPLICATION); /* icon style */
wcl.hCursor = LoadCursor(NULL, IDC_ARROW); /* cursor style */

/* Specify name of menu resource. */
wcl.lpszMenuName = "MYMENU"; /* main menu */

wcl.cbClsExtra = 0; /* no extra */
wcl.cbWndExtra = 0; /* information needed */

/* Make the window light gray. */
wcl.hbrBackground = GetStockObject(LTGRAY_BRUSH);

/* Register the window class. */
if(!RegisterClass (&wcl)) return 0;

/* Now that a window class has been registered, a window
   can be created. */
hwnd = CreateWindow(
  szWinName, /* name of window class */
  "Dialog Boxes", /* title */
  WS_OVERLAPPEDWINDOW, /* window style--normal */
  CW_USEDEFAULT, /* X coordinate--let Windows decide */
  CW_USEDEFAULT, /* Y coordinate--let Windows decide */
  CW_USEDEFAULT, /* width--let Windows decide */
  CW_USEDEFAULT, /* height--let Windows decide */
  HWND_DESKTOP, /* handle of parent window--there isn't one */
  NULL, /* no menu */
  hThisInst, /* handle of this instance of the program */
  NULL /* no additional arguments */
);

hInst = hThisInst; /* save the current instance handle */

/* Load accelerators. */
hAccel = LoadAccelerators(hThisInst, "MYMENU");
```

```c
  /* Display the window. */
  ShowWindow(hwnd, nWinMode);
  UpdateWindow(hwnd);

  /* Create the message loop. */
  while(GetMessage(&msg, NULL, 0, 0))
  {
    if(!TranslateAccelerator(hwnd, hAccel, &msg)) {
      TranslateMessage(&msg); /* allow use of keyboard */
      DispatchMessage(&msg); /* return control to Windows */
    }
  }
  return msg.wParam;
}

/* This function is called by Windows NT and is passed
   messages from the message queue.
*/
LRESULT CALLBACK WindowFunc(HWND hwnd, UINT message, WPARAM wParam,
                LPARAM lParam)
{
  char str[255];

  switch(message) {
    case WM_COMMAND:
      switch(LOWORD(wParam)) {
        case ID_DIALOG1:
          DialogBox(hInst, "MYDB", hwnd, DialogFunc);
          break;
        case ID_STATUS:
          if(cbstatus1) strcpy(str, "Check box 1 is checked\n");
          else strcpy(str, "Check box 1 is not checked\n");
          if(cbstatus2) strcat(str, "Check box 2 is checked\n");
          else strcat(str, "Check box 2 is not checked\n");
          if(rbstatus1) strcat(str, "Radio 1 is checked\n");
          else strcat(str, "Radio 1 is not checked\n");
          if(rbstatus2) strcat(str, "Radio 2 is checked");
          else strcat(str, "Radio 2 is not checked");
          MessageBox(hwnd, str, "", MB_OK);
          break;
        case ID_HELP:
          MessageBox(hwnd, "Help", "", MB_OK);
          break;
```

```
      }
    break;
  case WM_DESTROY: /* terminate the program */
    PostQuitMessage(0);
    break;
  default:
    /* Let Windows NT process any messages not specified in
    the preceding switch statement. */
    return DefWindowProc(hwnd, message, wParam, lParam);
  }
  return 0;
}

/* A simple dialog function. */
LRESULT CALLBACK DialogFunc(HWND hdwnd, UINT message,
                            WPARAM wParam, LPARAM lParam)
{
  switch(message) {
    case WM_INITDIALOG:
      /* The dialog box has just been displayed.  Set
         the check boxes and radio buttons appropriately. */
      SendDlgItemMessage(hdwnd, ID_CB1, BM_SETCHECK, cbstatus1, 0);
      SendDlgItemMessage(hdwnd, ID_CB2, BM_SETCHECK, cbstatus2, 0);
      SendDlgItemMessage(hdwnd, ID_RB1, BM_SETCHECK, rbstatus1, 0);
      SendDlgItemMessage(hdwnd, ID_RB2, BM_SETCHECK, rbstatus2, 0);
      return 1;
    case WM_COMMAND:
      switch(LOWORD(wParam)) {
        case IDCANCEL:
          EndDialog(hdwnd, 0);
          return 1;
        case IDOK:
          /* update global check box status variables */
          cbstatus1 = SendDlgItemMessage(hdwnd, ID_CB1,
            BM_GETCHECK, 0, 0);  // is box checked?
          cbstatus2 = SendDlgItemMessage(hdwnd, ID_CB2,
            BM_GETCHECK, 0, 0);  // is box checked?

          /* now, update global radio button status variables */
          rbstatus1 = SendDlgItemMessage(hdwnd, ID_RB1,
```

```
         BM_GETCHECK, 0, 0);  // is button checked?
       rbstatus2 = SendDlgItemMessage(hdwnd, ID_RB2,
         BM_GETCHECK, 0, 0);  // is button checked?

       EndDialog(hdwnd, 0);
       return 1;
     case ID_CB1: /* this is a manually managed check box */
       if(!SendDlgItemMessage(hdwnd, ID_CB1, BM_GETCHECK, 0, 0))
         SendDlgItemMessage(hdwnd, ID_CB1, BM_SETCHECK, 1, 0);
       else /* turn it off */
         SendDlgItemMessage(hdwnd, ID_CB1, BM_SETCHECK, 0, 0);
       return 1;
   }
 }
 return 0;
}
```

When you run this program, the dialog box will now look like that shown in Figure 7-3.

In the next chapter, you will learn more about outputting text to a window.

Figure 7-3

The dialog box with radio buttons

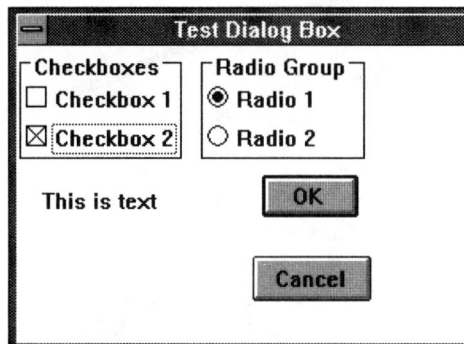

Chapter 8

Working with Text

INCE Chapter 4, we have been ouputting information using message and dialog boxes and ignoring the client area of the window. This chapter returns to the client area and explores various aspects of how Windows NT manages text. Also, some important techniques are developed that make it easier for you to restore the window when it has been overwritten. The use of different text fonts is also discussed.

As with most other aspects of the Windows NT environment, you, the programmer, have virtually unlimited control over the way that text is displayed and managed within the client area of a window. As such, it is far beyond the scope of this chapter to cover all aspects of text manipulation using Windows. However, you will easily be able to explore other aspects of text manipulation after understanding the basics introduced in this chapter.

This chapter begins with a discussion of the window coordinate system and how text is mapped onto it. Then some text and screen API functions are described. These functions help you control and manage text output to the screen.

Window Coordinates

As you know from Chapter 3, **TextOut()** is Windows NT's text output function. It displays a string, the upper left corner of which is located at the coordinates supplied to the function. The coordinates specified to **TextOut()** are always relative to the window. The position of the window on the screen has no effect on the coordinates passed to **TextOut()**. By default, the upper left corner of the client area of the window is location 0, 0. The X value increases to the right and the Y value increases downward.

So far, we have been using window coordinates for **TextOut()** and for positioning various elements within a dialog box without any specific mention of what those coordinates actually refer to. Now is the time to clarify a few details. First, the coordinates that are specified in **TextOut()** are *logical coordinates*. That is, the units used by **TextOut()** (and other window display functions, including the graphics functions described in the next chapter) are *logical units*. Windows NT maps these logical units onto pixels when output is actually displayed. The reason that we haven't had to worry about this distinction is that, by default, logical units are the same as pixels. In other words, by default, logical units are pixels. It is important to understand, however, that different mapping modes can be selected in which this convenient default will not be the case.

Setting the Text and Background Color

By default, when you output text to the window using **TextOut()**, it is shown as black text with a white background. However, you can determine both the color of the text and the background color using the API functions **Set-TextColor()** and **SetBkColor()**, whose prototypes are shown here:

COLORREF SetTextColor(HDC *hdc*, COLORREF *color*);

COLORREF SetBkColor(HDC *hdc*, COLORREF *color*);

The **SetTextColor()** function sets the current text color of the device associated with *hdc* to that specified by *color* (or to the closest color that the device is capable of displaying). The **SetBkColor()** function sets the current text background color to that specified by *color* (or to the nearest possible match). Both functions return the previous color setting. If an error occurs, then they return the value **CLR_INVALID**.

The color is specified as a value of type **COLORREF**, which is a long integer. Windows NT allows colors to be specified in three different ways. First, and by far most common, is as an RGB (red, green, blue) value. In an RGB value, the relative intensities of the three colors are combined to produce the actual color. The second way a color can be specified is as an index into a logical palette. The third is as an RGB value relative to a palette. In this chapter, only the first way will be discussed.

A long integer value that holds an RGB color is passed to either **Set-TextColor()** or **SetBkColor()** using the following encoding:

Byte		Color
byte 0 (low-order byte)		red
byte 1		green
byte 2		blue
byte 3 (high-order byte)		must be zero

Each color in an RGB value is in the range 0 through 255, with 0 being the lowest intensity and 255 being the brightest intensity. For example, the following long integer produces a bright pink:

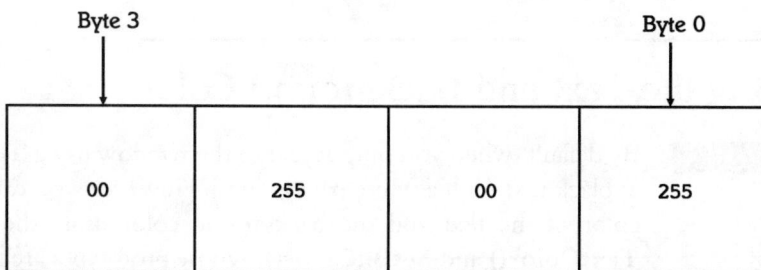

Byte 3   Byte 0

00	255	00	255

Although you are free to manually construct a **COLORREF** value, Windows NT defines the macro **RGB()** that does this for you. It has this general form:

COLORREF RGB(int *red,* int *green,* int *blue*);

Here, *red, green,* and *blue* must be values in the range 0 through 255. Therefore, to create bright pink, use **RGB(255, 0, 255)**. To create the color white, use **RGB(255, 255, 255)**. To create the color black use **RGB(0, 0, 0)**. To create other colors, you combine the three basic colors in varying intensities. For example, this creates a light aqua: **RGB(0, 100, 100)**. You can experiment to determine which colors are best for your application.

Setting the Background Display Mode

You can control the way that the background is affected when text is displayed on the screen by using the **SetBkMode()** API function, whose prototype is shown here:

int SetBkMode(HDC *hdc,* int *mode*);

This function determines what happens to the current background color when text (and some other types of output) is displayed. The device affected is specified by *hdc*. The background mode is specified in *mode* and must be one of these two macros: **OPAQUE** or **TRANSPARENT**. The function returns the previous setting or 0 if an error occurs.

If *mode* is **OPAQUE**, then each time text is output, the background is changed to that of the current text background color. If *mode* is **TRANSPARENT**, then the background is not altered. In this case, any effects of a call to **SetBkColor()** are effectively ignored. The default background mode is **OPAQUE**.

Obtaining the Text Metrics

As was mentioned in Chapter 3, characters are not all the same dimensions. That is, in Windows, most text fonts are proportional. Therefore, the character *i* is not as wide as the character *w*. Also, the height of each character and of descenders varies between fonts. The amount of space between horizontal lines is also changeable. That these (and other) attributes are variable would not be of too much consequence, except for the fact that Windows demands that you, the programmer, manually perform virtually all text output.

Windows provides only minimal support for text output to the client area of a window. The main output function is **TextOut()**. This function will only display a string of text, beginning at a specified location. It will not format output or even automatically perform a carriage return/linefeed sequence, for example. Managing output to the client window is completely your job.

Given that the size of each font may be different (and that fonts may be changed while your program is executing), there must be some way to determine the dimensions and various other attributes of the current font. For example, in order to write one line of text after another you must have some way of knowing how high the font is and how many pixels there are between lines. The API function that obtains information about the current font is called **GetTextMetrics()**, and it has this prototype:

BOOL GetTextMetrics(HDC *hdc,* LPTEXTMETRIC *lpTAttrib*);

Here, *hdc* is the handle of the output device, which is generally obtained using **GetDC()** or **BeginPaint()**, and *lpTAttrib* is a pointer to a structure of type **TEXTMETRIC**, which will, upon return, contain the text metrics for the currently selected font. The **TEXTMETRIC** structure is defined as shown here:

```
typedef struct tagTEXTMETRIC
{
    LONG tmHeight; /* total height of font */
    LONG tmAscent; /* height above baseline */
    LONG tmDescent; /* length of descenders */
    LONG tmInternalLeading; /* space above characters */
    LONG tmExternalLeading; /* space between rows */
    LONG tmAveCharWidth; /* average width */
    LONG tmMaxCharWidth; /* maximum width */
    LONG tmWeight; /* weight */
    LONG tmOverhang; /* extra width added to special fonts */
    LONG tmDigitizedAspectX; /* horizontal aspect */
    LONG tmDigitizedAspectY; /* vertical aspect */
    BYTE tmFirstChar; /* first character in font */
    BYTE tmLastChar; /* last character in font */
    BYTE tmDefaultChar; /* default character */
    BYTE tmBreakChar; /* character used to break words */
    BYTE tmItalic; /* non-zero if italic */
    BYTE tmUnderlined; /* non-zero if underlined */
    BYTE tmStruckOut; /* non-zero if struck out */
    BYTE tmPitchAndFamily; /* pitch and family of font */
    BYTE tmCharSet; /* character set identifier */
} TEXTMERIC;
```

While most of the values obtained by this function will not be used in this chapter, two are very important, because they let us output multiple lines of text to the window. Since the height of each font is possibly different, as is the amount of space required between lines, you need to find out in advance what vertical (Y) coordinate to call **TextOut()** with so that it begins on the next line. To accomplish this, you must first call **GetTextMetrics()** to determine two values: the height of each character and the amount of space between lines. These two values are given in the **tmHeight** and **tmExternalLeading** fields, respectively. These values are given in logical units that are mapped to the screen. Using this information, the following formula is used to compute the next value of Y, so that it will be the coordinate of the next line:

Y = Y + tmHeight + tmExternalLeading

You will see this formula applied, shortly.

note: *The value* **tmExternalLeading** *contains, in essence, the number of vertical units that should be left blank between lines of text. This value is separate from the height of the font.*

Computing the Length of a String

Because characters in the current font are not the same size, it is not possible to know the length of a string, in logical units, by simply knowing how many characters are in it. That is, the result returned by **strlen()** is not meaningful to managing output to a window, because characters are of differing widths. To solve this problem, Windows NT includes the API function **GetTextExtentPoint()**, whose prototype is shown here:

BOOL GetTextExtentPoint (HDC *hdc,* LPCSTR *lpszString,*
                                      int *len,* LPSIZE *lpSize*);

Here, *hdc* is the handle of the output device. The string that you want the length of is pointed to by *lpszString*. The number of characters in the string is specified in *len*. The width and height of the string, in logical units, is returned in the **SIZE** structure pointed to by *lpSize*. The **SIZE** structure is defined as shown here:

```
typedef struct tagSIZE {
  LONG cx; /* width */
  LONG cy; /* height */
} SIZE;
```

Upon return from a call to **GetTextExtentPoint()**, the **cx** field will contain the length of the string in logical units. Therefore, this value can be used to determine the starting point for the next string to be displayed if you want to continue from where the previous output left off.

Obtaining the System Metrics

Although Windows NT maintains and automatically translates logical coordinates into physical pixels, sometimes you will want to know the actual resolution of the video mode in effect when you run your application. To obtain this, and other information, use the **GetSystemMetrics()** API function, whose prototype is shown here:

    int GetSystemMetrics(int *value*);

Here, *value* will be a macro that specifies the value that you want to obtain, which is then returned by the function. **GetSystemMetrics()** can obtain 39 different values. The values for screen coordinates are returned in pixel units. Here are the macros for some common values:

Macro	Value Obtained
SM_CXFRAME	Width of frame
SM_CYFRAME	Height of frame
SM_CXFULLSCREEN	Width of maximized client area
SM_CYFULLSCREEN	Height of maximized client area
SM_CXICON	Width of icon
SM_CYICON	Height of icon
SM_CXSCREEN	Width of entire screen
SM_CYSCREEN	Height of entire screen

A Short Text Demonstration

Now that you have learned about some of Windows NT's text functions, a short demonstration of these features will be useful. Here is a short program that does just that:

```
/* A Windows NT skeleton that demonstrates
   text output. */

/* The following definition causes stricter type checking.
   This is optional, but suggested because it will help
   catch potential type mismatch errors--especially
   when porting from 16-bit Windows. */
#define STRICT

#include <windows.h>
#include <string.h>
#include <stdio.h>
#include "text.h"

LRESULT CALLBACK WindowFunc(HWND, UINT, WPARAM, LPARAM);

char szWinName[] = "MyWin"; /* name of window class */

char str[255]; /* holds output strings */

int X=0, Y=0; /* current output location */
int maxX, maxY; /* screen dimensions */

int WINAPI WinMain(HINSTANCE hThisInst, HINSTANCE hPrevInst,
                   LPSTR lpszArgs, int nWinMode)
{
  HWND hwnd;
  MSG msg;
  WNDCLASS wcl;
  HANDLE hAccel;

  /* Define a window class. */
  wcl.hInstance = hThisInst; /* handle to this instance */
  wcl.lpszClassName = szWinName; /* window class name */
  wcl.lpfnWndProc = WindowFunc; /* window function */
  wcl.style = 0; /* default style */

  wcl.hIcon = LoadIcon(NULL, IDI_APPLICATION); /* icon style */
  wcl.hCursor = LoadCursor(NULL, IDC_ARROW); /* cursor style */

  /* Specify name of menu resource. */
  wcl.lpszMenuName = "MYMENU"; /* main menu */
```

```
wcl.cbClsExtra = 0; /* no extra */
 wcl.cbWndExtra = 0; /* information needed */

 /* Make the window light gray. */
 wcl.hbrBackground = GetStockObject(LTGRAY_BRUSH);

 /* Register the window class. */
 if(!RegisterClass (&wcl)) return 0;

 /* Now that a window class has been registered, a window
    can be created. */
 hwnd = CreateWindow(
   szWinName, /* name of window class */
   "Fun with Text", /* title */
   WS_OVERLAPPEDWINDOW, /* window style--normal */
   CW_USEDEFAULT, /* X coordinate--let Windows decide */
   CW_USEDEFAULT, /* Y coordinate--let Windows decide */
   CW_USEDEFAULT, /* width--let Windows decide */
   CW_USEDEFAULT, /* height--let Windows decide */
   HWND_DESKTOP, /* handle of parent window--there isn't one */
   NULL, /* no menu */
   hThisInst, /* handle of this instance of the program */
   NULL /* no additional arguments */
 );

 /* Load accelerators. */
 hAccel = LoadAccelerators(hThisInst, "MYMENU");

 /* Display the window. */
 ShowWindow(hwnd, nWinMode);
 UpdateWindow(hwnd);

 /* Create the message loop. */
 while(GetMessage(&msg, NULL, 0, 0))
 {
   if(!TranslateAccelerator(hwnd, hAccel, &msg)) {
     TranslateMessage(&msg); /* allow use of keyboard */
     DispatchMessage(&msg); /* return control to Windows */
   }
 }
 return msg.wParam;
}
```

```
/* This function is called by Windows NT and is passed
   messages from the message queue.
*/
LRESULT CALLBACK WindowFunc(HWND hwnd, UINT message, WPARAM wParam,
               LPARAM lParam)
{
  HDC hdc;
  TEXTMETRIC tm;
  SIZE size;

  switch(message) {
    case WM_CREATE:
      /* get screen coordinates */
      maxX = GetSystemMetrics(SM_CXSCREEN);
      maxY = GetSystemMetrics(SM_CYSCREEN);
      break;
    case WM_COMMAND:
      switch(LOWORD(wParam)) {
        case ID_SHOW:
          hdc = GetDC(hwnd); /* get device context */

          /* set text color to black */
          SetTextColor(hdc, RGB(0, 0, 0));
          /* set background mode to transparent */
          SetBkColor(hdc, RGB(0, 255, 255));

          /* get text metrics */
          GetTextMetrics(hdc, &tm);

          sprintf(str, "The font is %ld pixels high.", tm.tmHeight);
          TextOut(hdc, X, Y, str, strlen(str)); /* output string */
          Y = Y + tm.tmHeight + tm.tmExternalLeading; /* next line */

          strcpy(str, "This is on the next line. ");
          TextOut(hdc, X, Y, str, strlen(str)); /* output string */

          /* compute length of a string */
          GetTextExtentPoint(hdc, str, strlen(str), &size);
          sprintf(str, "Previous string is %d units long", size.cx);
          X = size.cx; /* advance to end of previous string */
          TextOut(hdc, X, Y, str, strlen(str));
          Y = Y + tm.tmHeight + tm.tmExternalLeading; /* next line */
          X = 0; /* reset X */
```

```
                    sprintf(str, "Screen dimensions: %d %d", maxX, maxY);
                    TextOut(hdc, X, Y, str, strlen(str));
                    Y = Y + tm.tmHeight + tm.tmExternalLeading; /* next line */
                    ReleaseDC(hwnd, hdc); /* release DC */
                    break;
                  case ID_RESET:
                    X = Y = 0;
                    break;
                  case ID_HELP:
                    MessageBox(hwnd, "F2: Display\nF3: Reset", "Help", MB_OK);
                    break;
                }
              break;
          case WM_DESTROY: /* terminate the program */
            PostQuitMessage(0);
            break;
          default:
            /* Let Windows NT process any messages not specified in
            the preceding switch statement. */
            return DefWindowProc(hwnd, message, wParam, lParam);
        }
        return 0;
      }
```

This program requires the following resource file:

```
#include "text.h"
#include <windows.h>

MYMENU MENU
{
  MENUITEM "&Show", ID_SHOW
  MENUITEM "&Reset", ID_RESET
  MENUITEM "&Help", ID_HELP
}

MYMENU ACCELERATORS
{
  VK_F2, ID_SHOW, VIRTKEY
  VK_F3, ID_RESET, VIRTKEY
  VK_F1, ID_HELP, VIRTKEY
}
```

It also requires the header file **text.h**, which is shown here:

```
#define ID_SHOW    100
#define ID_RESET   101
#define ID_HELP    102
```

Enter these files and compile and run the program. Each time you select Show from the main menu, you will cause a few lines of text to be displayed. The text will be black and the background is turquoise. Sample output is shown in Figure 8-1.

When the window is first created and **WM_CREATE** is received, the global integers **maxX** and **maxY** are initialized to the coordinates of the screen using the **GetSystemMetrics()** function. While these values serve no real purpose in this program, they will be used in later examples.

Notice that the program declares two global variables called **X** and **Y** and initializes both to 0. These variables will contain the current window location at which text will be displayed. They will be continually updated by the program after each output sequence.

The interesting part of this program is mostly contained within the **WM_COMMAND** message. Let's examine it closely, beginning with the **ID_SHOW** case. Each time an **ID_SHOW** message is received, a device context is obtained. Then, the text color is set to black and the background color is set to turquoise. Since the device context is obtained each time an **ID_SHOW** message is received, the colors must be set each time. That is, they cannot be set only once (at the start of the program, for example).

After the colors have been set, the text metrics are obtained. Next, the first line of text is output. Notice that it is constructed using **sprintf()** and then actually displayed using **TextOut()**. As you know from earlier in this book,

Figure 8-1

Sample output from the text demonstration program

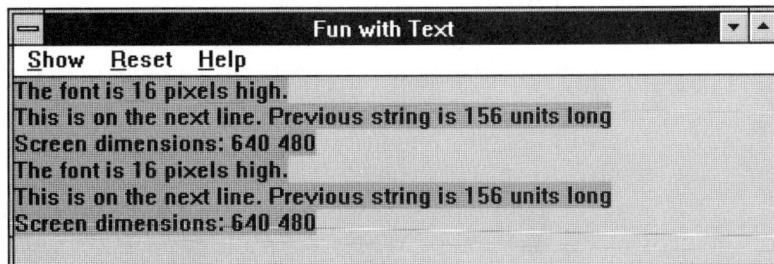

neither **TextOut()** nor any other API function performs text formatting, so it is up to you, the programmer, to construct your output first and then display it using **TextOut()**. After the string is displayed, the **Y** coordinate is advanced to the next line by applying the formula developed earlier.

The program continues by displaying the line "This is on the next line." Then, before that string is overwritten by the next call to **sprintf()**, its length is computed using a call to **GetTextExtentPoint()**. This value is then used to advance the **X** coordinate to the end of the previous line before the next line is printed. Notice that here the **Y** coordinate is unchanged. This causes the next string to be displayed immediately after the previous one. Before continuing, the program advances **Y** to the next line and resets **X** to 0, which is the leftmost coordinate. This causes subsequent output once again to be started at the beginning of the next line.

Finally, the screen dimensions are displayed and the **Y** coordinate is advanced to the next line.

Each time you select Show, the text is displayed lower in the window and does not overwrite the preceding text. Instead each set of lines is displayed beneath the previous one.

To start over, select Reset. This causes the coordinates to be reset to 0, 0. However, it does not erase what is already in the window.

Solving the Repaint Problem

While the preceding program demonstrates some text and system functions, it reintroduces a fundamental problem that was first discussed in Chapter 3. The problem is this: when you run the program, display some text, and then overwrite the window with another, the text is lost. When the window is then redisplayed, the part of the text that was covered will be missing. Of course, the reason for this is that each program must repaint its window when it receives a **WM_PAINT** message, and the preceding program does not do this. However, this raises the larger question: what mechanism should one use to restore the contents of a window that has been overwritten. As mentioned earlier, there are three basic methods. First, you can regenerate the output if that output is created by some computational method. Second, you can store a record of display events and "replay" those events. Third, you can maintain a virtual window and simply copy the contents of the virtual window into the actual window each time a **WM_CREATE** message is received. The most general of these is, of course, the third, and this is the method that will be developed here. As you will see, Windows NT provides substantial support for this method.

Virtual Window Theory

Before actually implementing a virtual window and using it to restore the contents of a window when a **WM_PAINT** message is received, it is important that you understand the theory behind this process. Once you understand the theory, it will be much easier for you to understand the details of an implementation using Windows NT.

In general, here is how output will be accomplished using a virtual window. First, a virtual device is created that is compatible with the actual device. Then, all output is written to the virtual device. Each time a **WM_PAINT** message is received, the contents of the virtual device are copied into the actual device, causing output to be displayed in the window. Therefore, there is always a record of the current contents of the window. If the window is overwritten and then uncovered, **WM_PAINT** will be sent and the window's contents will be automatically restored.

Some Additional API Functions

To implement a virtual window requires the use of several API functions. Three have been discussed already, in Chapter 6 when custom bitmaps were explained. These are **CreateCompatibleDC()**, **SelectObject()**, and **BitBlt()**. We will also be using **CreateCompatibleBitmap()**, **PatBlt()**, and **GetStockObject()**, which are described here. (Actually, you have been using **GetStockObject()** since Chapter 2 to load the default brush for the main window. However, it is described here for your convenience.)

The **CreateCompatibleBitmap()** function creates a bitmap that is compatible with the specified device. This bitmap can be used by any memory device (created by **CreateCompatibleDC()**) that is compatible with the specified device. Its prototype is shown here:

HBITMAP CreateCompatibleBitmap(HDC *hdc*, int *width*,
int *height*);

Here, *hdc* is the handle to the device with which the bitmap will be compatible. The dimensions of the bitmap are specified in *width* and *height*. These values are in pixels. The function returns a handle to the compatible bitmap.

The **PatBlt()** function fills a rectangle with the color and pattern of the currently selected *brush*. A brush is an object that specifies how a window (or region) will be filled. Filling an area using a brush is also commonly referred to as *painting* the region. **PatBlt()** has this prototype:

BOOL PatBlt (HDC *hdc,* int *X,* int *Y,* int *width,*
                   int *height,* DWORD *dwRaster*);

Here, *hdc* is the handle of the device to fill. The coordinates *X* and *Y* specify the upper left corner of the region to be filled. The width and height of the region are specified in *width* and *height.* The value passed in *dwRaster* determines how the brush will be applied. It must be one of these macros:

Macro	Meaning
BLACKNESS	Region is black (brush is ignored)
WHITENESS	Region is white (brush is ignored)
PATCOPY	Brush is copied to region
PATINVERT	Brush is ORed to region
DSTINVERT	Region is inverted (brush is ignored)

Therefore, if you wish to apply the current brush unaltered, you would select **PATCOPY** for the value for *dwRaster.* The function returns non-zero if successful; otherwise it returns zero.

As you learned in Chapter 2, the **GetStockObject()** function returns a handle to the specified standard object. Standard (or *stock*) objects include pens, brushes, and fonts. Its prototype is shown here:

HGDIOBJ GetStockObject(int *object*);

Here, *object* is a macro that specifies the standard object. The values for the standard brushes are shown here. For most, their names imply their meaning.

BLACK_BRUSH
DKGRAY_BRUSH
GRAY_BRUSH
HOLLOW_BRUSH
LTGRAY_BRUSH
NULL_BRUSH
WHITE_BRUSH

A hollow brush and a null brush take no action.

Now that you know about the functions that will be used, it is time to see how to implement a virtual window.

Creating and Using a Virtual Device

Let's begin by restating the procedure that will be implemented. To create an easy and convenient means of restoring a window after a **WM_PAINT** message has been received, a virtual device will be maintained and all output will be written to that virtual device. Each time a repaint request is received, the contents of that device are copied into the window that is physically on the screen. Now, let's implement this approach.

Creating the Virtual Device

First, a virtual device must be created that is compatible with the current device context. This will be done only once, when the program begins execution and a **WM_CREATE** message is received. This compatible device context will stay in existence the entire time the program is executing. Here is the code that performs this function:

```
case WM_CREATE:
  /* Get screen coordinates. */
  maxX = GetSystemMetrics(SM_CXSCREEN);
  maxY = GetSystemMetrics(SM_CYSCREEN);

  /* Make a compatible memory image. */
  hdc = GetDC(hwnd);
  memdc = CreateCompatibleDC(hdc);
  hbit = CreateCompatibleBitmap(hdc, maxX, maxY);
  SelectObject(memdc, hbit);
  hbrush = GetStockObject(LTGRAY_BRUSH);
  SelectObject(memdc, hbrush);
  PatBlt(memdc, 0, 0, maxX, maxY, PATCOPY);
  ReleaseDC(hwnd, hdc);
  break;
```

Let's examine this code closely. First, the dimensions of the screen are obtained. They will be used to create a compatible bitmap. Then, the current device context is obtained. Next, a compatible device context is created in memory, using **CreateCompatibleDC()**. The handle to this device context is stored in **memdc**, which is a global variable. Then, a compatible bitmap is created. The dimensions of the bitmap are those of the maximum screen size. This ensures that the bitmap will always be large enough to fully restore the window no matter how large the window is. (Actually, slightly smaller values could be used, since the borders aren't repainted, but this minor improvement is left to you, as an exercise.) This establishes a one-to-one mapping between the memory device and the physical device. The handle to the bitmap is stored in the global variable **hbit**. Next, a stock light gray brush is obtained and its handle is stored in the global variable **hbrush**. The reason that the light gray brush is used is that it is also the background color of the physical window created by the program in the full program that will follow. This brush is selected into the memory device and then **PatBlt()** paints the entire virtual window using the brush. Thus, the memory device will have a light gray background that matches the background of the physical window. (Remember, these colors are under your control. The colors used here are arbitrary.) Finally, the physical device context is released. However, the memory device stays in existence until the program ends.

Using the Virtual Device

Once the virtual device has been created, all output is directed to it. (The only time output is actually directed to the physical device is when a **WM_PAINT** message is received.) For example, here is a reworked version of the **ID_SHOW** message from the previous program that uses the virtual device:

```
case ID_SHOW:
  /* Set text color to black. */
  SetTextColor(memdc, RGB(0, 0, 0));
  /* Set background mode to transparent. */
  SetBkMode(memdc, TRANSPARENT);

  /* Get text metrics. */
  GetTextMetrics(memdc, &tm);

  sprintf(str, "The font is %ld pixels high.", tm.tmHeight);
  TextOut(memdc, X, Y, str, strlen(str)); /* output string */
  Y = Y + tm.tmHeight + tm.tmExternalLeading; /* next line */
```

```
strcpy(str, "This is on the next line. ");
TextOut(memdc, X, Y, str, strlen(str)); /* output string */

/* Compute length of a string. */
GetTextExtentPoint(memdc, str, strlen(str), &size);
sprintf(str, "Previous string is %d units long", size.cx);
X = size.cx; /* advance to end of previous string */
TextOut(memdc, X, Y, str, strlen(str));
Y = Y + tm.tmHeight + tm.tmExternalLeading; /* next line */
X = 0; /* reset X */

sprintf(str, "Screen dimensions: %d %d", maxX, maxY);
TextOut(memdc, X, Y, str, strlen(str));
Y = Y + tm.tmHeight + tm.tmExternalLeading; /* next line */
InvalidateRect(hwnd, NULL, 1);
break;
```

This version directs all output to **memdc** and then calls **InvalidateRect()** to cause the physical window to be updated.

Notice that this version also sets the background mode to **TRANSPARENT**. This causes the text to be displayed in the window without the background color being altered.

Each time a **WM_PAINT** message is received, the contents of the virtual device are copied into the physical device. This is accomplished by the following code:

```
case WM_PAINT: /* process a repaint request */
  hdc = BeginPaint(hwnd, &paintstruct); /* get DC */

  /* Now, copy memory image onto screen. */
  BitBlt(hdc, 0, 0, maxX, maxY, memdc, 0, 0, SRCCOPY);

  EndPaint(hwnd, &paintstruct); /* release DC */
  break;
```

As you can see, the **BitBlt()** function is used to copy the image from **memdc** into **hdc**. Remember, the parameter **SRCCOPY** simply means to copy the image as-is without alteration directly from the source to the target. Because all output has been stored in **memdc**, this statement causes that output to actually be displayed. More importantly, if the window is covered and then uncovered, **WM_PAINT** will be received and this code causes the contents of that window to be automatically restored.

As stated earlier, there are many ways to approach the restoring of a window, but the method just developed is applicable to a wide range of situations and is, generally, quite efficient. Also, since your program is passed the coordinates of the region that must be repainted, you can actually make the preceding routine more efficient by restoring only that part of the window that had been destroyed. (You might want to try implementing this enhancement on your own.)

The Entire Virtual Device Demonstration Program

Here is the complete program that demonstrates using a virtual device to hold output and repaint the window:

```
/* A Windows NT skeleton that demonstrates
   a virtual device. */

/* The following definition causes stricter type checking.
   This is optional, but suggested because it will help
   catch potential type mismatch errors--especially
   when porting from 16-bit Windows. */
#define STRICT

#include <windows.h>
#include <string.h>
#include <stdio.h>
#include "text.h"

LRESULT CALLBACK WindowFunc(HWND, UINT, WPARAM, LPARAM);

char szWinName[] = "MyWin"; /* name of window class */

char str[255]; /* holds output strings */

int X=0, Y=0; /* current output location */
int maxX, maxY; /* screen dimensions */

HDC memdc; /* store the virtual device handle */
HBITMAP hbit; /* store the virtual bitmap */
HBRUSH hbrush; /* store the brush handle */

int WINAPI WinMain(HINSTANCE hThisInst, HINSTANCE hPrevInst,
                   LPSTR lpszArgs, int nWinMode)
{
```

```
HWND hwnd;
MSG msg;
WNDCLASS wcl;
HANDLE hAccel;

/* Define a window class. */
wcl.hInstance = hThisInst; /* handle to this instance */
wcl.lpszClassName = szWinName; /* window class name */
wcl.lpfnWndProc = WindowFunc; /* window function */
wcl.style = 0; /* default style */

wcl.hIcon = LoadIcon(NULL, IDI_APPLICATION); /* icon style */
wcl.hCursor = LoadCursor(NULL, IDC_ARROW); /* cursor style */

/* Specify name of menu resource. */
wcl.lpszMenuName = "MYMENU"; /* main menu */

wcl.cbClsExtra = 0; /* no extra */
wcl.cbWndExtra = 0; /* information needed */

/* Make the window light gray. */
wcl.hbrBackground = GetStockObject(LTGRAY_BRUSH);

/* Register the window class. */
if(!RegisterClass (&wcl)) return 0;

/* Now that a window class has been registered, a window
   can be created. */
hwnd = CreateWindow(
  szWinName, /* name of window class */
  "Fun with Text", /* title */
  WS_OVERLAPPEDWINDOW, /* window style--normal */
  CW_USEDEFAULT, /* X coordinate--let Windows decide */
  CW_USEDEFAULT, /* Y coordinate--let Windows decide */
  CW_USEDEFAULT, /* width--let Windows decide */
  CW_USEDEFAULT, /* height--let Windows decide */
  HWND_DESKTOP, /* handle of parent window--there isn't one */
  NULL, /* no menu */
  hThisInst, /* handle of this instance of the program */
  NULL /* no additional arguments */
);

/* Load accelerators. */
hAccel = LoadAccelerators(hThisInst, "MYMENU");
```

```c
      /* Display the window. */
      ShowWindow(hwnd, nWinMode);
      UpdateWindow(hwnd);

      /* Create the message loop. */
      while(GetMessage(&msg, NULL, 0, 0))
      {
        if(!TranslateAccelerator(hwnd, hAccel, &msg)) {
          TranslateMessage(&msg); /* allow use of keyboard */
          DispatchMessage(&msg); /* return control to Windows */
        }
      }
      return msg.wParam;
}

/* This function is called by Windows NT and is passed
   messages from the message queue.
*/
LRESULT CALLBACK WindowFunc(HWND hwnd, UINT message, WPARAM wParam,
                LPARAM lParam)
{
  HDC hdc;
  PAINTSTRUCT paintstruct;
  TEXTMETRIC tm;
  SIZE size;

  switch(message) {
    case WM_CREATE:
      /* Get screen coordinates. */
      maxX = GetSystemMetrics(SM_CXSCREEN);
      maxY = GetSystemMetrics(SM_CYSCREEN);

      /* Make a compatible memory image. */
      hdc = GetDC(hwnd);
      memdc = CreateCompatibleDC(hdc);
      hbit = CreateCompatibleBitmap(hdc, maxX, maxY);
      SelectObject(memdc, hbit);
      hbrush = GetStockObject(LTGRAY_BRUSH);
      SelectObject(memdc, hbrush);
      PatBlt(memdc, 0, 0, maxX, maxY, PATCOPY);
      ReleaseDC(hwnd, hdc);
      break;
```

```
case WM_COMMAND:
  switch(LOWORD(wParam)) {
    case ID_SHOW:
      /* Set text color to black. */
      SetTextColor(memdc, RGB(0, 0, 0));
      /* Set background mode to transparent. */
      SetBkMode(memdc, TRANSPARENT);

      /* Get text metrics. */
      GetTextMetrics(memdc, &tm);

      sprintf(str, "The font is %ld pixels high.", tm.tmHeight);
      TextOut(memdc, X, Y, str, strlen(str)); /* output string */
      Y = Y + tm.tmHeight + tm.tmExternalLeading; /* next line */

      strcpy(str, "This is on the next line. ");
      TextOut(memdc, X, Y, str, strlen(str)); /* output string */

      /* Compute length of a string. */
      GetTextExtentPoint(memdc, str, strlen(str), &size);
      sprintf(str, "Previous string is %d units long", size.cx);
      X = size.cx; /* advance to end of previous string */
      TextOut(memdc, X, Y, str, strlen(str));
      Y = Y + tm.tmHeight + tm.tmExternalLeading; /* next line */
      X = 0; /* reset X */

      sprintf(str, "Screen dimensions: %d %d", maxX, maxY);
      TextOut(memdc, X, Y, str, strlen(str));
      Y = Y + tm.tmHeight + tm.tmExternalLeading; /* next line */
      InvalidateRect(hwnd, NULL, 1);
      break;
    case ID_RESET:
      X = Y = 0;
      /* Erase by repainting background. */
      PatBlt(memdc, 0, 0, maxX, maxY, PATCOPY);
      InvalidateRect(hwnd, NULL, 1);
      break;
    case ID_HELP:
      MessageBox(hwnd, "F2: Display\nF3: Reset", "Help", MB_OK);
      break;
  }
  break;
```

```
    case WM_PAINT: /* process a repaint request */
      hdc = BeginPaint(hwnd, &paintstruct); /* get DC */

      /* Now, copy memory image onto screen. */
      BitBlt(hdc, 0, 0, maxX, maxY, memdc, 0, 0, SRCCOPY);
      EndPaint(hwnd, &paintstruct); /* release DC */
      break;
    case WM_DESTROY: /* terminate the program */
      DeleteDC(memdc); /* delete the memory device */
      PostQuitMessage(0);
      break;
    default:
      /* Let Windows NT process any messages not specified in
      the preceding switch statement. */
      return DefWindowProc(hwnd, message, wParam, lParam);
  }
  return 0;
}
```

When you run this program you will see two immediate improvements. First, each time you cover and then uncover the window, the contents are restored. Secondly, when you select Reset, the window is cleared. This occurs because the call to **BitBlt()** inside the **ID_RESET** message causes the light gray brush to be used to paint the window, thus erasing any preexisting contents.

Changing Fonts

As you probably know, one of the main purposes of Windows in general and Windows NT, specifically, is to provide complete control over the user interface. As such, Windows NT has a rich and varied set of text-based features that you can use. One of its strongest text-based features is its collection of various type fonts. In Windows NT you have several built-in type fonts to choose from. (You can also use custom fonts, but this is beyond the scope of this chapter.) This section shows how to select and switch between Windows NT's built-in text fonts.

The built-in fonts are stock objects that are selected using **GetStockObject()** (a function that was described earlier). At the time of this writing, Windows NT supports six built-in fonts. The macros associated with these fonts are shown here:

Macro	Font Description
ANSI_FIXED_FONT	Fixed pitch font
ANSI_VAR_FONT	Variable pitch font
DEVICE_DEFAULT_FONT	Default device font
OEM_FIXED_FONT	OEM defined font
SYSTEM_FONT	Font used by Windows NT
SYSTEM_FIXED_FONT	Font used by older versions of Windows

The system fonts are those character fonts used by Windows for things like menus and dialog boxes. Older versions of Windows used a fixed pitch system font, but, beginning with Windows 3.0, a variable font is used. Windows NT also uses the variable font.

Selecting and using a built-in font is very easy. To do so, your program must first create a font handle, which is of type **HFONT**. Next, it must load the desired font, using **GetStockObject()**, which returns a handle to the font. To switch to the font, select the font using **SelectObject()** with the new font as a parameter. **SelectObject()** will return a handle to the old font, which you may want to save so that you can switch back to it after you are done using the other font.

The following program demonstrates changing fonts. It adds another menu selection called Font. Each time it is selected, the font is toggled between the default system font and the ANSI variable font.

```
/* A Windows NT skeleton that demonstrates
   built-in fonts. */

/* The following definition causes stricter type checking.
   This is optional, but suggested because it will help
   catch potential type mismatch errors--especially
   when porting from 16-bit Windows. */
#define STRICT

#include <windows.h>
#include <string.h>
#include <stdio.h>
#include "text.h"

LRESULT CALLBACK WindowFunc(HWND, UINT, WPARAM, LPARAM);

char szWinName[] = "MyWin"; /* name of window class */
```

```
char str[255]; /* holds output strings */

int X=0, Y=0; /* current output location */
int maxX, maxY; /* screen dimensions */

HDC memdc; /* store the virtual device handle */
HBITMAP hbit; /* store the virtual bitmap */
HBRUSH hbrush; /* store the brush handle */
HFONT holdf, hnewf; /* store the font handles */

int WINAPI WinMain(HINSTANCE hThisInst, HINSTANCE hPrevInst,
                   LPSTR lpszArgs, int nWinMode)
{
  HWND hwnd;
  MSG msg;
  WNDCLASS wcl;
  HANDLE hAccel;

  /* Define a window class. */
  wcl.hInstance = hThisInst; /* handle to this instance */
  wcl.lpszClassName = szWinName; /* window class name */
  wcl.lpfnWndProc = WindowFunc; /* window function */
  wcl.style = 0; /* default style */

  wcl.hIcon = LoadIcon(NULL, IDI_APPLICATION); /* icon style */
  wcl.hCursor = LoadCursor(NULL, IDC_ARROW); /* cursor style */

  /* Specify name of menu resource. */
  wcl.lpszMenuName = "MYMENU"; /* main menu */

  wcl.cbClsExtra = 0; /* no extra */
  wcl.cbWndExtra = 0; /* information needed */

  /* Make the window light gray. */
  wcl.hbrBackground = GetStockObject(LTGRAY_BRUSH);

  /* Register the window class. */
  if(!RegisterClass (&wcl)) return 0;

  /* Now that a window class has been registered, a window
     can be created. */
  hwnd = CreateWindow(
    szWinName, /* name of window class */
```

```
    "Fun with Text", /* title */
    WS_OVERLAPPEDWINDOW, /* window style--normal */
    CW_USEDEFAULT, /* X coordinate--let Windows decide */
    CW_USEDEFAULT, /* Y coordinate--let Windows decide */
    CW_USEDEFAULT, /* width--let Windows decide */
    CW_USEDEFAULT, /* height--let Windows decide */
    HWND_DESKTOP, /* handle of parent window--there isn't one */
    NULL, /* no menu */
    hThisInst, /* handle of this instance of the program */
    NULL /* no additional arguments */
  );

  /* Load accelerators. */
  hAccel = LoadAccelerators(hThisInst, "MYMENU");

  /* Display the window. */
  ShowWindow(hwnd, nWinMode);
  UpdateWindow(hwnd);

  /* Create the message loop. */
  while(GetMessage(&msg, NULL, 0, 0))
  {
    if(!TranslateAccelerator(hwnd, hAccel, &msg)) {
      TranslateMessage(&msg); /* allow use of keyboard */
      DispatchMessage(&msg); /* return control to Windows */
    }
  }
  return msg.wParam;
}

/* This function is called by Windows NT and is passed
   messages from the message queue.
*/
LRESULT CALLBACK WindowFunc(HWND hwnd, UINT message, WPARAM wParam,
                  LPARAM lParam)
{
  HDC hdc;
  PAINTSTRUCT paintstruct;
  static TEXTMETRIC tm;
  SIZE size;
  static fontswitch = 0;

  switch(message) {
    case WM_CREATE:
```

```
      /* Get screen coordinates. */
      maxX = GetSystemMetrics(SM_CXSCREEN);
      maxY = GetSystemMetrics(SM_CYSCREEN);

      /* Make a compatible memory image device. */
      hdc = GetDC(hwnd);
      memdc = CreateCompatibleDC(hdc);
      hbit = CreateCompatibleBitmap(hdc, maxX, maxY);
      SelectObject(memdc, hbit);
      hbrush = GetStockObject(LTGRAY_BRUSH);
      SelectObject(memdc, hbrush);
      PatBlt(memdc, 0, 0, maxX, maxY, PATCOPY);

      /* Get the new font. */
      hnewf = GetStockObject(ANSI_VAR_FONT);

    ReleaseDC(hwnd, hdc);
    break;
case WM_COMMAND:
  switch(LOWORD(wParam)) {
    case ID_SHOW:
      /* Set text to black and background to transparent. */
      SetTextColor(memdc, RGB(0, 0, 0));
      SetBkMode(memdc, TRANSPARENT);

      /* Get text metrics. */
      GetTextMetrics(memdc, &tm);

      sprintf(str, "The font is %ld pixels high.", tm.tmHeight);
      TextOut(memdc, X, Y, str, strlen(str)); /* output string */
      Y = Y + tm.tmHeight + tm.tmExternalLeading; /* next line */

      strcpy(str, "This is on the next line. ");
      TextOut(memdc, X, Y, str, strlen(str)); /* output string */

      /* Compute length of a string. */
      GetTextExtentPoint(memdc, str, strlen(str), &size);
      sprintf(str, "Previous string is %d units long", size.cx);
      X = size.cx; /* advance to end of previous string */
      TextOut(memdc, X, Y, str, strlen(str));
      Y = Y + tm.tmHeight + tm.tmExternalLeading; /* next line */
      X = 0; /* reset X */
```

```
      sprintf(str, "Screen dimensions: %d %d", maxX, maxY);
      TextOut(memdc, X, Y, str, strlen(str));
      Y = Y + tm.tmHeight + tm.tmExternalLeading; /* next line */
      InvalidateRect(hwnd, NULL, 1);
      break;
    case ID_RESET:
      X = Y = 0;
      /* Erase by repainting background. */
      PatBlt(memdc, 0, 0, maxX, maxY, PATCOPY);
      InvalidateRect(hwnd, NULL, 1);
      break;
    case ID_FONT:
      if(!fontswitch) {  /* switch to new font */
        holdf = SelectObject(memdc, hnewf);
        fontswitch = 1;
      }
      else { /* switch to old font */
        SelectObject(memdc, holdf);
        fontswitch = 0;
      }
      break;
    case ID_HELP:
      MessageBox(hwnd, "F2: Display\nF3: Change font\nF4: Reset",
                 "Text Fun", MB_OK);
      break;
  }
  break;
case WM_PAINT: /* process a repaint request */
  hdc = BeginPaint(hwnd, &paintstruct); /* get DC */

  /* Now, copy memory image onto screen. */
  BitBlt(hdc, 0, 0, maxX, maxY, memdc, 0, 0, SRCCOPY);
  EndPaint(hwnd, &paintstruct); /* release DC */
  break;
case WM_DESTROY: /* terminate the program */
  DeleteDC(memdc);
  PostQuitMessage(0);
  break;
default:
 /* Let Windows NT process any messages not specified in
  the preceding switch statement. */
  return DefWindowProc(hwnd, message, wParam, lParam);
}
```

```
    return 0;
}
```

Before you compile this program, change your resource file to the following:

```
#include "text.h"
#include <windows.h>

MYMENU MENU
{
  MENUITEM "&Show", ID_SHOW
  MENUITEM "&Font", ID_FONT
  MENUITEM "&Reset", ID_RESET
  MENUITEM "&Help", ID_HELP
}

MYMENU ACCELERATORS
{
  VK_F2, ID_SHOW, VIRTKEY
  VK_F3, ID_FONT, VIRTKEY
  VK_F4, ID_RESET, VIRTKEY
  VK_F1, ID_HELP, VIRTKEY
}
```

Finally, add this line to the **text.h** header file:

```
#define ID_FONT      103
```

Sample output produced by this program is shown in Figure 8-2.

In the next chapter, we will continue exploring window output by working with graphics.

Figure 8-2

Sample output
from the font
program

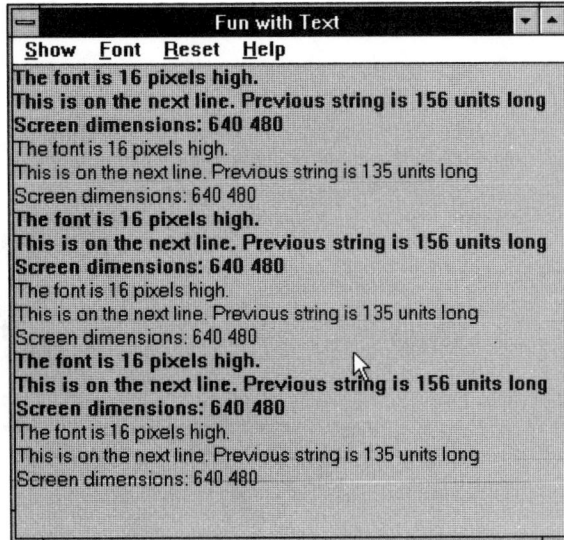

```
┌──────────────────────────────────────────────┐
│ ▬            Fun with Text              ▼  ▲  │
├──────────────────────────────────────────────┤
│  Show   Font   Reset   Help                  │
├──────────────────────────────────────────────┤
│ The font is 16 pixels high.                   │
│ This is on the next line. Previous string is 156 units long│
│ Screen dimensions: 640 480                    │
│ The font is 16 pixels high.                   │
│ This is on the next line. Previous string is 135 units long│
│ Screen dimensions: 640 480                    │
│ The font is 16 pixels high.                   │
│ This is on the next line. Previous string is 156 units long│
│ Screen dimensions: 640 480                    │
│ The font is 16 pixels high.                   │
│ This is on the next line. Previous string is 135 units long│
│ Screen dimensions: 640 480                    │
│ The font is 16 pixels high.                   │
│ This is on the next line. Previous string is 156 units long│
│ Screen dimensions: 640 480                    │
│ The font is 16 pixels high.                   │
│ This is on the next line. Previous string is 135 units long│
│ Screen dimensions: 640 480                    │
│                                              │
│                                              │
└──────────────────────────────────────────────┘
```

Chapter 9

Working with Graphics

WINDOWS NT has a rich and flexible set of graphics functions available to the programmer. This is not surprising, since Windows NT is a graphical operating system. However, what you might find surprising is how tightly integrated graphics are into the Windows NT display system. In fact, much of what you learned in the preceding chapter about text is applicable to graphics. For example, the same brush that is used to paint the window is used to fill an object.

This chapter explores the most commonly used API graphics functions. Keep in mind, however, that the discussion of graphics in this chapter only scratches the surface. The Windows NT graphics system is quite powerful and you will want to explore it further on your own.

This chapter begins by discussing the basic graphics functions and concludes with a program that demonstrates them.

16-Bit Conversion Note In 16-bit Windows, graphics coordinates are 16-bit values. However, in Windows NT, graphics coordinates are stored as 32-bit values. This has required that some of the graphics functions be expanded to accommodate this increase in size. The main difference is found in those functions that return coordinates. In 16-bit Windows, these values were packed in one double word. While a double word can hold two 16-bit values, it can only hold one 32-bit value. In Windows NT, coordinates are returned in a **POINT** structure, which holds two 32-bit values. Because of this difference, new functions needed to be created. To provide, as far as possible, name compatibility with 16-bit Windows, when a function returns a **POINT** value, the old 16-bit Windows name is kept, but the suffix **Ex** is added. When converting from 16-bit Windows, you will need to make the appropriate changes when these functions are encountered.

The Graphics Coordinate System

The graphics coordinate system is the same as that used by the text-based functions (discussed in Chapter 8). This means that, by default, the upper left corner is location 0, 0 and that logical units are equivalent to pixels. Remember that the coordinate system and the mapping of logical units to pixels are under your control and may be changed. (However, the manipulation of coordinate systems and mapping modes is beyond the scope of this book.)

Windows NT (and Windows in general) maintains a *current position* that is used and updated by certain graphics functions. When your program begins, the current location is set to 0, 0. Keep in mind that the location of the current position is completely invisible. That is, no graphics "cursor" is displayed. Instead, the current position is simply the next place in the window at which certain graphics functions will begin.

Pens and Brushes

The Windows NT graphics system is based upon two important objects: pens and brushes. You learned about brushes in Chapter 8. All of that information applies to the graphics functions described here, as well. By default, closed graphics shapes, such as rectangles and ellipses, are filled using the currently selected brush. *Pens* are resources that draw the lines and curves specified by the various graphics functions. The default pen is black and one pixel thick. However, you can alter these attributes.

Until now, we have only been working with stock objects, which are objects automatically included with Windows NT. In this chapter you will learn how to create custom brushes and pens. There is one important thing to remember about custom objects: they must be deleted before your program ends. This is accomplished using **DeleteObject()**, which is described later in this chapter.

Setting a Pixel

You can set the color of any specific pixel using the API function **SetPixel()**, whose prototype is shown here:

COLORREF SetPixel(HDC *hdc*, int *X*, int *Y*, COLORREF *color*);

Here, *hdc* is the handle of the desired device context. The coordinates of the point to set are specified by *X*, *Y*, and the color is specified in *color*. (**COLORREF** is discussed in Chapter 8.) The function returns the original color of the pixel, **COLOR_INVALID**, if an error occurs, or –1 if the location specified is outside the window.

Drawing a Line

To draw a line, use the **LineTo()** function. This function draws a line using the currently selected pen. Its prototype is shown here:

BOOL LineTo(HDC *hdc*, int *X*, int *Y*);

The handle of the device context in which to draw the line is specified by *hdc*. The line is drawn from the current graphics position to the coordinates specified by *X*, *Y*. The current position is then changed to *X*, *Y*. The function returns non–zero if successful (that is, the line is drawn) and zero on failure.

Some programmers are surprised by the fact that **LineTo()** uses the current position as its starting location and then sets the current position to the end point of the line that is drawn (instead of leaving it unchanged). However, there is a good reason for this. Many times, when displaying lines, one line will begin at the end of the previous line. When this is the case, the **LineTo()** operates extremely efficiently by avoiding the additional overhead of passing an extra set of coordinates. When this is not the case, you can set the current location to any position you like using the **MoveToEx()** function, described next, prior to calling **LineTo()**.

Setting the Current Location

To set the current position, use the **MoveToEx()** function, whose prototype is shown here:

BOOL MoveToEx(HDC *hdc*, int *X*, int *Y*, LPPOINT *lpCoord*);

The handle of the device context affected is specified in *hdc*. The coordinates of the new current position are specified by *X, Y*. The previous current position is returned in the **POINT** structure pointed to by *lpCoord*. **POINT** is defined like this:

```
typedef struct tagPOINT {
  LONG x;
  LONG y;
} POINT;
```

However, if you pass a NULL pointer in the *lpCoord* parameter, then **Move-ToEx()** does not return the previous current position.

   MoveToEx() returns non-zero if successful and zero on failure.

16-bit Conversion Note In 16-bit Windows, the function that moves the current location is called **MoveTo()**. It has only three parameters, which are the same as the first three parameters of **MoveToEx()**. It returns the previous location as a double word. This function is not supported by Windows NT. If you are porting code that uses this function, make appropriate changes. If you don't use the previous location, simply make the *lpCoord* parameter NULL.

Drawing an Arc

You can draw an elliptical arc (a portion of an ellipse) in the current pen color using the **Arc()** function. Its prototype is shown here:

BOOL Arc(HDC *hdc*, int *upX*, int *upY*, int *lowX*, int *lowY*,
         int *startX*, int *startY*, int *endX*, int *endY*);

Here, *hdc* is the handle of the device context in which the arc will be drawn. The arc is defined by two objects. First, the arc is a portion of an ellipse bounded by the rectangle whose upper left corner is at *upX, upY* and whose lower right corner is at *lowX, lowY*. The portion of the ellipse that is actually drawn (that is, the arc) starts at the intersection of a line from the center of the rectangle to the point specified by *startX, startY*. The arc ends at the intersection of the line from the center of the rectangle to the point specified by *endX, endY*. The arc is drawn counterclockwise starting from *startX, startY*. Figure 9-1 illustrates how **Arc()** works.

Arc() returns non-zero if successful and zero on failure.

Displaying Rectangles

You can display a rectangle in the current pen using the **Rectangle()** function, whose prototype is shown here:

BOOL Rectangle(HDC *hdc,* int *upX,* int *upY,*
          int *lowX,* int *lowY*);

As usual, *hdc* is the handle of the device context. The upper left corner of the rectangle is specified by *upX, upY* and the lower right corner is specified by *lowX, lowY*. The function returns non-zero if successful and zero if an error occurs. The rectangle is automatically filled using the current brush.

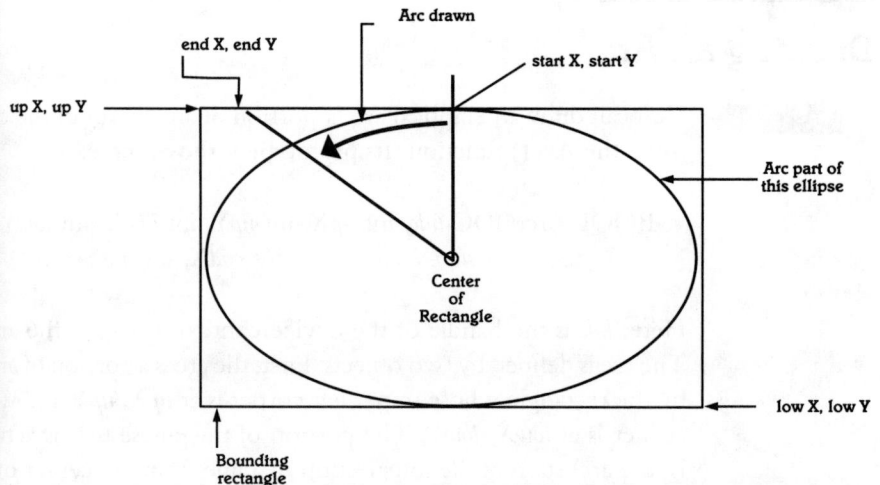

Figure 9-1

How the Arc() function operates

You can display a rounded rectangle using the **RoundRect()** function. A rounded rectangle has its corners rounded slightly. The prototype for **Round Rect()** is shown here:

BOOL RoundRect(HDC *hdc*, int *upX*, int *upY*,
              int *lowX*, int *lowY*,
              int *curveX*, int *curveY*);

The first five parameters are the same as for **Rectangle()**. How the corners are curved is determined by the values of *curveX* and *curveY*, which define the width and the height of the ellipse that describe the curve. The function returns non–zero if successful and zero if a failure occurs. The rounded rectangle is automatically filled using the current brush.

Drawing Ellipses and Pie Slices

To draw an ellipse or a circle in the current pen, use the **Ellipse()** function, whose prototype is shown here:

BOOL Ellipse(HDC *hdc*, int *upX*, int *upY*, int *lowX*, int *lowY*);

Here, *hdc* is the handle of the device context in which the ellipse will be drawn. The ellipse is defined by specifying its bounding rectangle. The upper left corner of the rectangle is specified by *upX*, *upY* and the lower right corner is specified by *lowX*, *lowY*. To draw a circle, specify a square rectangle.

The function returns non–zero if successful and zero if a failure occurs. The ellipse is filled using the current brush.

Related to the ellipse is the pie slice. A pie slice is an object that includes an arc and lines from each end point of the arc to the center of the ellipse. To draw a pie slice use the **Pie()** function, whose prototype is shown here:

BOOL Pie(HDC *hdc*, int *upX*, int *upY*,
        int *lowX*, int *lowY*,
        int *startX*, int *startY*,
        int *endX*, int *endY*);

Here, *hdc* is the handle of the device context in which the pie slice will be drawn. The arc of the slice is defined by two objects. First, the arc is a portion of an ellipse that is bounded by the rectangle whose upper left corner is at *upX, upY* and whose lower right corner is at *lowX, lowY.* The portion of the ellipse that is actually drawn (i.e., the arc of the slice) starts at the intersection of a line that includes the center of the rectangle and the point specified by *startX, startY* and ends at the intersection of the line that includes the center of the rectangle and the point *endX, endY.*

The slice is drawn in the current pen and filled using the current brush. The **Pie()** function returns non-zero if successful and zero if an error occurs.

Working with Pens

Graphic objects are drawn using the current pen. By default, this is a black pen that is one pixel wide. There are three stock pens: black, white, and null. A handle to each of these can be obtained using **GetStockObject()**, discussed earlier in this book. The macros for these stock pens are **BLACK_PEN**, **WHITE_PEN**, and **NULL_PEN**, respectively. Pen handles are of type **HPEN**.

Frankly, the stock pens are quite limited and usually you will want to define your own pens for your application. This is accomplished using the function **CreatePen()**, whose prototype is shown here:

HPEN CreatePen(int *style*, int *width*, COLORREF *color*);

The *style* parameter determines what type of pen is created. It must be one of these values:

Macro	Pen style
PS_DASH	dashed
PS_DASHDOT	dash-dot
PS_DASHDOTDOT	dash-dot-dot
PS_DOT	dotted
PS_INSIDEFRAME	solid pen that is within a bounded region
PS_NULL	none
PS_SOLID	solid line

The dotted and/or dashed styles may only be applied to pens that are one unit thick. The **PS_INSIDEFRAME** pen is a solid pen that will be completely within the dimensions of any object that is drawn, even when that pen is more than one unit thick. For example, if a pen with **PS_INSIDEFRAME** style and width greater than one is used to draw a rectangle, then the outside of the line will be within the coordinates of the rectangle. (When a wide pen of a different style is used, the line may be partially outside the dimensions of the object.)

The thickness of a pen is specified by *width,* which is in logical units. The color of the pen is specified by *color,* which is a **COLORREF** value (discussed in Chapter 8). For the examples in this chapter, all colors are specified as RGB values.

Once a pen has been created, it is selected into a device context using **SelectObject()**. For example, the following fragment creates a red pen and then selects it for use:

```
HPEN hRedpen;
hRedpen = CreatePen(PS_SOLID, 1, RGB(255,0,0));
SelectObject(dc, hRedpen);
```

Remember, you must delete any custom pens you create by calling **DeleteObject()** before your program terminates.

Creating Custom Brushes

Custom brushes are created in a way similar to custom pens. There are various styles of brushes. The most common custom brush is a *solid brush*. A solid brush is created using the **CreateSolidBrush()** API function, whose prototype is shown here:

HBRUSH CreateSolidBrush(COLORREF *color*);

The color of the brush is specified in *color*. The function returns a handle to the brush.

Once a custom brush has been created, it is selected into the device context using **SelectObject()**. For example, the following fragment creates a green brush and then selects it for use:

```
HBRUSH hGreenbrush
hGreenbrush = CreateSolidBrush(RGB(0, 255 ,0));
SelectObject(dc, hGreenbrush);
```

Like custom pens, custom brushes must be deleted before your program terminates.

Other types of brushes you might want to explore on your own are hatch and pattern brushes, which are created using **CreateHatchBrush()** and **CreatePatternBrush()**, respectively.

Deleting Custom Objects

Typically, you must delete custom objects before your program terminates. You do this using the **DeleteObject()** API function. Its prototype is shown here:

BOOL DeleteObject(HGDIOBJ *hObject*);

Here, *hObject* is the handle to the custom object to be deleted. Remember, you cannot (and must not) delete stock objects. The object being deleted must not be currently selected into any device context.

DeleteObject() returns non-zero if successful and zero on failure.

A Graphics Demonstration

The following program demonstrates the various graphics functions discussed in this chapter. The program uses the virtual window technique developed in Chapter 8. It directs output to a memory device context, which is then copied to the physical window when a **WM_PAINT** message is received. (Remember, this approach to output allows a window's contents to be automatically updated each time a **WM_PAINT** message is received.)

```
/* A Windows NT skeleton that demonstrates
   the basic graphics functions. */
```

```c
/* The following definition causes stricter type checking.
   This is optional, but suggested because it will help
   catch potential type mismatch errors--especially
   when porting from 16-bit Windows. */
#define STRICT

#include <windows.h>
#include <string.h>
#include <stdio.h>
#include "graph.h"

LRESULT CALLBACK WindowFunc(HWND, UINT, WPARAM, LPARAM);

char szWinName[] = "MyWin"; /* name of window class */

char str[255]; /* holds output strings */

int maxX, maxY; /* screen dimensions */

HDC memdc; /* handle of memory DC */
HBITMAP hbit; /* handle of compatible bitmap */
HBRUSH hbrush, hOldbrush; /* handles of brushes */

/* Create pens. */
HPEN hOldpen; /* handle of old pen */
HPEN hRedpen, hGreenpen, hBluepen, hYellowpen;

int WINAPI WinMain(HINSTANCE hThisInst, HINSTANCE hPrevInst,
                   LPSTR lpszArgs, int nWinMode)
{
  HWND hwnd;
  MSG msg;
  WNDCLASS wcl;
  HANDLE hAccel;

  /* Define a window class. */
  wcl.hInstance = hThisInst; /* handle to this instance */
  wcl.lpszClassName = szWinName; /* window class name */
  wcl.lpfnWndProc = WindowFunc; /* window function */
  wcl.style = 0; /* default style */
```

```
wcl.hIcon = LoadIcon(NULL, IDI_APPLICATION); /* icon style */
wcl.hCursor = LoadCursor(NULL, IDC_ARROW); /* cursor style */

/* Specify name of menu resource. */
wcl.lpszMenuName = "MYMENU"; /* main menu */

wcl.cbClsExtra = 0; /* no extra */
wcl.cbWndExtra = 0; /* information needed */

/* Make the window white. */
wcl.hbrBackground = GetStockObject(WHITE_BRUSH);

/* Register the window class. */
if(!RegisterClass (&wcl)) return 0;

/* Now that a window class has been registered, a window
   can be created. */
hwnd = CreateWindow(
  szWinName, /* name of window class */
  "Fun with Graphics", /* title */
  WS_OVERLAPPEDWINDOW, /* window style--normal */
  CW_USEDEFAULT, /* X coordinate--let Windows decide */
  CW_USEDEFAULT, /* Y coordinate--let Windows decide */
  CW_USEDEFAULT, /* width--let Windows decide */
  CW_USEDEFAULT, /* height--let Windows decide */
  HWND_DESKTOP, /* handle of parent window--there isn't one */
  NULL, /* no menu */
  hThisInst, /* handle of this instance of the program */
  NULL /* no additional arguments */
);

/* Load accelerators. */
hAccel = LoadAccelerators(hThisInst, "MYMENU");

/* Display the window. */
ShowWindow(hwnd, nWinMode);
UpdateWindow(hwnd);

/* Create the message loop. */
while(GetMessage(&msg, NULL, 0, 0))
```

```
    {
      if(!TranslateAccelerator(hwnd, hAccel, &msg)) {
        TranslateMessage(&msg); /* allow use of keyboard */
        DispatchMessage(&msg); /* return control to Windows */
      }
    }
    return msg.wParam;
}


/* This function is called by Windows NT and is passed
   messages from the message queue.
*/
LRESULT CALLBACK WindowFunc(HWND hwnd, UINT message, WPARAM wParam,
                 LPARAM lParam)
{
  HDC hdc;
  PAINTSTRUCT paintstruct;
  SIZE size;

  switch(message) {
    case WM_CREATE:
      /* Get screen coordinates. */
      maxX = GetSystemMetrics(SM_CXSCREEN);
      maxY = GetSystemMetrics(SM_CYSCREEN);

      /* Make a compatible memory image device. */
      hdc = GetDC(hwnd);
      memdc = CreateCompatibleDC(hdc);
      hbit = CreateCompatibleBitmap(hdc, maxX, maxY);
      SelectObject(memdc, hbit);
      hbrush = GetStockObject(WHITE_BRUSH);
      SelectObject(memdc, hbrush);
      PatBlt(memdc, 0, 0, maxX, maxY, PATCOPY);

      hRedpen = CreatePen(PS_SOLID, 1, RGB(255,0,0));
      hGreenpen = CreatePen(PS_SOLID, 2, RGB(0,255,0));
      hBluepen = CreatePen(PS_SOLID, 3, RGB(0,0,255));
      hYellowpen = CreatePen(PS_SOLID, 4, RGB(255, 255, 0));

      /* Save default pen. */
```

```
      hOldpen = SelectObject(memdc, hRedpen);
      SelectObject(memdc, hOldpen);

      ReleaseDC(hwnd, hdc);
      break;
    case WM_COMMAND:
      switch(LOWORD(wParam)) {
        case ID_LINES:
          /* Set two pixels. */
          SetPixel(memdc, 40, 14, RGB(0, 0, 0));
          SetPixel(memdc, 40, 15, RGB(0, 0, 0));

          LineTo(memdc, 100, 50);
          MoveToEx(memdc, 100, 50, NULL);

          /* Change to green pen. */
          hOldpen = SelectObject(memdc, hGreenpen);
          LineTo(memdc, 200, 100);

          /* Change to yellow pen. */
          SelectObject(memdc, hYellowpen);
          LineTo(memdc, 0, 200);

          /* Change to blue pen. */
          SelectObject(memdc, hBluepen);
          LineTo(memdc, 200, 200);

          /* Change to red pen. */
          SelectObject(memdc, hRedpen);
          LineTo(memdc, 0, 0);

          /* Return to default pen. */
          SelectObject(memdc, hOldpen);

          Arc(memdc, 0, 0, 300, 300, 0, 50, 200, 50);
          /* Show intersecting lines that define arc. */
          MoveToEx(memdc, 150, 150, NULL);
          LineTo(memdc, 0, 50);
          MoveToEx(memdc, 150, 150, NULL);
          LineTo(memdc, 200, 50);
```

```
    InvalidateRect(hwnd, NULL, 1);
    break;
case ID_RECTANGLES:
  /* Display, but don't fill. */
  hOldbrush = SelectObject(memdc,
                          GetStockObject(HOLLOW_BRUSH));

  /* Draw some rectangles. */
  Rectangle(memdc, 50, 50, 300, 300);
  RoundRect(memdc, 125, 125, 220, 240, 15, 13);

  /* Use a red pen. */
  SelectObject(memdc, hRedpen);
  Rectangle(memdc, 100, 100, 200, 200);
  SelectObject(memdc, hOldpen); /* return to default pen */

  /* Restore default brush. */
  SelectObject(memdc, hOldbrush);

  InvalidateRect(hwnd, NULL, 1);
  break;
case ID_ELLIPSES:
  /* Make blue brush. */
  hbrush = CreateSolidBrush(RGB(0, 0, 255));
  hOldbrush = SelectObject(memdc, hbrush);

  /* Fill these ellipses with blue. */
  Ellipse(memdc, 50, 200, 100, 280);
  Ellipse(memdc, 75, 25, 280, 100);

  /* Use a red pen and fill with green. */
  SelectObject(memdc, hRedpen);
  DeleteObject(hbrush); /* delete brush */
  /* Create green brush. */
  hbrush = CreateSolidBrush(RGB(0, 255, 0));
  SelectObject(memdc, hbrush); /* select green brush */
  Ellipse(memdc, 100, 100, 200, 200);

  /* Draw a pie slice. */
  Pie(memdc, 200, 200, 340, 340, 225, 200, 200, 250);
```

```
            SelectObject(memdc, hOldpen); /* return to default pen */
            SelectObject(memdc, hOldbrush); /* select default brush *.
            DeleteObject(hbrush); /* delete green brush */

            InvalidateRect(hwnd, NULL, 1);
            break;
          case ID_RESET:
            /* Reset current position to 0,0. */
            MoveToEx(memdc, 0, 0, NULL);
            /* Erase by repainting background. */
            PatBlt(memdc, 0, 0, maxX, maxY, PATCOPY);
            InvalidateRect(hwnd, NULL, 1);
            break;
          case ID_HELP:
            MessageBox(hwnd, "F2: Lines\nF3: Rectangles\n"
                      "F4: Ellipses\nF5: Reset",
                      "Graphics Fun", MB_OK);
            break;
        }
      break;
    case WM_PAINT: /* Process a repaint request. */
      hdc = BeginPaint(hwnd, &paintstruct); /* get DC */

      /* Now, copy memory image onto screen. */
      BitBlt(hdc, 0, 0, maxX, maxY, memdc, 0, 0, SRCCOPY);
      EndPaint(hwnd, &paintstruct); /* release DC */
      break;
    case WM_DESTROY: /* terminate the program */
      DeleteObject(hRedpen); /* delete pens */
      DeleteObject(hGreenpen);
      DeleteObject(hBluepen);
      DeleteObject(hYellowpen);

      DeleteDC(memdc);
      PostQuitMessage(0);
      break;
    default:
     /* Let Windows NT process any messages not specified in
     the preceding switch statement. */
     return DefWindowProc(hwnd, message, wParam, lParam);
```

```
    }
  return 0;
}
```

This program requires the resource file shown here:

```
#include "graph.h"
#include <windows.h>

MYMENU MENU
{
  MENUITEM "&Lines", ID_LINES
  MENUITEM "&Rectangles", ID_RECTANGLES
  MENUITEM "&Ellipses", ID_ELLIPSES
  MENUITEM "&Reset", ID_RESET
  MENUITEM "&Help", ID_HELP
}

MYMENU ACCELERATORS
{
  VK_F2, ID_LINES, VIRTKEY
  VK_F3, ID_RECTANGLES, VIRTKEY
  VK_F4, ID_ELLIPSES, VIRTKEY
  VK_F5, ID_RESET, VIRTKEY
  VK_F1, ID_HELP, VIRTKEY
}
```

It also requires the header file **graph.h**, shown here:

```
#define ID_LINES       100
#define ID_RECTANGLES  101
#define ID_ELLIPSES    102
#define ID_RESET       103
#define ID_HELP        104
```

The program displays a main menu that lets you display lines (plus two pixels), rectangles, and ellipses. It also lets you reset the window, which erases its contents and resets the current position, and start over. Sample output is shown in Figure 9-2.

Figure 9-2

Sample output from the Graphics Demonstration program

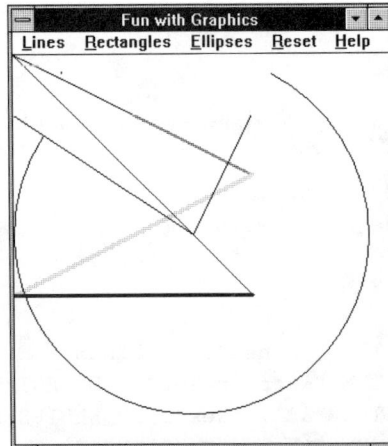

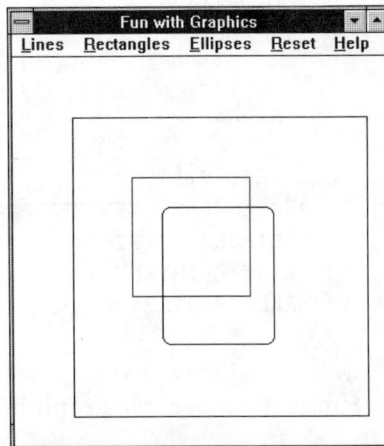

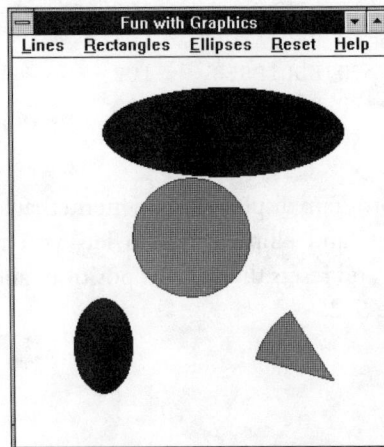

In the next chapter we will continue exploring output to the window by examining *consoles,* Windows NT's mechanism that supports text-based applications.

Chapter 10

Working with Consoles

WHILE Windows is, in general, an excellent operating system for most types of programs, it has had one traditional failing: it has been cumbersome when it comes to writing character mode programs. A *character mode* program is one that uses mainly the ASCII character set and assumes a character-based device, such as an 80-character by 25-line display system. That is, a character mode application is the type that is commonly written for DOS. Frankly, it has been difficult to write character-based programs for Windows, which is optimized for graphics, menus, and dialog boxes. However, as you will see in this chapter, Windows NT changes this.

In order to provide better support for character mode programs, Windows NT provides several new API functions that support the console-style interface. These API functions are collectively called *console functions*. By including support for consoles, Windows NT makes it easier for a character mode program to coexist with a Windows program. For example, it is now possible to write character mode programs that:

♦ Respond to Windows mouse events.

♦ Run in their own console session.

♦ Have access to the (relevant) API functions.

♦ Use pipes and I/O redirection.

♦ Allow Windows-based control over keyboard activity, if desired.

Also, supporting consoles makes it is easier for Windows NT to emulate character-based operating systems.

While graphical programs will always be the most popular type written for Windows NT, the support of consoles is the final brick in the wall that completes the Windows environment. Often, a program is needed that is short, requires little user interaction, and has to be written quickly. For example, short file utility programs fall into this category. For these types of programs, the overhead of implementing them as full-blown Windows applications is difficult to justify. However, now these types of programs can be created as console programs. As such, they will use the simple character mode interface, yet still be fully integrated into the Windows NT environment.

remember: *DOS programs that run under Windows are not fully integrated within Windows, and the "marriage" between DOS and Windows was never a happy one.*

This chapter describes how to write a character mode program and demonstrates several of the console API functions.

16-Bit Conversion Note The console API functions discussed in this chapter are not available in 16-bit Windows. Therefore, the programs shown here are not downward compatible.

Character Mode Theory

Character mode programs resemble traditional, non-windowed programs that you almost certainly have written. That is, in a character mode program no window is created. Also, there is no window function. Further, a character mode program begins with a call to **main()**, not **WinMain()**. In fact, there will generally not be a function called **WinMain()** in your program. (If there is, it is simply treated as just another function with no special meaning.) For the most part, character mode programs do not use most of the Windows features discussed in the first nine chapters of this book.

Given the preceding paragraph, you might be wondering two things. First, what general support does Windows NT give to a character mode program? Second, since a character mode program is not a Windows program in the usual sense, why not just write a DOS-style program instead? The answers are interrelated. First, as mentioned earlier, Windows NT supplies a number of API functions that allow your character mode program to be fully integrated into the Windows NT environment. Mouse support, for example, is provided by Windows NT for character mode programs. Second, a character mode program can access other useful API functions which a DOS-style program does not.

If you execute a character mode program from the command prompt, it will inherit that console session. However, as you will soon see, it is possible for each character mode program to allocate its own console. In fact, allocating a console is the recommended practice. One advantage of this is that a character mode program can control several attributes of its console that are generally beyond the control of a DOS-style program.

All Windows NT consoles maintain a visible cursor marking the place at which the next output to the console will begin. The cursor is automatically updated after each output operation. It is also possible to set the cursor location within a console to any (legal) location you desire.

Allocating a Console

By default, a character mode program either inherits the current console or is given a console if none exists when it is run. However, a better approach is for a character mode program to acquire its own console. The reason for this is simple: any changes to the program's console affect only that console and do not affect an inherited console. Therefore, the cleanest way to implement a character mode program is to have it create its own console. To do this, use the API function **AllocConsole()**, whose prototype is shown here:

    BOOL AllocConsole(void);

This function acquires a new console session for the program that calls it. The function returns non-zero if successful and zero otherwise. An allocated console is freed automatically when the program terminates.

Once a console has been allocated, it creates a window that behaves, more or less, like any other window. It includes a title, a system menu, minimize and maximize boxes, and, if needed, scroll bars.

If the character mode program is executed from within a console session, then before a new one can be allocated, the old one inherited by the program must be freed, using **FreeConsole()**. Its prototype is shown here:

    BOOL FreeConsole(void);

The function returns non-zero if successful and zero otherwise.

When creating your character mode application, the best approach is to execute this sequence as the first actions taken by **main()**.

```
FreeConsole();
AllocConsole();
```

Even if no parent console was previously in effect, no harm is done by calling **FreeConsole()** and, in any case, a new console is allocated.

Giving a Title to a Console

You can give the current console window a title using the **SetConsoleTitle()** API function, shown here:

BOOL SetConsoleTitle(LPTSTR *lpszTitle*);

Here, the string pointed to by *lpszTitle* becomes the title of the console window. The function returns non-zero if successful and zero otherwise.

Acquiring Handles to Standard Input and Output

Many of the console API functions require a standard handle to perform I/O. The standard handles are linked to standard input, standard output, and standard error. By default, these handles are linked to the keyboard and the screen. (However, they may be redirected.) For example, when you write to a console, you will write to standard output. Handles to console input and output are of type **HANDLE**.

To acquire a standard handle, use the **GetStdHandle()** function, whose prototype is shown here:

HANDLE GetStdHandle(DWORD *dwStdDev*);

Here, *dwSTdDev* must be one of these macros: **STD_INPUT_HANDLE**, **STD_OUTPUT_HANDLE**, or **STD_ERROR_HANDLE**, which correspond to standard input, standard output, and standard error, respectively. The function returns a handle to the device. On failure, **INVALID_HANDLE_VALUE** is returned.

Outputting Text to the Console

One way to output text to the console is to use the **WriteConsole()** API function, whose prototype is shown here:

BOOL WriteConsole(HANDLE *hConOut*, CONST VOID **lpString*,
         DWORD *dwLen*, LPDWORD *lpdwNumWritten*,
         LPVOID *lpNotUsed*);

Here, *hConOut* is the handle of console output, generally obtained through a call to **GetStdHandle()**. The string to be output is pointed to by *lpString*. The number of characters in *lpString* to output is passed in *dwLen*, and the actual number of characters written is returned in the long integer pointed to by *lpdwNumWritten*. *lpNotUsed* is reserved for future use by Windows NT.

The string is output using the current text and background colors. The output begins at the current cursor location, and the cursor location is automatically updated.

The function returns non-zero if successful and zero otherwise.

It is important to understand that **WriteConsole()** does not provide any formatting capabilities. This means that you will still need to use a function like **sprintf()** to first construct the string that you want to output if you want to use **WriteConsole()** to output formatted data.

Inputting from the Console

To input information entered at the keyboard, use the **ReadConsole()** function, shown here:

BOOL ReadConsole(HANDLE *hConIn*, LPVOID *lpBuf*,
         DWORD *dwLen*, LPDWORD *lpdwNumRead*,
         LPVOID *lpNotUsed*);

Here, *hConIn* is the handle linked to console input. The character array that will receive the characters typed by the user is pointed to by *lpBuf*. The function will read up to *dwLen* characters or until ENTER is pressed. The number of characters actually read is returned in the long integer pointed to by *lpdwNum-Read*. The *lpNotUsed* parameter is reserved for future use by Windows NT.

note: *The string read by **ReadConsole()** is not automatically null-terminated.*

The exact operation of **ReadConsole()** is determined by the current console mode. (The console mode can be set using **SetConsoleMode()**.)

Setting the Cursor Position

To position the cursor, use the **SetConsoleCursorPosition()** function. Its prototype is shown here:

BOOL SetConsoleCursorPosition(HANDLE *hConOut, COORD XY*);

Here, *hConOut* is the output handle of the console and *XY* is a **COORD** structure that contains the coordinates of the desired cursor location. **COORD** is defined like this:

```
typedef struct _COORD {
    SHORT X;
    SHORT Y;
} COORD;
```

The function returns non-zero if successful and zero on failure.

Setting Text and Background Colors

When using a console, by default text is white and the background is black. You can change this, if you want, by using **SetConsoleTextAttribute()**, whose prototype is shown here:

BOOL SetConsoleTextAttribute(HANDLE *hConOut*, WORD *color*);

Here, *hConOut* is the handle linked to console output, and *color* is the value that determines the text and background colors. The value of *color* is constructed by ORing together two or more of the following macros, which are defined in

wincon.h. (**wincon.h** is automatically included when you include **windows.h**.)

Macro	Meaning
FOREGROUND_BLUE	Text includes blue
FOREGROUND_RED	Text includes red
FOREGROUND_GREEN	Text includes green
FOREGROUND_INTENSITY	Text is shown in high intensity
BACKGROUND_BLUE	Background includes blue
BACKGROUND_RED	Background includes red
BACKGROUND_GREEN	Background includes green
BACKGROUND_INTENSITY	Background is shown in high intensity

The actual color will be a combination of the color components that you specify. To create white, combine all three colors. For black, specify no color.

Consoles and the C/C++ Standard I/O Functions

Once you have obtained a console it is permissible (indeed, completely valid) to use the C/C++ standard I/O functions and operators with it. However, using the console API functions does give your application more control over the console in many situations. Also, in the case of monitoring console events, only the API functions allow full integration with Windows NT. For example, mouse events are not accessible using the standard C/C++ I/O systems. They are accessible, however, by using the console API functions (as you will soon see).

In the example that follows, the standard C/C++ I/O functions are used only to illustrate their validity.

A Console Demonstration Program

Before continuing, the operation of the console functions just described is demonstrated by the following program. Its operation should be clear.

```c
/* Demonstrate consoles */

/* The following definition causes stricter type checking.
   This is optional, but suggested because it will help
   catch potential type mismatch errors--especially
   when porting from 16-bit Windows. */
#define STRICT

#include <windows.h>
#include <string.h>
#include <stdio.h>

main()
{
  HANDLE hStdin, hStdout;
  char str[255] = "This is an example of output to a console.";
  DWORD result;
  COORD coord;
  int x=0, y=0;
  int i;

  /* Free old console and start fresh with new one. */
  FreeConsole();
  AllocConsole();

  /* Give console window a title. */
  SetConsoleTitle("Console Demonstration");

  /* Get standard handles. */
  hStdin = GetStdHandle(STD_INPUT_HANDLE);
  hStdout = GetStdHandle(STD_OUTPUT_HANDLE);

  WriteConsole(hStdout, str, strlen(str), &result, NULL);

  /* Demonstrate cursor positioning. */
  for(x=0, y=1; y<10; x+=5, y++) {
    coord.X = x;
    coord.Y = y;
    sprintf(str, "At location %d %d", x, y);
    SetConsoleCursorPosition(hStdout, coord);
    WriteConsole(hStdout, str, strlen(str), &result, NULL);
  }
```

```
/* Change the colors. */
coord.X = 0;
coord.Y = 12;
strcpy(str, "This is in blue on green background.");
SetConsoleCursorPosition(hStdout, coord);
SetConsoleTextAttribute(hStdout,
                   FOREGROUND_BLUE | BACKGROUND_GREEN);
WriteConsole(hStdout, str, strlen(str), &result, NULL);

coord.X = 0;
coord.Y = 14;
strcpy(str, "Enter a string: ");
SetConsoleCursorPosition(hStdout, coord);
WriteConsole(hStdout, str, strlen(str), &result, NULL);

/* Read input. */
ReadConsole(hStdin, str, 80, &result, NULL);
str[result] = '\0'; /* null terminate */
/* display ASCII code of each character in str */
for(i=0; str[i]; i++) printf("%d ", str[i]);
/* now, display as string */
WriteConsole(hStdout, str, strlen(str), &result, NULL);

/* can use printf(), gets(), etc. */
printf("This is a test.  Enter another string:");
gets(str);
printf("%s\n", str);
printf("Press ENTER: ");

getchar(); /* wait for keypress */

return 0;
}
```

To compile a console program, you may need to use a different set of compiler and linker commands than you have been using to compile Windows-style programs. You will need to check your compiler's user manual for instructions.

Sample output from this program is shown in Figure 10-1. Notice that when a string is input, the carriage return/linefeed sequence is automatically appended. (These are shown as decimal values 13, 10 when the string is displayed by its ASCII values.)

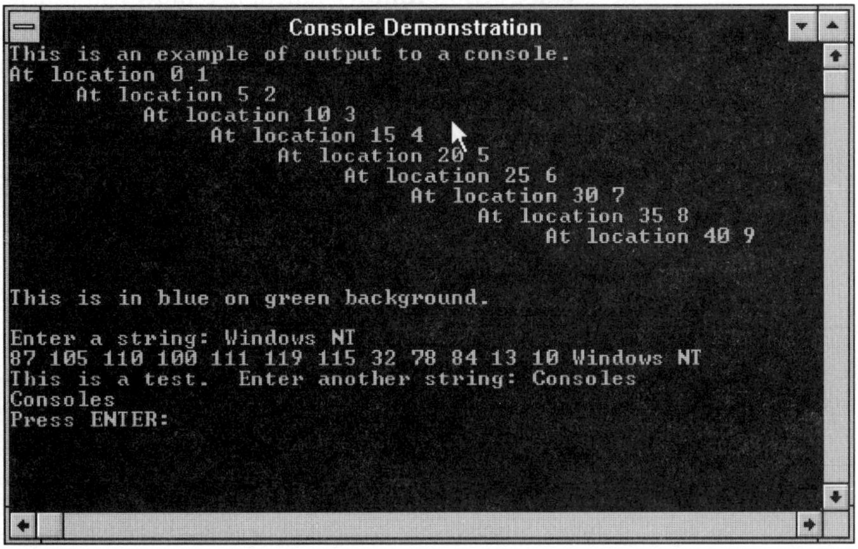

Figure 10-1

Sample output
from the
Console
Demonstration
program

Managing the Mouse

One of the main advantages of using Windows NT consoles and writing character mode Windows NT programs over simply letting DOS-style programs execute in a window is that a console gives you access to the mouse. To obtain mouse events (and other information) when using a console you must use an API console input function called **ReadConsoleInput()**, whose prototype is shown here:

```
BOOL ReadConsoleInput(HANDLE hConIn,
                      PINPUT_RECORD pBuf,
                      DWORD dwNum,
                      LPDWORD lpdwNumRead);
```

Here, *hConIn* is the handle of the console you want information about. The parameter *pBuf* is a pointer to a structure of type **INPUT_RECORD** which will receive the information regarding the requested input event or events. The number of event records to input is specified in *dwNum*, and the amount actually read by the function is returned in *lpdwNumRead*. The function returns non-zero if successful or zero otherwise.

The **ReadConsoleInput()** function removes information about one or more input events from the console's input buffer. Each time you strike a key or use the mouse an input event is generated and the information associated with this event is stored in an **INPUT_RECORD** structure. (Certain other input events may also occur, but the keyboard and mouse events are the only ones of interest to us in this chapter.) The **ReadConsoleInput()** function reads one or more of these events and makes the input event information available to your program.

Each event record is returned in a structure of type **INPUT_RECORD**, which is shown here:

```
typedef struct _INPUT_RECORD {
  WORD EventType;
  union {
    KEY_EVENT_RECORD KeyEvent;
    MOUSE_EVENT_RECORD MouseEvent;
    WINDOW_BUFFER_SIZE_RECORD WindowBufferSizeEvent;
    MENU_EVENT_RECORD MenuEvent;
    FOCUS_EVENT_RECORD FocusEvent;
  } Event;
} INPUT_RECORD;
```

The contents of **EventType** determine what type of event has occurred. It can be one of these macros:

Macro	Event
KEY_EVENT	Keypress
MOUSE_EVENT	Mouse action
WINDOW_BUFFER_SIZE_EVENT	Window resized
FOCUS_EVENT	Used by Windows NT
MENU_EVENT	Used by Windows NT

Only mouse and keyboard events are examined in this chapter. Briefly, focus and menu events are for the internal use of Windows NT only. A resize event may be of interest to your program in some situations. In this case, **Window-BufferSizeEvent** contains a **COORD** structure that holds the dimensions of the window.

Each time a mouse event occurs, the **EventType** field contains **MOUSE_EVENT** and the **Event** union contains a **MOUSE_EVENT_RE-CORD** structure that describes the mouse event. This structure is shown here:

```
typedef struct _MOUSE_EVENT_RECORD {
    COORD dwMousePosition;
    DWORD dwButtonState;
    DWORD dwControlKeyState;
    DWORD dwEventFlags;
} MOUSE_EVENT_RECORD;
```

The **dwMousePosition** field contains the coordinates of the mouse when the event took place. Since a console is a text-based device, the coordinates are in terms of character position and line, not pixels.

dwButtonState describes the state of the mouse buttons when the event was generated. If bit one is on, then the left mouse button is pressed. If bit two is on, then the right mouse button is pressed. If bit three is on, the middle button (if it exists) is pressed. More than one bit will be set when more than one button is pressed at the same time.

The **dwControlKeyState** field contains the state of the various control keys when the event occurred. It may contain one or more of the following macros:

SHIFT_PRESSED
RIGHT_CTRL_PRESSED
LEFT_CTRL_PRESSED
RIGHT_ALT_PRESSED
LEFT_ALT_PRESSED
ENHANCED_KEY
CAPSLOCK_ON
NUMLOCK_ON
SCROLLLOCK_ON

An enhanced key is one of those added to the standard keyboard by the IBM enhanced keyboard. (For example, the extra arrow keys are enhanced keys.)

dwEventFlags contains either **MOUSE_MOVED** (the mouse has moved) or **DOUBLE_CLICK** (a mouse button has been double-clicked).

Demonstrating the Console Mouse

The following program illustrates how to manage mouse events when using a console.

```
/* Managing the mouse from a console. */
```

```
/* The following definition causes stricter type checking.
   This is optional, but suggested because it will help
   catch potential type mismatch errors--especially
   when porting from 16-bit Windows. */
#define STRICT

#include <windows.h>
#include <string.h>
#include <stdio.h>

main()
{
  HANDLE hStdin, hStdout;
  char str[80] = "Press a key to stop.";
  DWORD result;
  COORD coord;
  int x=0, y=0;
  INPUT_RECORD inBuf;

  /* Free old console and start fresh with new one. */
  FreeConsole();
  AllocConsole();

  /* Give console window a title. */
  SetConsoleTitle("Mouse with Console Demonstration");

  /* Get standard handles. */
  hStdin = GetStdHandle(STD_INPUT_HANDLE);
  hStdout = GetStdHandle(STD_OUTPUT_HANDLE);

  WriteConsole(hStdout, str, strlen(str), &result, NULL);

  /* Show mouse events until a key is pressed. */
  do {
    ReadConsoleInput(hStdin, &inBuf, 1, &result);
    /* If mouse event occurs, report it. */
    if(inBuf.EventType==MOUSE_EVENT) {
      sprintf(str, "Button state: %lu, X,Y: %3lu,%3lu\n",
              inBuf.Event.MouseEvent.dwButtonState,
              inBuf.Event.MouseEvent.dwMousePosition.X,
              inBuf.Event.MouseEvent.dwMousePosition.Y);
      coord.X = 0;
      coord.Y = 1;
      SetConsoleCursorPosition(hStdout, coord);
```

```
        WriteConsole(hStdout, str, strlen(str), &result, NULL);

        /* If a double click occurs, report it. */
        if(inBuf.Event.MouseEvent.dwEventFlags==DOUBLE_CLICK) {
          sprintf(str, "Double click\a");
          coord.X = inBuf.Event.MouseEvent.dwMousePosition.X;
          coord.Y = inBuf.Event.MouseEvent.dwMousePosition.Y;
          SetConsoleCursorPosition(hStdout, coord);
          WriteConsole(hStdout, str, strlen(str), &result,
                    NULL);
          Sleep(600); /* wait */
          SetConsoleCursorPosition(hStdout, coord);
          strcpy(str, "                    "); /* erase message */
          WriteConsole(hStdout, str, strlen(str), &result,
                    NULL);
        }
      }
  } while(inBuf.EventType!=KEY_EVENT);

  return 0;
}
```

This program displays the current location of the mouse when it is within the console window and the state of the mouse buttons. It also reports when the mouse is double-clicked. The program continues to execute until a key event is generated when you press a key.

The API function **Sleep()** is used to provide a short delay before the **Double Click** message is erased. This function takes as its argument a value that specifies the number of milliseconds to suspend the execution of the program.

Responding to Keyboard Events

As you know from your previous programming experience, it is quite common for text-based programs to need to respond to key presses in a more subtle fashion than by simply inputting the keystroke. For example, sometimes your program will need to know if a control key is pressed, or the state of the shift key. Sometimes it is useful to know if a key stroke has been automatically repeated by holding the key down. Also, some applications make use of the *scan code* that corresponds to the key. When you press a key, a scan code (sometimes called a position code) is generated that corresponds to the key's position on the keyboard, which is then translated into an ASCII character. Whatever the need, Windows NT gives character mode, console-based applications access to all the information associated with a keyboard event. Like mouse events, keyboard events are obtained by calling **ReadConsoleInput()**, described earlier.

Each time a key is pressed, a keyboard event is generated. When this event is obtained using **ReadConsoleInput()**, the **EventType** field of the **IN-PUT_RECORD** structure contains the **KEY_EVENT** value. When this is the case, then the **Event** union holds a **KEY_EVENT_:RECORD** structure, which describes the event. This structure is shown here.

```
typedef struct _KEY_EVENT_RECORD {
  BOOL bKeyDown;
  WORD wRepeatCount;
  WORD wVirtualKeyCode;
  WORD wVirtualScanCode;
  union {
    WCHAR UnicodeChar;
    CHAR   AsciiChar;
  } uChar;
  DWORD dwControlKeyState;
} KEY_EVENT_RECORD;
```

If **bKeyDown** is nonzero, then a key was being pressed when the key event was generated. If it is zero, the key was being released.

The number of times a key stroke is generated when a key is held down and autorepeat takes over is returned in **wRepeatCount**.

The virtual key code, which is a device-independent key code, is returned in **wVirtualKeyCode**.

The scan (position) code of the key is returned in **wVirtualScanCode**.

The union **uChar** contains the ASCII code of the key being pressed. (It may also contain a wide (16-bit) character for languages that have large character sets.)

The state of the control keys (and other keys) is returned in **dwControlKeyState**. The values are the same as those described for mouse events.

A Sample Key Event Program

The following program demonstrates keyboard events. This program reports each character typed and the state of the various control keys, when one is pressed. It continues to execute until you click the left mouse button.

```
/* Managing the keyboard from a console. */

/* The following definition causes stricter type checking.
   This is optional, but suggested because it will help
   catch potential type mismatch errors--especially
   when porting from 16-bit Windows. */
#define STRICT

#include <windows.h>
#include <string.h>
#include <stdio.h>

main()
{
  HANDLE hStdin, hStdout;
  char str[255] = "Press the left mouse button to stop.";
  DWORD result;
  COORD coord;
  int x=0, y=0;
  int i;
  int done = 0;
  INPUT_RECORD inBuf;

  /* Free old console and start fresh with new one. */
  FreeConsole();
  AllocConsole();

  /* Give console window a title. */
  SetConsoleTitle("Keyboard Demonstration");

  /* Get standard handles. */
  hStdin = GetStdHandle(STD_INPUT_HANDLE);
  hStdout = GetStdHandle(STD_OUTPUT_HANDLE);

  WriteConsole(hStdout, str, strlen(str), &result, NULL);

  /* Show keyboard events until left
     mouse button is pressed. */
  do {
    ReadConsoleInput(hStdin, &inBuf, 1, &result);
    /* If key is pressed, report it. */
    if(inBuf.EventType==KEY_EVENT) {
      sprintf(str, "Key pressed is: %c\n",
              inBuf.Event.KeyEvent.uChar);
```

```c
coord.X = 0;
coord.Y = 1;
SetConsoleCursorPosition(hStdout, coord);
WriteConsole(hStdout, str, strlen(str), &result, NULL);

/* If a control, alt, etc. key is pressed, report it. */
if(inBuf.Event.KeyEvent.dwControlKeyState &&
   inBuf.Event.KeyEvent.bKeyDown) {
  coord.X = 0;
  coord.Y = 10;
  *str = '\0';
  if(inBuf.Event.KeyEvent.dwControlKeyState
    & RIGHT_ALT_PRESSED)
      strcat(str, "Right alt key is pressed. ");
  if(inBuf.Event.KeyEvent.dwControlKeyState
    & LEFT_ALT_PRESSED)
      strcat(str, "Left alt key is pressed. ");
  if(inBuf.Event.KeyEvent.dwControlKeyState
    & RIGHT_CTRL_PRESSED)
      strcat(str, "Right control key is pressed. ");
  if(inBuf.Event.KeyEvent.dwControlKeyState
    & LEFT_CTRL_PRESSED)
      strcat(str, "Left control key is pressed. ");
  if(inBuf.Event.KeyEvent.dwControlKeyState
    & SHIFT_PRESSED)
      strcat(str, "Shift key is pressed. ");
  if(inBuf.Event.KeyEvent.dwControlKeyState
    & NUMLOCK_ON)
      strcat(str, "Num lock key on. ");
  if(inBuf.Event.KeyEvent.dwControlKeyState
    & SCROLLLOCK_ON)
      strcat(str, "Scroll lock key is on. ");
  if(inBuf.Event.KeyEvent.dwControlKeyState
    & CAPSLOCK_ON)
      strcat(str, "Caps lock key is on. ");
  if(inBuf.Event.KeyEvent.dwControlKeyState
    & ENHANCED_KEY)
      strcat(str, "Enhanced key is pressed. ");

  SetConsoleCursorPosition(hStdout, coord);
  strcat(str, "\a");
  WriteConsole(hStdout, str, strlen(str), &result,
               NULL);
  SetConsoleCursorPosition(hStdout, coord);
```

```
        /* wait, then erase the message */
        Sleep(1000);
        coord.X = 0;
        coord.Y = 10;
        i = strlen(str);
        for(*str='\0'; i; i--) strcat(str, " ");
        WriteConsole(hStdout, str, strlen(str), &result,
                    NULL);
      }
    }
    if(inBuf.EventType==MOUSE_EVENT)
      if(inBuf.Event.MouseEvent.dwButtonState==1) done = 1;

  } while(!done);

  return 0;
}
```

As this chapter has shown, creating character mode programs using Windows NT is quite easy. Therefore, while Windows NT can execute DOS programs, when creating new character mode applications, you should always use a Windows NT console and employ its character mode functions.

In the next chapter, Windows NT multitasking is examined.

Chapter 11

Multitasking Processes and

Threads

223

HIS final chapter discusses how you can use multitasking within your Windows NT programs. As such, it covers two important and interrelated Windows NT topics: processes and threads. The main emphasis is on threads.

As mentioned in Chapter 1, Windows NT supports two forms of multitasking. The first type is process-based. This is the type of multiprocessing that Windows has supported from its inception. A process is, essentially, a program that is executing. In process-based multitasking, two or more processes can execute concurrently. The second type of multitasking is thread-based. Thread-based multitasking is new to Windows NT. A thread is a path (or *thread*) of execution within a process. In Windows NT, every process has at least one thread, but it may have two or more. Thread-based multitasking allows two or more parts of a single program to execute concurrently. This added tasking dimension allows extremely efficient programs to be written, because you, the programmer, can define the separate threads of execution and thus manage the way that your program executes.

The inclusion of support for thread-based multitasking has increased the need for a special type of tasking feature called *synchronization,* which allows the execution of threads (and processes) to be coordinated in certain well-defined ways. Windows NT has added a complete subsystem devoted to synchronization.

Frankly, the Windows NT tasking system is far too complex to cover fully in a single chapter. However, the most important features and commonly used functions are examined and several examples are included which will give you a firm basis upon which to build.

This chapter begins by exploring process-based multitasking and then concentrates on thread-based tasking. It ends with an overview of thread and process synchronization.

16-Bit Conversion Note 16-bit Windows supports only process-based multitasking. It does not support thread-based multitasking. As such, all of the material in this chapter relating to threads is specific to Windows NT. Also, Windows NT's approach to process-based multitasking differs from that used by 16-bit Windows.

Creating a Separate Task

By far the simplest type of multitasking that your program can engage in is process-based. In this case, one program simply starts the execution of another and then (more or less) ignores it. In Windows NT, it is possible for one process to start the execution of another using the **CreateProcess()** API function, whose prototype is shown here.

BOOL CreateProcess(LPCSTR *lpszName,* LPCSTR *lpszComLine,*
            LPSECURITY_ATTRIBUTES *lpProcAttr,*
            LPSECURITY_ATTRIBUTES *lpThreadAttr,*
            BOOL *InheritAttr,* DWORD *How,*
            LPVOID *lpEnv,* LPSTR *lpszDir,*
            LPSTARTUPINFO *lpStartInfo,*
            LPPROCESS_INFORMATION *lpPInfo);*

Don't let the rather long parameter list worry you. As you will soon see, it is possible for most of these parameters to default.

The name of the program to execute, which may include a full path name, is specified in the string pointed to by *lpszName.* Any command-line parameters required by the program are specified in the string pointed to by *lpszComLine.* However, if you specify *lpszName* as NULL, then the first token in the string pointed to by *lpszComLine* will be used as the program name. Thus, typically, *lpszName* is specified as NULL, and the program name and any required parameters are specified in the string pointed to by *lpszComLine.*

The *lpProcAttr* and *lpThreadAttr* parameters are used to specify any security attributes related to the process being created. These may be specified as NULL, in which case no security attributes are used. Since the security system is both complex and not applicable to all situations, no security attributes will be used when creating processes or threads in this chapter. However, be aware that you may specify security attributes for the new process if your situation demands it.

If *InheritAttr* is **TRUE** (non-zero), handles in use by the creating process are inherited by the new process. If this parameter is **FALSE** (zero), then handles are not inherited. (**TRUE** and **FALSE** are macros defined by Windows NT by including **windows.h**.)

By default, the new process is run "normally." However, the *How* parameter can be used to specify certain additional attributes that affect how the new process will be created. If *How* is zero, then the defaults apply. The examples in this chapter simply use the defaults supplied by Windows NT, so this parameter is set to zero.

The *lpEnv* parameter points to a buffer that contains the new process's environmental parameters. If this parameter is NULL, then the new process inherits the creating process's environment.

The current drive and directory of the new process can be specified in the string pointed to by *lpszDir*. If this parameter is NULL, then the current drive and directory of the creating process are used.

The structure **STARTUPINFO** contains information that determines how the main window of the new process will look. The **STARTUPINFO** structure is defined as shown here:

```
typedef struct _STARTUPINFO {
  DWORD   cb; /* size of STARTUPINFO */
  LPSTR   lpReserved;
  LPSTR   lpDesktop; /* name of desktop */
  LPSTR   lpTitle; /* title of console (consoles only) */
  DWORD   dwX; /* upper left corner */
  DWORD   dwY; /* of new window */
  DWORD   dwXSize; /* size of new window */
  DWORD   dwYSize; /* size of new window */
  DWORD   dwXCountChars; /* console buffer size */
  DWORD   dwYCountChars; /* console buffer size */
  DWORD   dwFillAttribute; /* initial text color */
  DWORD   dwFlags; /* determines which fields are active */
  WORD    wShowWindow; /* how window is shown */
  WORD    cbReserved2;
  LPBYTE  lpReserved2;
  HANDLE  hStdInput; /* standard handles */
  HANDLE  hStdOutput;
  HANDLE  hStdError;
} STARTUPINFO;
```

As this structure suggests, Windows NT gives you more control over how a process will be created than you will normally ever want! Generally, you will want to use the standard defaults that Windows NT supplies. In fact, the fields **dwX, dwY, dwXSize, dwYSize, dwXCountChars, dwYCountChars,**

dwFillAttribute, and **wShowWindow** are ignored unless they are enabled by including the proper value as part of the **dwFlags** field. The values for **dwFlags** are shown here:

Macro	Enables
STARTF_USESHOWWINDOW	dwShowWindow
STARTF_USESIZE	dwXSize and dwYSize
STARTF_USEPOSITION	dwX and dwY
STARTF_USECOUNTCHARS	dwXCountChars and dwYCountChars
STARTF_USEFILLATTRIBUTE	dwFillAttribute

Generally, you will not need to use most of the fields in **STARTUPINFO** and you can allow most to be ignored. However, you must specify **cb**, which contains the size of the structure, and several other fields must be set to NULL. For the purposes of this chapter, the new process information specified in the **STARTUPINFO** structure will be set as shown here:

```
STARTUPINFO startin;
/* ... */
/* Start a new process. */
startin.cb = sizeof(STARTUPINFO);
startin.lpReserved = NULL;
startin.lpDesktop = NULL;
startin.lpTitle = NULL;
startin.dwFlags = STARTF_USESHOWWINDOW;
startin.cbReserved2 = 0;
startin.lpReserved2 = NULL;
startin.wShowWindow = SW_SHOWMINIMIZED;
```

Here, the process will be started as a minimized window, because **dwFlags** is set to **STARTF_USESHOWWINDOW**, which allows the **wShowWindow** field to be used. (By default, the new process's window is shown in a size deemed appropriate by Windows NT.)

The final parameter to **CreateProcess()** is *lpPInfo,* which is a pointer to a structure of type **PROCESS_INFORMATION**, shown here:

```
typedef struct _PROCESS_INFORMATION {
  HANDLE hProcess; /* handle to new process */
  HANDLE hThread; /* handle to main thread */
  DWORD dwProcessId; /* ID of new process */
  DWORD dwThreadId; /* ID of new thread */
} PROCESS_INFORMATION;
```

Handles to the new process and the main thread of that process are passed back to the creating process in **hProcess** and **hThread**. The new process and thread IDs are returned in **dwProcessId** and **dwThreadId**. Your program can make use of this information or choose to ignore it.

CreateProcess() returns non-zero if successful and zero otherwise.

Once created, the new process is largely independent from the creating process. It is possible for the parent process to terminate the child, however. To do so, use the **TerminateProcess()** API function, shown here:

BOOL TerminateProcess(HANDLE *hProcess,* UINT *status*);

Here, *hProcess* is the handle to the child process obtained from the **hProcess** field of *lpPInfo* when the process is created. The value of *status* becomes the exit code of the terminated process.

16-Bit Conversion Note To start a new process in 16-bit Windows, use the **WinExec()** function. Windows NT still includes this function for compatibility, but describes it as obsolete. When porting code, you should convert **WinExec()** calls to **CreateProcess()**.

A Sample Multiprocess Program

The following program demonstrates creating and terminating processes. The program allows you to create up to five child processes. You may also terminate the processes in the reverse order in which they are created.

remember: *You can always terminate a process by activating its system menu and choosing **Close**.*

The program starts another program called **TEST.EXE**, but you can change this to any other Windows NT program you like.

note: *This program, and the others in this chapter, use a virtual window to hold and restore output to the physical window. This procedure was discussed in Chapter 8.*

```
/* A Windows NT skeleton that demonstrates processes. */

/* The following definition causes stricter type checking.
   This is optional, but suggested because it will help
   catch potential type mismatch errors--especially
   when porting from 16-bit Windows. */
#define STRICT

#include <windows.h>
#include <string.h>
#include <stdio.h>
#include "proc.h"

#define PROCMAX 5 /* max of five processes */

LRESULT CALLBACK WindowFunc(HWND, UINT, WPARAM, LPARAM);

char szWinName[] = "MyWin"; /* name of window class */

char str[255]; /* holds output strings */

int X=0, Y=0; /* current output location */
int maxX, maxY; /* screen dimensions */

int procnum = 0; /* number of active processes */

HDC memdc;
HBITMAP hbit;
HBRUSH hbrush;

PROCESS_INFORMATION pinfo[PROCMAX];

int WINAPI WinMain(HINSTANCE hThisInst, HINSTANCE hPrevInst,
                   LPSTR lpszArgs, int nWinMode)
{
  HWND hwnd;
  MSG msg;
  WNDCLASS wcl;
  HANDLE hAccel;

  /* Define a window class. */
  wcl.hInstance = hThisInst; /* handle to this instance */
  wcl.lpszClassName = szWinName; /* window class name */
  wcl.lpfnWndProc = WindowFunc; /* window function */
  wcl.style = 0; /* default style */
```

```
wcl.hIcon = LoadIcon(NULL, IDI_APPLICATION); /* icon style */
wcl.hCursor = LoadCursor(NULL, IDC_ARROW); /* cursor style */

/* Specify name of menu resource. */
wcl.lpszMenuName = "MYMENU"; /* main menu */

wcl.cbClsExtra = 0; /* no extra */
wcl.cbWndExtra = 0; /* information needed */

/* Make the window white. */
wcl.hbrBackground = GetStockObject(WHITE_BRUSH);

/* Register the window class. */
if(!RegisterClass (&wcl)) return 0;

/* Now that a window class has been registered, a window
   can be created. */
hwnd = CreateWindow(
  szWinName, /* name of window class */
  "Demonstrate Processes", /* title */
  WS_OVERLAPPEDWINDOW, /* window style--normal */
  CW_USEDEFAULT, /* X coordinate--let Windows decide */
  CW_USEDEFAULT, /* Y coordinate--let Windows decide */
  CW_USEDEFAULT, /* width--let Windows decide */
  CW_USEDEFAULT, /* height--let Windows decide */
  HWND_DESKTOP, /* handle of parent window--there isn't one */
  NULL, /* no menu */
  hThisInst, /* handle of this instance of the program */
  NULL /* no additional arguments */
);

/* Load accelerators. */
hAccel = LoadAccelerators(hThisInst, "MYMENU");

/* Display the window. */
ShowWindow(hwnd, nWinMode);
UpdateWindow(hwnd);

/* Create the message loop. */
```

```
  while(GetMessage(&msg, NULL, 0, 0))
  {
    if(!TranslateAccelerator(hwnd, hAccel, &msg)) {
      TranslateMessage(&msg); /* allow use of keyboard */
      DispatchMessage(&msg); /* return control to Windows */
    }
  }
  return msg.wParam;
}


/* This function is called by Windows NT and is passed
   messages from the message queue.
*/
LRESULT CALLBACK WindowFunc(HWND hwnd, UINT message, WPARAM wParam,
                 LPARAM lParam)
{
  HDC hdc;
  PAINTSTRUCT paintstruct;
  TEXTMETRIC tm;
  SIZE size;
  STARTUPINFO startin;
  char mess[80];

  switch(message) {
    case WM_CREATE:
      /* Get screen coordinates. */
      maxX = GetSystemMetrics(SM_CXSCREEN);
      maxY = GetSystemMetrics(SM_CYSCREEN);

      /* Make a compatible memory image device. */
      hdc = GetDC(hwnd);
      memdc = CreateCompatibleDC(hdc);
      hbit = CreateCompatibleBitmap(hdc, maxX, maxY);
      SelectObject(memdc, hbit);
      hbrush = GetStockObject(WHITE_BRUSH);
      SelectObject(memdc, hbrush);
      PatBlt(memdc, 0, 0, maxX, maxY, PATCOPY);
      ReleaseDC(hwnd, hdc);
      break;
    case WM_COMMAND:
      switch(LOWORD(wParam)) {
        case ID_PROCESS:
          if(procnum==PROCMAX) {
```

```
        MessageBox(hwnd, "Can't Create", "", MB_OK);
        break; /* no more than PROCMAX */
  }

  /* Get text metrics. */
  GetTextMetrics(memdc, &tm);

  sprintf(str, "Execute Process %d.", procnum);
  TextOut(memdc, X, Y, str, strlen(str)); /* output string */
  Y = Y + tm.tmHeight + tm.tmExternalLeading; /* next line */
  InvalidateRect(hwnd, NULL, 1);

  /* Start a new process. */
  startin.cb = sizeof(STARTUPINFO);
  startin.lpReserved = NULL;
  startin.lpDesktop = NULL;
  startin.lpTitle = NULL;
  startin.dwFlags = STARTF_USESHOWWINDOW;
  startin.cbReserved2 = 0;
  startin.lpReserved2 = NULL;
  startin.wShowWindow = SW_SHOWMINIMIZED;

  CreateProcess(NULL, "test.exe",
               NULL, NULL, FALSE, 0,
               NULL, NULL, &startin, &pinfo[procnum]);
  procnum++;
  break;
case ID_KILLPROC:
  if(procnum) procnum − −;
  else MessageBox(hwnd, "No process to terminate.",
               "", MB_OK);
  TerminateProcess(pinfo[procnum].hProcess, 0);
  sprintf(str, "Terminate Process %d.", procnum);
  TextOut(memdc, X, Y, str, strlen(str)); /* output string */
  Y = Y + tm.tmHeight + tm.tmExternalLeading; /* next line */
  InvalidateRect(hwnd, NULL, 1);
  break;
case ID_HELP:
  MessageBox(hwnd, "F2: Start Process\nF3: Kill Process",
            "Help", MB_OK);
```

```
        break;
  }
  break;
case WM_PAINT: /* process a repaint request */
  hdc = BeginPaint(hwnd, &paintstruct); /* get DC */

        /* Now, copy memory image onto screen. */
        BitBlt(hdc, 0, 0, maxX, maxY, memdc, 0, 0, SRCCOPY);
        EndPaint(hwnd, &paintstruct); /* release DC */
        break;
      case WM_DESTROY: /* terminate the program */
        DeleteDC(memdc); /* delete the memory device */
        PostQuitMessage(0);
        break;
      default:
        /* Let Windows NT process any messages not specified in
        the preceding switch statement. */
        return DefWindowProc(hwnd, message, wParam, lParam);
  }
  return 0;
}
```

Before you can compile this program, you will need to create the header file **proc.h**, shown here. (The **ID_THREAD** value will be used by later examples.)

```
#define ID_PROCESS   100
#define ID_KILLPROC  101
#define ID_THREAD    102
#define ID_HELP      103
```

You will also need to create this resource file:

```
#include "proc.h"
#include <windows.h>

MYMENU MENU
{
  MENUITEM "&Execute Process", ID_PROCESS
  MENUITEM "&Kill Process", ID_KILLPROC
  MENUITEM "&Help", ID_HELP
}
```

```
MYMENU ACCELERATORS
{
  VK_F2, ID_PROCESS, VIRTKEY
  VK_F3, ID_KILLPROC, VIRTKEY
  VK_F1, ID_HELP, VIRTKEY
}
```

Sample output is shown in Figure 11-1.

Creating Multithread Programs

While multiprocess programming using Windows NT is more flexible and contains more programmer-controlled features, it does not represent any major advance. However, Windows NT support for multithread programs does! Multithread multitasking adds a new dimension to your programming, because it lets you, the programmer, more fully control how pieces of your program

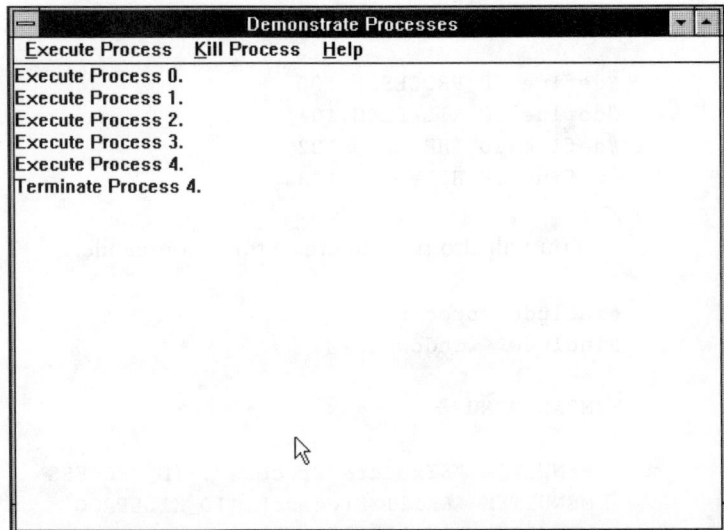

Figure 11-1

Sample output from the process demonstration program

execute. This allows you to implement more efficient programs. For example, you could assign one thread of a program the job of sorting a file, another thread the job of gathering information from some remote source, and another thread the task of performing user input. Because of multithread multitasking, each thread can execute concurrently and no CPU time is wasted.

It is important to understand that all processes have at least one thread of execution. For the sake of discussion, this is called the *main thread*. However, it is possible to create more than one thread of execution within the same process. In general, once a new thread is created, it also begins execution. Thus, each process starts with one thread of execution and may create one or more additional threads. In this way, thread-based multitasking is supported.

In this section you will see how to create a multithread program.

Creating a Thread

To create a thread, use the API function **CreateThread()**. Its prototype is shown here:

```
HANDLE CreateThread(LPSECURITY_ATTRIBUTES lpAttr,
                    DWORD dwStack,
                    LPTHREAD_START_ROUTINE lpFunc,
                    LPVOID lpParam,
                    DWORD dwFlags,
                    LPDWORD lpdwID);
```

Here, *lpAttr* is a pointer to a set of security attributes pertaining to the thread. However, if *lpAttr* is NULL, then no security is used.

Each thread has its own stack. You can specify the size of the new thread's stack, in bytes, using the *dwStack* parameter. If this value is 0, then the thread will be given a stack that is the same size as the main thread of the process that creates it. (This is the common approach taken to thread stack size.)

Each thread of execution begins with a call to a function, called the *thread function*, within the process. Execution of the thread continues until the thread function returns. The address of this function (the entry point to the thread) is specified in *lpFunc*. All thread functions must have this prototype:

```
DWORD threadfunc(LPVOID param);
```

Any argument that you need to pass to the new thread is specified in **CreateThread()**'s *lpParam*. This 32-bit value is received by the thread's entry function in its parameter. This parameter may be used for any purpose.

The *dwFlags* parameter determines the execution state of the thread. If it is 0, the thread begins execution immediately. If it is **CREATE_SUSPEND**, the thread is created in a suspended state, awaiting execution. (It may be started using a call to **ResumeThread()**.)

The identifier associated with a thread is returned in the double word pointed to by *lpdwID*.

The function returns a handle to the thread if successful or 0 if a failure occurs.

Terminating a Thread

As stated, a thread of execution terminates when its entry function returns. The process may also terminate the thread manually, using **TerminateThread()**, whose prototype is shown here:

BOOL TerminateThread(HANDLE *hThread*, DWORD *dwStatus*);

Here, *hThread* is the handle of the thread to be terminated and *dwStatus* is the termination status. The function returns non-zero if successful and zero otherwise.

When a thread is terminated using **TerminateThread()**, it is stopped immediately and does not perform any special cleanup activities. Also, **TerminateThread()** may stop a thread during an important operation. For these reasons, it is usually best (and easiest) to let a thread terminate normally when its entry function returns. This is the approach used by the example programs in this chapter.

A Short Multithread Example

The following program creates a thread each time the Execute Thread menu option is selected. The thread beeps ten times and displays the number of each beep along with its thread ID on the screen. Another thread can be started before the first is finished.

The computer's beep is sounded using the **MessageBeep()** API function. When called with a parameter of –1, it uses the standard beep.

```
/* A very simple multithread program. */

/* The following definition causes stricter type checking.
   This is optional, but suggested because it will help
   catch potential type mismatch errors--especially
   when porting from 16-bit Windows. */
#define STRICT

#define PROCMAX 5 /* maximum number of processes */

#include <windows.h>
#include <string.h>
#include <stdio.h>
#include "proc.h"

LRESULT CALLBACK WindowFunc(HWND, UINT, WPARAM, LPARAM);
DWORD MyThread(LPVOID param);

char szWinName[] = "MyWin"; /* name of window class */

char str[255]; /* holds output strings */

int X=0, Y=0; /* current output location */
int maxX, maxY; /* screen dimensions */

int procnum = 0; /* number of active processes */

DWORD Tid; /* thread ID */

HDC memdc;
HBITMAP hbit;
HBRUSH hbrush;

PROCESS_INFORMATION pinfo[PROCMAX];

int WINAPI WinMain(HINSTANCE hThisInst, HINSTANCE hPrevInst,
                   LPSTR lpszArgs, int nWinMode)
{
  HWND hwnd;
  MSG msg;
  WNDCLASS wcl;
  HANDLE hAccel;

  /* Define a window class. */
```

```
wcl.hInstance = hThisInst; /* handle to this instance */
wcl.lpszClassName = szWinName; /* window class name */
wcl.lpfnWndProc = WindowFunc; /* window function */
wcl.style = 0; /* default style */

wcl.hIcon = LoadIcon(NULL, IDI_APPLICATION); /* icon style */
wcl.hCursor = LoadCursor(NULL, IDC_ARROW); /* cursor style */

/* Specify name of menu resource. */
wcl.lpszMenuName = "MYMENU"; /* main menu */

wcl.cbClsExtra = 0; /* no extra */
wcl.cbWndExtra = 0; /* information needed */

/* Make the window white. */
wcl.hbrBackground = GetStockObject(WHITE_BRUSH);

/* Register the window class. */
if(!RegisterClass (&wcl)) return 0;

/* Now that a window class has been registered, a window
   can be created. */
hwnd = CreateWindow(
  szWinName, /* name of window class */
  "Demonstrate Threads and Processes", /* title */
  WS_OVERLAPPEDWINDOW, /* window style--normal */
  CW_USEDEFAULT, /* X coordinate--let Windows decide */
  CW_USEDEFAULT, /* Y coordinate--let Windows decide */
  CW_USEDEFAULT, /* width--let Windows decide */
  CW_USEDEFAULT, /* height--let Windows decide */
  HWND_DESKTOP, /* handle of parent window--there isn't one */
  NULL, /* no menu */
  hThisInst, /* handle of this instance of the program */
  NULL /* no additional arguments */
);

/* Load accelerators. */
hAccel = LoadAccelerators(hThisInst, "MYMENU");

/* Display the window. */
ShowWindow(hwnd, nWinMode);
```

```
  UpdateWindow(hwnd);

  /* Create the message loop. */
  while(GetMessage(&msg, NULL, 0, 0))
  {
    if(!TranslateAccelerator(hwnd, hAccel, &msg)) {
      TranslateMessage(&msg); /* allow use of keyboard */
      DispatchMessage(&msg); /* return control to Windows */
    }
  }
  return msg.wParam;
}


/* This function is called by Windows NT and is passed
   messages from the message queue.
*/
LRESULT CALLBACK WindowFunc(HWND hwnd, UINT message, WPARAM wParam,
                LPARAM lParam)
{
  HDC hdc;
  PAINTSTRUCT paintstruct;
  TEXTMETRIC tm;
  SIZE size;
  STARTUPINFO startin;

  switch(message) {
    case WM_CREATE:
      /* Get screen coordinates. */
      maxX = GetSystemMetrics(SM_CXSCREEN);
      maxY = GetSystemMetrics(SM_CYSCREEN);

      /* Make a compatible memory image device. */
      hdc = GetDC(hwnd);
      memdc = CreateCompatibleDC(hdc);
      hbit = CreateCompatibleBitmap(hdc, maxX, maxY);
      SelectObject(memdc, hbit);
      hbrush = GetStockObject(WHITE_BRUSH);
      SelectObject(memdc, hbrush);
      PatBlt(memdc, 0, 0, maxX, maxY, PATCOPY);
      ReleaseDC(hwnd, hdc);
      break;
    case WM_COMMAND:
      switch(LOWORD(wParam)) {
```

```
case ID_PROCESS:
  if(procnum==PROCMAX) {
    MessageBox(hwnd, "Can't Create", "", MB_OK);
    break; /* no more than PROCMAX */
  }

  /* Get text metrics. */
  GetTextMetrics(memdc, &tm);

  sprintf(str, "Execute Process %d.", procnum);
  TextOut(memdc, X, Y, str, strlen(str)); /* output string */
  Y = Y + tm.tmHeight + tm.tmExternalLeading; /* next line */
  InvalidateRect(hwnd, NULL, 1);

  /* Start a new process. */
  startin.cb = sizeof(STARTUPINFO);
  startin.lpReserved = NULL;
  startin.lpDesktop = NULL;
  startin.lpTitle = NULL;
  startin.dwFlags = STARTF_USESHOWWINDOW;
  startin.cbReserved2 = 0;
  startin.lpReserved2 = NULL;
  startin.wShowWindow = SW_SHOWMINIMIZED;

  CreateProcess(NULL, "test.exe",
                NULL, NULL, FALSE, 0,
                NULL, NULL, &startin, &pinfo[procnum]);
  procnum++;
  break;
case ID_KILLPROC:
  if(procnum) procnum − −;
  else MessageBox(hwnd, "No process to terminate.",
                  "", MB_OK);
  TerminateProcess(pinfo[procnum].hProcess, 0);
  sprintf(str, "Terminate Process %d.", procnum);
  TextOut(memdc, X, Y, str, strlen(str)); /* output string */
  Y = Y + tm.tmHeight + tm.tmExternalLeading; /* next line */
  InvalidateRect(hwnd, NULL, 1);
  break;
case ID_THREAD:
```

```
            CreateThread(NULL, 0, (LPTHREAD_START_ROUTINE)MyThread,
                        (LPVOID) NULL, 0, &Tid);
            InvalidateRect(hwnd, NULL, 1);
            break;
          case ID_HELP:
            MessageBox(hwnd,
                      "F2: Start Process\nF3: Kill Process\n"
                      "F4: Start Thread",
                      "Help", MB_OK);
            break;
      }
      break;
    case WM_PAINT: /* process a repaint request */
      hdc = BeginPaint(hwnd, &paintstruct); /* get DC */

      /* Now, copy memory image onto screen. */
      BitBlt(hdc, 0, 0, maxX, maxY, memdc, 0, 0, SRCCOPY);
      EndPaint(hwnd, &paintstruct); /* release DC */
      break;
    case WM_LBUTTONDOWN: /* process left button */
      X = LOWORD(lParam); /* set X,Y to */
      Y = HIWORD(lParam); /* mouse location */
      break;
    case WM_DESTROY: /* terminate the program */
      DeleteDC(memdc); /* delete the memory device */
      PostQuitMessage(0);
      break;
    default:
      /* Let Windows NT process any messages not specified in
      the preceding switch statement. */
      return DefWindowProc(hwnd, message, wParam, lParam);
  }
  return 0;
}


/* A thread of execution within the process. */
DWORD MyThread(LPVOID param)
{
  int i;
  DWORD curTid = Tid;
  TEXTMETRIC tm;
```

```
/* Get text metrics. */
GetTextMetrics(memdc, &tm);

for(i=0; i<10; i++) {
  Sleep(500);
  sprintf(str, "Thread ID #%d, beep #%d",
          curTid, i);
  TextOut(memdc, X, Y, str, strlen(str)); /* output string */
  Y = Y + tm.tmHeight + tm.tmExternalLeading; /* next line */
  InvalidateRect((HWND) param, NULL, 1);
  MessageBeep(-1);
}
}
```

This program uses the same **proc.h** file as the previous example, but you will need to enter this resource file:

```
#include "proc.h"
#include <windows.h>

MYMENU MENU
{
  MENUITEM "&Execute Process", ID_PROCESS
  MENUITEM "&Kill Process", ID_KILLPROC
  MENUITEM "Execute &Thread", ID_THREAD
  MENUITEM "&Help", ID_HELP
}

MYMENU ACCELERATORS
{
  VK_F2, ID_PROCESS, VIRTKEY
  VK_F3, ID_KILLPROC, VIRTKEY
  VK_F4, ID_THREAD, VIRTKEY
  VK_F1, ID_HELP, VIRTKEY
}
```

Sample output from the program is shown in Figure 11-2.

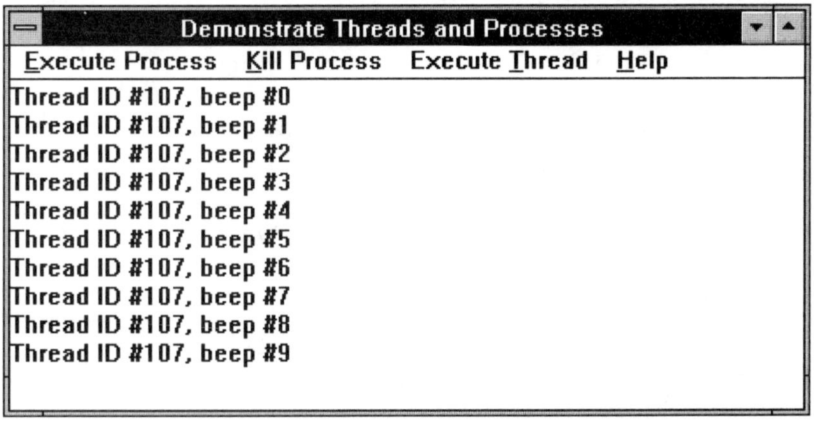

Figure 11-2

Sample output from the multithread program

```
┌─────────────────────────────────────────────────────────┐
│ ─    Demonstrate Threads and Processes          ▼ ▲     │
├─────────────────────────────────────────────────────────┤
│ Execute Process   Kill Process   Execute Thread   Help  │
├─────────────────────────────────────────────────────────┤
│ Thread ID #107, beep #0                                  │
│ Thread ID #107, beep #1                                  │
│ Thread ID #107, beep #2                                  │
│ Thread ID #107, beep #3                                  │
│ Thread ID #107, beep #4                                  │
│ Thread ID #107, beep #5                                  │
│ Thread ID #107, beep #6                                  │
│ Thread ID #107, beep #7                                  │
│ Thread ID #107, beep #8                                  │
│ Thread ID #107, beep #9                                  │
│                                                          │
└─────────────────────────────────────────────────────────┘
```

Using Multiple Threads

A program can have, within reason, as many threads of execution as the system will support. For example, this version of the preceding program starts two threads:

```
/* Another multithread program. */

/* The following definition causes stricter type checking.
   This is optional, but suggested because it will help
   catch potential type mismatch errors--especially
   when porting from 16-bit Windows. */
#define STRICT

#define PROCMAX 5 /* maximum number of processes */

#include <windows.h>
#include <string.h>
#include <stdio.h>
#include "proc.h"

LRESULT CALLBACK WindowFunc(HWND, UINT, WPARAM, LPARAM);
DWORD MyThread1(LPVOID param);
DWORD MyThread2(LPVOID param);
```

```
char szWinName[] = "MyWin"; /* name of window class */

char str[255]; /* holds output strings */

int X=0, Y=0; /* current output location */
int maxX, maxY; /* screen dimensions */

int procnum = 0; /* number of active processes */

DWORD Tid1, Tid2; /* thread IDs */

HDC memdc;
HBITMAP hbit;
HBRUSH hbrush;

PROCESS_INFORMATION pinfo[PROCMAX];

int WINAPI WinMain(HINSTANCE hThisInst, HINSTANCE hPrevInst,
                   LPSTR lpszArgs, int nWinMode)
{
  HWND hwnd;
  MSG msg;
  WNDCLASS wcl;
  HANDLE hAccel;

  /* Define a window class. */
  wcl.hInstance = hThisInst; /* handle to this instance */
  wcl.lpszClassName = szWinName; /* window class name */
  wcl.lpfnWndProc = WindowFunc; /* window function */
  wcl.style = 0; /* default style */

  wcl.hIcon = LoadIcon(NULL, IDI_APPLICATION); /* icon style */
  wcl.hCursor = LoadCursor(NULL, IDC_ARROW); /* cursor style */

  /* Specify name of menu resource. */
  wcl.lpszMenuName = "MYMENU"; /* main menu */

  wcl.cbClsExtra = 0; /* no extra */
  wcl.cbWndExtra = 0; /* information needed */

  /* Make the window white. */
  wcl.hbrBackground = GetStockObject(WHITE_BRUSH);
```

```
/* Register the window class. */
if(!RegisterClass (&wcl)) return 0;

/* Now that a window class has been registered, a window
   can be created. */
hwnd = CreateWindow(
  szWinName, /* name of window class */
  "Demonstrate Threads and Processes", /* title */
  WS_OVERLAPPEDWINDOW, /* window style--normal */
  CW_USEDEFAULT, /* X coordinate--let Windows decide */
  CW_USEDEFAULT, /* Y coordinate--let Windows decide */
  CW_USEDEFAULT, /* width--let Windows decide */
  CW_USEDEFAULT, /* height--let Windows decide */
  HWND_DESKTOP, /* handle of parent window--there isn't one */
  NULL, /* no menu */
  hThisInst, /* handle of this instance of the program */
  NULL /* no additional arguments */
);

/* Load accelerators. */
hAccel = LoadAccelerators(hThisInst, "MYMENU");

/* Display the window. */
ShowWindow(hwnd, nWinMode);
UpdateWindow(hwnd);

/* Create the message loop. */
while(GetMessage(&msg, NULL, 0, 0))
{
  if(!TranslateAccelerator(hwnd, hAccel, &msg)) {
    TranslateMessage(&msg); /* allow use of keyboard */
    DispatchMessage(&msg); /* return control to Windows */
  }
}
return msg.wParam;
}


/* This function is called by Windows NT and is passed
   messages from the message queue.
*/
LRESULT CALLBACK WindowFunc(HWND hwnd, UINT message, WPARAM wParam,
                 LPARAM lParam)
```

```
    {
      HDC hdc;
      PAINTSTRUCT paintstruct;
      TEXTMETRIC tm;
      SIZE size;
      STARTUPINFO startin;

      switch(message) {
        case WM_CREATE:
          /* Get screen coordinates. */
          maxX = GetSystemMetrics(SM_CXSCREEN);
          maxY = GetSystemMetrics(SM_CYSCREEN);

          /* Make a compatible memory image device. */
          hdc = GetDC(hwnd);
          memdc = CreateCompatibleDC(hdc);
          hbit = CreateCompatibleBitmap(hdc, maxX, maxY);
          SelectObject(memdc, hbit);
          hbrush = GetStockObject(WHITE_BRUSH);
          SelectObject(memdc, hbrush);
          PatBlt(memdc, 0, 0, maxX, maxY, PATCOPY);
          ReleaseDC(hwnd, hdc);
          break;
        case WM_COMMAND:
          switch(LOWORD(wParam)) {
            case ID_PROCESS:
              if(procnum==PROCMAX) {
                MessageBox(hwnd, "Can't Create", "", MB_OK);
                break; /* no more than PROCMAX */
              }

              /* Get text metrics. */
              GetTextMetrics(memdc, &tm);

              sprintf(str, "Execute Process %d.", procnum);
              TextOut(memdc, X, Y, str, strlen(str)); /* output string */
              Y = Y + tm.tmHeight + tm.tmExternalLeading; /* next line */
              InvalidateRect(hwnd, NULL, 1);

              /* Start a new process. */
              startin.cb = sizeof(STARTUPINFO);
```

```
            startin.lpReserved = NULL;
            startin.lpDesktop = NULL;
            startin.lpTitle = NULL;
            startin.dwFlags = STARTF_USESHOWWINDOW;
            startin.cbReserved2 = 0;
            startin.lpReserved2 = NULL;
            startin.wShowWindow = SW_SHOWMINIMIZED;

            CreateProcess(NULL, "test.exe",
                        NULL, NULL, FALSE, 0,
                        NULL, NULL, &startin, &pinfo[procnum]);
            procnum++;
            break;
          case ID_KILLPROC:
            if(procnum) procnum − −;
            else MessageBox(hwnd, "No process to terminate.",
                          "", MB_OK);
            TerminateProcess(pinfo[procnum].hProcess, 0);
            sprintf(str, "Terminate Process %d.", procnum);
            TextOut(memdc, X, Y, str, strlen(str)); /* output string */
            Y = Y + tm.tmHeight + tm.tmExternalLeading; /* next line */
            InvalidateRect(hwnd, NULL, 1);
            break;
          case ID_THREAD:
            CreateThread(NULL, 0, (LPTHREAD_START_ROUTINE)MyThread1,
                        (LPVOID) hwnd, 0, &Tid1);
            CreateThread(NULL, 0, (LPTHREAD_START_ROUTINE)MyThread2,
                        (LPVOID) hwnd, 0, &Tid2);
            break;
          case ID_HELP:
            MessageBox(hwnd,
                        "F2: Start Process\nF3: Kill Process\n"
                        "F4: Start Thread",
                        "Help", MB_OK);
            break;
        }
      break;
    case WM_PAINT: /* process a repaint request */
      hdc = BeginPaint(hwnd, &paintstruct); /* get DC */
```

```
      /* Now, copy memory image onto screen. */
      BitBlt(hdc, 0, 0, maxX, maxY, memdc, 0, 0, SRCCOPY);
      EndPaint(hwnd, &paintstruct); /* release DC */
      break;
    case WM_LBUTTONDOWN: /* process left button */
      X = LOWORD(lParam); /* set X,Y to */
      Y = HIWORD(lParam); /* mouse location */
      break;
    case WM_DESTROY: /* terminate the program */
      DeleteDC(memdc); /* delete the memory device */
      PostQuitMessage(0);
      break;
    default:
      /* Let Windows NT process any messages not specified in
      the preceding switch statement. */
      return DefWindowProc(hwnd, message, wParam, lParam);
  }
  return 0;
}


/* First thread of execution. */
DWORD MyThread1(LPVOID param)
{
  int i;
  DWORD curTid = Tid1;
  TEXTMETRIC tm;

  /* Get text metrics. */
  GetTextMetrics(memdc, &tm);

  for(i=0; i<10; i++) {
    Sleep(500);
    sprintf(str, "Thread ID #%d, beep #%d",
            curTid, i);
    TextOut(memdc, X, Y, str, strlen(str)); /* output string */
    Y = Y + tm.tmHeight + tm.tmExternalLeading; /* next line */
    InvalidateRect((HWND) param, NULL, 1);
    MessageBeep(-1);
  }
}
```

```
/* Second thread of execution. */
DWORD MyThread2(LPVOID param)
{
  int i;
  DWORD curTid = Tid2;
  TEXTMETRIC tm;

  /* Get text metrics. */
  GetTextMetrics(memdc, &tm);

  for(i=0; i<10; i++) {
    Sleep(200);
    sprintf(str, "Thread 2");
    TextOut(memdc, X, Y, str, strlen(str)); /* output string */
    Y = Y + tm.tmHeight + tm.tmExternalLeading; /* next line */
    InvalidateRect((HWND) param, NULL, 1);
  }
}
```

As this program illustrates, when using multiple threads, simply define a thread function for each thread and then start each thread separately. All the threads in the process will then execute concurrently.

Synchronization

It is sometimes necessary to synchronize the activities of two or more threads or processes. The most common reason for this is that sometimes two or more threads need access to a shared resource that may only be used by one thread at a time. For example, when one thread is writing to a file, a second thread must be prevented from doing so at the same time. The mechanism that prevents this is called *serialization*. Synchronization is also required when one thread is waiting for an event that is caused by another thread. In this case, there must be some means by which the first thread is held in a suspended state until the event has occurred. Then, the waiting thread must resume execution.

There are two general states that a task may be in. First, it may be *executing* (or, ready to execute as soon as it obtains its time slice). Second, a task may be *blocked,* awaiting some resource or event in which case its execution is *suspended* until the needed resource is available or until the required event occurs.

If you are not familiar with the need for synchronization and the serialization problem or its most common solution, the semaphore, the next section discusses it. (If this is familiar territory for you, skip ahead.)

Understanding the Serialization Problem

Windows NT must provide special services that allow access to a shared resource to be serialized, because without help from the operating system, there is no way for one process or thread to know that it has sole access to a resource. To understand this, imagine that you are writing programs for a multitasking operating system that does not provide any serialization support. Further imagine that you have two concurrently executing processes, A and B, both of which, from time to time, require access to some resource R (such as a disk file) that must only be accessed by one task at a time. As a means of preventing one program from accessing R while the other is using it, you try the following solution. First, you establish a variable called **flag**, which can be accessed by both programs. Your programs initialize **flag** to 0. Next, before using each piece of code that accesses R, you wait for the flag to be cleared, then set the flag, access R, and finally clear the flag. That is, before either program accesses R it executes this piece of code:

```
while(flag) ; /* wait for flag to be cleared */
flag = 1; /* set flag */

/* ... access resource R ... */

flag = 0; /* clear the flag */
```

The idea behind this code is that neither process will access R if **flag** is set. Conceptually, this approach is in the spirit of the correct solution. However, in actual fact it leaves much to be desired for one simple reason: it won't always work! Let's see why.

Using the code just given, it is possible for both processes to access R at the same time. The **while** loop is, in essence, performing related load and compare instructions on **flag** or, in other words, it is testing the flag's value. When the flag is cleared, the next line of code sets the flag's value. The trouble is that it is possible for these two operations to be performed in two different time slices. Between the two time slices, the value of **flag** might have been changed by a different process, thus allowing R to be accessed by both processes at the same time. To understand this, imagine that process A enters the **while** loop and finds that **flag** is 0, which is the green light to access R. However, before it can set **flag** to 1, its time slice expires and process B resumes execution. If B executes its **while**, it too will find that **flag** is not set and assume that it is safe to access R. However, when A resumes it will also begin accessing R. The crucial point of the problem is that the testing and setting of **flag** do not comprise one uninterruptable operation. Rather, as just illustrated, they can be separated by a time slice. No matter how you try, there is no way, using only application-level code, that you can absolutely guarantee that one and only one process will access R at one time.

The solution to the serialization problem is as elegant as it is simple. The operating system (in this case Windows NT) provides a routine that in one uninterrupted operation, tests and, if possible, sets a flag. In the language of operating systems engineers, this is called a *test and set* operation. For historical reasons, the flags used to control serialization and provide synchronization between processes (and threads) are called *semaphores*. The core Windows NT functions that support semaphores are discussed in the next section.

Windows NT Synchronization Objects

Windows NT supports four types of synchronization objects. All are based, in one way or another, on the concept of the semaphore. The first type is the classic semaphore. A semaphore can be used to allow a limited number of processes or threads access to a resource. When using a semaphore, the resource can be either completely serialized, in which case one and only one thread or process can access it at any one time, or the semaphore can be used to allow no more than a small number of processes or threads access to the resource at any one time. Semaphores are implemented using a counter that is decremented when a task is granted the semaphore and incremented when the task releases it.

The second synchronization object is the *mutex* semaphore. A mutex semaphore is used to serialize a resource so that one and only one thread or process can access it at one time. In essence, a mutex semaphore is a special case version of a standard semaphore.

The third synchronization object is the *event object*. It can be used to block access to a resource until some other thread or process signals that it may be used.

Finally, you can prevent a section of code from being used by more than one thread at a time by making it into a *critical section*, using a critical section object. Once a critical section is entered by one thread, no other thread may use it until the first thread has left the critical section. (Critical sections only apply to threads within a process.)

With the exception of critical sections, the other synchronization objects can be used either to serialize threads within a process or to serialize processes themselves. In fact, semaphores are a common means of interprocess communication.

This chapter describes how to create and use a semaphore and an event object. After you understand these two synchronization objects, the other two will be easy for you to explore on your own.

Using a Semaphore to Synchronize Threads

Before you can use a semaphore, you must create one using **CreateSemaphore()**, whose prototype is shown here:

```
HANDLE CreateSemaphore(LPSECURITY_ATTRIBUTES lpAttr,
                       LONG InitialCount,
                       LONG MaxCount,
                       LPSTR lpszName);
```

Here, *lpAttr* is a pointer to the security attributes, or NULL if no security attributes are used.

A semaphore can allow one or more tasks access to an object. The number of tasks allowed to simultaneously access an object is determined by the value of *MaxCount*. If this value is 1, then the semaphore acts much like a mutex semaphore, allowing one and only one thread or process access to the resource at any one time.

Semaphores use a counter to keep track of how many tasks have currently been granted access. If the count is zero, then no further access can be granted until one task releases the semaphore. The initial count of the semaphore is specified in *InitialCount*. If this value is zero, then initially all objects waiting on the semaphore will be blocked until the semaphore is released elsewhere by your program. Typically, *InitialCount* is set initially to 1 or more, indicating that the semaphore can be granted to at least one task. In any event, *InitialCount* must be non-negative and less than or equal to the value specified in *MaxCount*.

lpszName points to a string that becomes the name of the semaphore object. Semaphores are global objects that may be used by other processes. As such, when two processes each open a semaphore using the same name, both are referring to the same semaphore. In this way, two processes can be synchronized. The name may also be NULL, in which case, the semaphore is localized to one process.

The **CreateSemaphore()** function returns a handle to the semaphore if successful or NULL on failure.

Once you have created a semaphore, you use it by calling two related functions: **WaitForSingleObject()** and **ReleaseSemaphore()**. The prototypes for these functions are shown here:

DWORD WaitForSingleObject(HANDLE *hObject*,
                          DWORD *dwHowLong*);

BOOL ReleaseSemaphore(HANDLE *hSema*, LONG *Count*,
                        LPLONG *lpPrevCount*);

WaitForSingleObject() waits on a semaphore (or on some other type of object). Here, *hObject* is the handle to the semaphore created earlier. The *dwHowLong* parameter specifies, in milliseconds, how long the calling routine will wait. Once that time has elapsed, a time-out error will be returned. To wait indefinitely, use the value **INFINITE**. The function returns zero when successful (that is, when access is granted). It returns **WAIT_TIMEOUT** when time out is reached. Each time **WaitForSingleObject()** succeeds, the counter associated with the semaphore is decremented.

ReleaseSemaphore() releases the semaphore and allows another thread to use it. Here, *hSema* is the handle to the semaphore. *Count* determines what value will be added to the semaphore counter. Typically, this value is 1.

The *lpPrevCount* parameter points to a variable that will contain the previous semaphore count. If you don't need this count, pass NULL for this parameter.

The following program demonstrates how to use a semaphore. It prevents the threads from executing concurrently. That is, it forces the threads to be serialized. Notice that the semaphore handle is a global variable that is created when the window is first created. This allows it to be used by all threads (including the main thread) in the program.

```
/* A multithread program that illustrates synchronization
   using a standard semaphore. */

/* The following definition causes stricter type checking.
   This is optional, but suggested because it will help
   catch potential type mismatch errors--especially
   when porting from 16-bit Windows. */
```

```c
#define STRICT

#define PROCMAX 5 /* maximum number of processes */

#include <windows.h>
#include <string.h>
#include <stdio.h>
#include "proc.h"

LRESULT CALLBACK WindowFunc(HWND, UINT, WPARAM, LPARAM);
DWORD MyThread1(LPVOID param);
DWORD MyThread2(LPVOID param);

char szWinName[] = "MyWin"; /* name of window class */

char str[255]; /* holds output strings */

int X=0, Y=0; /* current output location */
int maxX, maxY; /* screen dimensions */

int procnum = 0;

DWORD Tid1, Tid2; /* thread IDs */

HDC memdc;
HBITMAP hbit;
HBRUSH hbrush;

PROCESS_INFORMATION pinfo[PROCMAX];

HANDLE hSema; /* handle to semaphore */

TEXTMETRIC tm;

int WINAPI WinMain(HINSTANCE hThisInst, HINSTANCE hPrevInst,
                   LPSTR lpszArgs, int nWinMode)
{
  HWND hwnd;
  MSG msg;
  WNDCLASS wcl;
  HANDLE hAccel;

  /* Define a window class. */
  wcl.hInstance = hThisInst; /* handle to this instance */
```

```
wcl.lpszClassName = szWinName; /* window class name */
wcl.lpfnWndProc = WindowFunc; /* window function */
wcl.style = 0; /* default style */

wcl.hIcon = LoadIcon(NULL, IDI_APPLICATION); /* icon style */
wcl.hCursor = LoadCursor(NULL, IDC_ARROW); /* cursor style */

/* Specify name of menu resource. */
wcl.lpszMenuName = "MYMENU"; /* main menu */

wcl.cbClsExtra = 0; /* no extra */
wcl.cbWndExtra = 0; /* information needed */

/* Make the window white. */
wcl.hbrBackground = GetStockObject(WHITE_BRUSH);

/* Register the window class. */
if(!RegisterClass (&wcl)) return 0;

/* Now that a window class has been registered, a window
   can be created. */
hwnd = CreateWindow(
  szWinName, /* name of window class */
  "Demonstrate Semaphores Synchronization", /* title */
  WS_OVERLAPPEDWINDOW, /* window style--normal */
  CW_USEDEFAULT, /* X coordinate--let Windows decide */
  CW_USEDEFAULT, /* Y coordinate--let Windows decide */
  CW_USEDEFAULT, /* width--let Windows decide */
  CW_USEDEFAULT, /* height--let Windows decide */
  HWND_DESKTOP, /* handle of parent window--there isn't one */
  NULL, /* no menu */
  hThisInst, /* handle of this instance of the program */
  NULL /* no additional arguments */
);

/* Load accelerators. */
hAccel = LoadAccelerators(hThisInst, "MYMENU");

/* Display the window. */
ShowWindow(hwnd, nWinMode);
UpdateWindow(hwnd);
```

```
      /* Create the message loop. */
      while(GetMessage(&msg, NULL, 0, 0))
      {
        if(!TranslateAccelerator(hwnd, hAccel, &msg)) {
          TranslateMessage(&msg); /* allow use of keyboard */
          DispatchMessage(&msg); /* return control to Windows */
        }
      }
      return msg.wParam;
    }


    /* This function is called by Windows NT and is passed
       messages from the message queue.
    */
    LRESULT CALLBACK WindowFunc(HWND hwnd, UINT message, WPARAM wParam,
                    LPARAM lParam)
    {
      HDC hdc;
      PAINTSTRUCT paintstruct;
      SIZE size;
      STARTUPINFO startin;

      switch(message) {
        case WM_CREATE:
          hSema = CreateSemaphore(NULL, 1, 1, "mysem");

          /* Get screen coordinates. */
          maxX = GetSystemMetrics(SM_CXSCREEN);
          maxY = GetSystemMetrics(SM_CYSCREEN);

          /* Make a compatible memory image device. */
          hdc = GetDC(hwnd);
          memdc = CreateCompatibleDC(hdc);
          hbit = CreateCompatibleBitmap(hdc, maxX, maxY);
          SelectObject(memdc, hbit);
          hbrush = GetStockObject(WHITE_BRUSH);
          SelectObject(memdc, hbrush);
          PatBlt(memdc, 0, 0, maxX, maxY, PATCOPY);
          ReleaseDC(hwnd, hdc);
          break;
        case WM_COMMAND:
          switch(LOWORD(wParam)) {
```

```
case ID_PROCESS:
  if(procnum==PROCMAX) {
    MessageBox(hwnd, "Can't Create", "", MB_OK);
    break; /* no more than PROCMAX */
  }

  /* Get text metrics. */
  GetTextMetrics(memdc, &tm);

  sprintf(str, "Execute Process %d.", procnum);
  TextOut(memdc, X, Y, str, strlen(str)); /* output string */
  Y = Y + tm.tmHeight + tm.tmExternalLeading; /* next line */
  InvalidateRect(hwnd, NULL, 1);

  /* Start a new process. */
  startin.cb = sizeof(STARTUPINFO);
  startin.lpReserved = NULL;
  startin.lpDesktop = NULL;
  startin.lpTitle = NULL;
  startin.dwFlags = STARTF_USESHOWWINDOW;
  startin.cbReserved2 = 0;
  startin.lpReserved2 = NULL;
  startin.wShowWindow = SW_SHOWMINIMIZED;

  CreateProcess(NULL, "test.exe",
                NULL, NULL, FALSE, 0,
                NULL, NULL, &startin, &pinfo[procnum]);
  procnum++;
  break;
case ID_KILLPROC:
  if(procnum) procnum - -;
  else MessageBox(hwnd, "No process to terminate.",
                  "", MB_OK);
  TerminateProcess(pinfo[procnum].hProcess, 0);
  sprintf(str, "Terminate Process %d.", procnum);
  TextOut(memdc, X, Y, str, strlen(str)); /* output string */
  Y = Y + tm.tmHeight + tm.tmExternalLeading; /* next line */
  InvalidateRect(hwnd, NULL, 1);
  break;
```

```
        case ID_THREAD:
          CreateThread(NULL, 0, (LPTHREAD_START_ROUTINE)MyThread1,
                     (LPVOID) hwnd, 0, &Tid1);
          CreateThread(NULL, 0, (LPTHREAD_START_ROUTINE)MyThread2,
                     (LPVOID) hwnd, 0, &Tid2);
          break;
        case ID_HELP:
          MessageBox(hwnd,
                   "F2: Start Process\nF3: Kill Process\n"
                   "F4: Start Thread",
                   "Help", MB_OK);
          break;
      }
      break;
    case WM_PAINT: /* process a repaint request */
      hdc = BeginPaint(hwnd, &paintstruct); /* get DC */

      /* Now, copy memory image onto screen. */
      BitBlt(hdc, 0, 0, maxX, maxY, memdc, 0, 0, SRCCOPY);
      EndPaint(hwnd, &paintstruct); /* release DC */
      break;
    case WM_LBUTTONDOWN: /* process left button */
      X = LOWORD(lParam); /* set X,Y to */
      Y = HIWORD(lParam); /* mouse location */
      break;
    case WM_DESTROY: /* terminate the program */
      DeleteDC(memdc); /* delete the memory device */
      PostQuitMessage(0);
      break;
    default:
     /* Let Windows NT process any messages not specified in
      the preceding switch statement. */
      return DefWindowProc(hwnd, message, wParam, lParam);
  }
  return 0;
}


/* First thread of execution. */
DWORD MyThread1(LPVOID param)
{
  int i;
  DWORD curTid = Tid1;
```

```c
   /* Get text metrics. */
   GetTextMetrics(memdc, &tm);

   /* Wait for access to be granted. */
   if(WaitForSingleObject(hSema, 10000)==WAIT_TIMEOUT)
         MessageBox((HWND)param, "Time Out Thread 1",
                    "Semaphore Error", MB_OK);

   for(i=0; i<10; i++) {
     Sleep(500);
     sprintf(str, "Thread 1, ID #%d, beep #%d",
             curTid, i);
     TextOut(memdc, X, Y, str, strlen(str)); /* output string */
     Y = Y + tm.tmHeight + tm.tmExternalLeading; /* next line */
     InvalidateRect((HWND) param, NULL, 1);
     MessageBeep(-1);
   }
   ReleaseSemaphore(hSema, 1, NULL);
}

/* Second thread of execution. */
DWORD MyThread2(LPVOID param)
{
   int i;
   DWORD curTid = Tid2;

   /* Get text metrics. */
   GetTextMetrics(memdc, &tm);

   /* Wait for access to be granted. */
   if(WaitForSingleObject(hSema, 10000)==WAIT_TIMEOUT)
         MessageBox((HWND)param, "Time Out Thread 2",
                    "Semaphore Error", MB_OK);

   for(i=0; i<10; i++) {
     Sleep(200);
     sprintf(str, "Thread 2");
     TextOut(memdc, X, Y, str, strlen(str)); /* output string */
     Y = Y + tm.tmHeight + tm.tmExternalLeading; /* next line */
     InvalidateRect((HWND) param, NULL, 1);
```

```
    }
    ReleaseSemaphore(hSema, 1, NULL);
}
```

Using an Event Object

As explained earlier, an event object is used to notify one thread or process when an event has occurred. To create an event object, use the **CreateEvent()** API function shown here:

> HANDLE CreateEvent(LPSECURITY_ATTRIBUTES *lpAttr*,
>   BOOL *Manual*,
>   BOOL *Initial*,
>   LPSTR *lpszName*);

Here, *lpAttr* is a pointer to security attributes. If it is NULL, then no security attributes are used. The value of *Manual* determines how the event object will be affected after the event has occurred. If *Manual* is **TRUE** (non-zero) then the event object is reset only by a call to the **ResetEvent()** function. Otherwise, the event object is reset automatically after a blocked thread is granted access. The value of *Initial* specifies the initial state of the object. If it is **TRUE**, the event object is set (the event is signaled). If it is **FALSE**, the event object is cleared (the event is not signaled).

lpszName points to a string that becomes the name of the event object. Event objects are global objects that may be used by other processes. As such, when two processes each open an event object using the same name, both are referring to the same object. In this way, two processes can be synchronized. The name may also be NULL, in which case, the object is localized to one process.

The **CreateEvent()** function returns a handle to the event object if successful and NULL otherwise.

Once an event object has been created, the thread (or process) that is waiting for the event to occur simply calls **WaitForSingleObject()** using the handle to the event object as the first parameter. This causes execution of that thread or process to suspend until the event occurs.

To signal that an event has occurred, use the **SetEvent()** function, shown here:

> BOOL SetEvent(HANDLE *hEventObject*);

Here, *hEventObject* is a handle to a previously created event object. When this function is called, the first thread or process waiting for the event will return from **WaitForSingleObject()** and begin execution.

To see how an event object operates, modify the preceding program so that an event object is created inside the **WM_CREATE** message using this statement:

```
hEvent = CreateEvent(NULL, FALSE, FALSE, "myevent");
```

Next, change **MyThread1()** and **MyThread2()** to the following:

```
/* First thread of execution. */
DWORD MyThread1(LPVOID param)
{
  int i;
  DWORD curTid = Tid;

  /* Get text metrics. */
  GetTextMetrics(memdc, &tm);

  /* Wait for event. */
  if(WaitForSingleObject(hEvent, 10000)==WAIT_TIMEOUT)
        MessageBox((HWND)param, "Time Out Thread 1",
                  "Event Error", MB_OK);

  for(i=0; i<10; i++) {
    Sleep(500);
    sprintf(str, "Thread ID #%d, beep #%d",
          curTid, i);
    TextOut(memdc, X, Y, str, strlen(str)); /* output string */
    Y = Y + tm.tmHeight + tm.tmExternalLeading; /* next line */
    InvalidateRect((HWND) param, NULL, 1);
    MessageBeep(-1);
  }

}

/* Second thread of execution. */
DWORD MyThread2(LPVOID param)
{
  int i;
```

```
DWORD curTid = Tid;

/* Get text metrics. */
GetTextMetrics(memdc, &tm);

for(i=0; i<10; i++) {
  Sleep(200);
  sprintf(str, "Thread 2");
  TextOut(memdc, X, Y, str, strlen(str)); /* output string */
  Y = Y + tm.tmHeight + tm.tmExternalLeading; /* next line */
  InvalidateRect((HWND) param, NULL, 1);
}

/* Send event notification. */
SetEvent(hEvent);
}
```

In this situation, **MyThread1()** is blocked until **MyThread2()** completes its execution and signals that it is done.

Things to Try

This chapter really just scratches the surface of Windows NT's multitasking and synchronization subsystems and capabilities. Some areas that you will want to explore on your own include setting and changing the scheduling priority of a thread or process. A task's priority partially determines how much CPU time it is given. You may also want to examine the security system if your environment requires a secure system.

You have come a long way in your study of Windows NT since the first chapter. Keep in mind that this book only discusses a fraction of the total API functions available for you to use. If you are going to be doing serious programming in Windows NT, you must have an API function reference and you must take some time to study it. If you are coming from a DOS environment, remember that Windows, in general, and Windows NT, specifically, are exponentially more complex. Becoming an excellent Windows programmer requires significant dedication, but the rewards are worth it.

Index

SPECIAL OFFER

WINDOWS DEVELOPER LETTER

THE TECHNICAL NEWSLETTER FOR ADVANCED WINDOWS PROGRAMMING

Windows Developer Letter is a new and unique newsletter for advanced Microsoft Windows developers. It is neither a marketing letter nor an introduction to basic Windows programming. Rather, it is packed with in-depth technical know-how, tips, techniques, secrets, and undocumented knowledge that will turn you into a Windows guru. The sort of knowledge only a few individuals possess, and even fewer are willing to share. The know-how that will give you and your programs a unique advantage in the market. *Windows Developer Letter* is a hands-on newsletter that explains new and complex issues in complete detail, with full source-code examples. No hand waving, no fluff, no ads, no reviews, just the facts – and lots of them.

Each issue of *Windows Developer Letter* takes a detailed look at some of Windows' newest and most advanced features, with special emphasis on 32-bit programming. It covers such topics as: OLE, TrueType, Hooks, Toolhelp, advanced debugging techniques, intercepting DLL calls, and much more. The *Windows Developer Letter* includes in-depth discussions of Windows architecture and internals, articles on how to extend and modify Windows, the underlying hardware and how to access it, unconventional uses for device drivers, fully utilizing the Win32 API, issues and pitfalls of multitasking, taking advantage of virtual device drivers, and similar cutting-edge topics.

Written exclusively by developers, for developers, the *Windows Developer Letter* is like no other publication. It provides original and useful information (not reprints of the manuals) that you cannot afford to be without. Articles include a discussion and full working source code that show exactly how to use each advanced feature. In addition, each issue includes a diskette with the royalties-free source code for all the examples, so that you can put your new knowledge to work at once, building on the examples to create your own powerful programs. It is this type of innovation and thoroughness that has already earned the *Windows Developer Letter* top praise:

"... a new one-of-a-kind, highly technical newsletter ... not for the faint of heart. The three issues I've seen so far have presented more detailed discussions (including source code on disk) of a range of useful and important topics than I have ever seen before. ... designed, and written for the heavy-duty Windows technical guru who is searching for cutting-edge solutions to tomorrow's Windows application problems."

> Steve Gibson
> *Tech Talk* Column
> *InfoWorld,* October 12, 1992

Special offer to Osborne/McGraw-Hill readers
Get 12 issues of the *Windows Developer Letter* for only $250.00 (regular subscription rate is $300.00).

No-risk double guarantee:
We are so sure you will find *Windows Developer Letter* to be an indispensable source of advanced technical information that we guarantee your complete satisfaction in two ways:
1. We will not charge your credit card or cash your check until 21 days after we mail your first issue. If it falls short of your expectations, simply drop us a note within 21 days and we will cancel your subscription, without charging your credit card or cashing your check. The first issue, including the diskette, is yours to keep – **free!**
2. If you decide to cancel your subscription at any time after 21 days, you will receive a refund for all unmailed issues.

OMH1

SUBSCRIPTION ORDER FORM – Special limited time offer!
Please start my subscription to *Windows Developer Letter* at the special rate of $250.00 (12 issues). **In California** add applicable **sales tax. Outside the U.S. and Canada** add $50.00 for airmail shipping and handling.

Start my subscription with: ❑ The premiere issue (July '92)   ❑ The current issue
Diskette size: ❑ 3½"   ❑ 5¼"
❑ Check enclosed (U.S. funds drawn on a U.S. bank) - made payable to: Wisdom Software, Inc.
Charge my: ❑Visa ❑MasterCard ❑AmEx   Card number: _____ Exp. date: _____
Name on card: _____   Signature: _____
Name: _____   Company: _____
Address: _____
City: _____   State: _____ ZIP: _____
Phone: _____   FAX: _____

Mail order form to:
Wisdom Software, Inc., 322 Eureka Street, San Francisco, CA 94114 Telephone: (415) 824-8482